HOW DARK THE HEAVENS

1400 Days In the Grip of Nazi Terror

HOW DARK THE HEAVENS

1400 Days In the Grip of Nazi Terror

by SIDNEY IWENS

Shengold Publishers, Inc.
New York

Copyright © 1990 by Sidney Iwens

Published by Shengold Publishers, Inc.
18 West 45th Street, New York, N.Y. 10036

Second Edition 1992

Library of Congress Cataloging-in-Publication Data

Iwens, Sidney, 1924–
   How dark the heavens: 1400 days in the grip of Nazi terror/by
Sidney Iwens.
      p.   cm.
   ISBN 0-88400-147-4
   1. Iwens, Sidney, 1924–   . 2. Jews—Lithuania—Biography.
3. Jews—Latvia—Biography. 4. Holocaust, Jewish (1939–1945)—
Lithuania—Personal narratives. 5. Holocaust, Jewish (1939–1945)—
Latvia—Personal narratives. 6. World War, 1939–1945—Underground
movements, Jewish—Byelorussian S.S.R. 7. Lithuania—Biography.
8. Latvia—Biography.   I. Title.
DS135.R95I945   1990
940.53'18'094743092—dc20   90-52879
                                 CIP

Printed in the United States of America

To my children and my children's children.

May the memories of those whose lives
were cut short continue to live in
your minds as they have always lived
in mine.

U.S.S.R

BALTIC SEA

LATVIA

● RIGA

DAUGAVA RIVER

● DAUGAVPILS

GRIVA

LITHUANIA

● SIAULIAI

● RADVILISKIS

ZARASAI

● PANEVEZYS

● UTENA

● OPSA

■ AKSIUTOVA

● BOBILY

● UKMERGE

● JONAVA

BORDER UNTIL 1939

● KAUNAS

● VILNIUS

WHITE RUSSIA

PREFACE

Throughout the war it seemed very important to me, as it did to many others, that there be left an authentic record of what actually happened to us. And although we had very little hope of survival and the ability to tell all, something compelled me to record dates and make notations on scraps of paper. In effect this became a crude sort of diary.

Even in the midst of these experiences, part of my mind seemed to be observing, and committing to memory in sharp detail, the events I was witnessing. My personal reactions often surprised me. I was struck by the fact that, in extreme situations, people don't always react in the expected way. The scraps of paper, along with all my other personal effects, disappeared when I arrived at Concentration Camp Stutthoff, thirty kilometers east of Danzig (now Gdansk), in July of 1944, but the memories have always remained clear and sharp in my mind.

I was liberated on the last day of April in 1945, and about a month later, as soon as I was well enough, I once again compiled the dates and began to record all that had happened to me during the war. My primary concern then was to get everything down on paper, and though the diary was written in an irregular and rambling fashion—I could only work at it when time permitted—after some years I managed to set down a great deal of relevant information.

It was always my hope that I could some day arrange the material in a manner that would make clear exactly what had happened to us. But it was not until 1983 that my personal circumstances finally permitted me to devote the necessary time to the work I had started thirty-eight years earlier.

I knew full well that there were great difficulties in trying to convey everything I saw, experienced, and thought during those years. To simplify this task, I decided to record everything in chronological order

7

as the events unfolded. The entries document events occurring between June 22, 1941, in Janova, Lithuania, and April 30, 1945, in Camp Allach near Munich. These events were a microcosm of the Jewish experience throughout the Baltic states, during which, especially in the first few months of the war, most of the Baltic Jews were murdered.

The notes I took down in 1945 were a major resource. But there is no discrepancy between what I remember now and what I wrote shortly after the war. For, on a certain level, I have never really left those times behind. I relive them every day.

•   •   •

I am grateful for the support and encouragement of my wife Ita, and of my children, Ilana and Richard Kennell, and Judy and Roy Eidelson.

S.I.

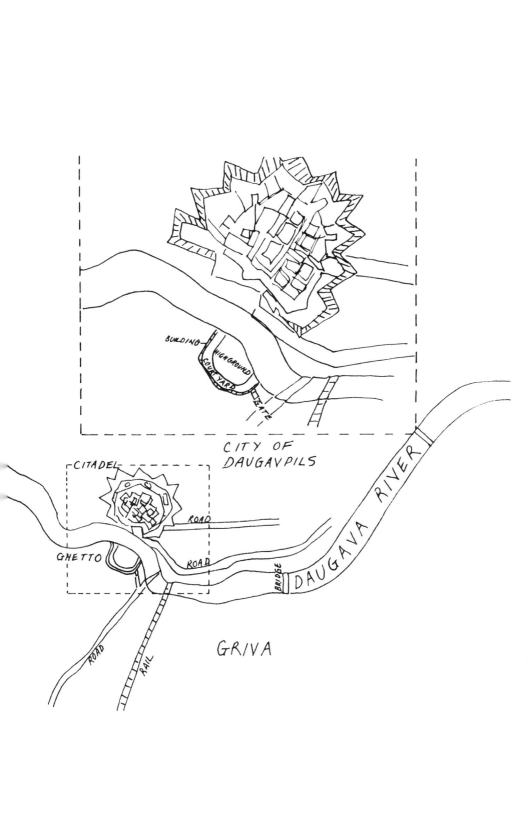

BUILDING HIGH GROUND COURT YARD GATE

CITY OF DAUGAVPILS

CITADEL ROAD

GHETTO ROAD

BRIDGE DAUGAVA RIVER

ROAD RAIL GRIVA

BEFORE THE FIRST DAY

I always enjoyed Saturday night dances at the Firemen's Hall in Jonava. But tonight it seemed more exciting than ever. Everyone was there—the fellows, the girls—and though Sheinale was surrounded by a circle of boys most of the time, I managed to dance with her while the band was playing "*U Menya Yest Szerdza* (Inside Me There Is a Heart)." I wanted the music to go on and on. . . . I was seventeen.

The dance did not end until very late, and when I left with Leib and Motke, the air was mild and the sky full of stars. We walked slowly and hardly talked but—still under the spell of the girls, the dancing, and the music—we each hummed or whistled softly "U Menya." In our ears, the romantic tango music still played, the girls still whirled in our arms. We dawdled, not wanting the mood to end, but we only had a few blocks to walk.

Finally Leib said, "See you tomorrow!" and I answered, "You mean today." For it was after midnight, and it was already the twenty-second of June.

Sunday, June 22, 1941: The first day

The war started this morning.

I awoke to my mother's voice. She and Father were having breakfast and talking about rumors that Mother had heard while buying rolls at the bakery. I didn't pay much attention until I heard her say, "There are posters—precautions to be taken. In case of war."

I dressed quickly and was out on Kaunas Street in a few minutes. It was a nice morning—blue skies, the sun hot and pleasant as it can only be in June. The street seemed crowded for a Sunday morning, and at the next corner, I ran into Leib and Motke. But before I could ask them if they had any news, we saw three planes flying high in formation. We gaped at them—Silvery-looking, majestic, unwavering. Then suddenly, delicate puffs of smoke materialized all around them—antiaircraft shells bursting. We looked at one another.

Those were German planes. This must be war.

I ran home quickly, and a little later, at about eleven o'clock, we heard V. M. Molotov address the country over the radio—a speech that was rebroadcast throughout the day. The Soviet foreign minister said that at four o'clock on that morning, the Germans had attacked the Soviet Union and bombed many cities. The attack had occurred, he said, "with no declaration of war and no demands made." The speech concluded with the words, "The enemy will be defeated, victory will be ours!"

We had lived in the shadow of war for a long time, but now that it had actually erupted, the event seemed unexpected. It reminded me of the shock I had experienced when my grandfather, who had been incurably ill for a long time, finally died.

For as long as I could remember, there had been international crises, one after the other. Many times in the past, war had seemed inevitable, yet it had somehow been avoided. In September of 1939, Germany and the Soviet Union attacked and occupied Poland, and the refugees appearing among us made war seem more real. Then, Germany began to invade one country after another, and in June of 1940 Soviet troops marched into Lithuania and annexed it. I stood by the highway watching what seemed like an unending stream of huge tanks that kept rolling toward Kaunas, the former capital, about thirty-five kilometers away; I watched for hours, and there seemed to be no end to them. But we were still at peace in Jonava.

Now the war was really here. German planes were in the skies, fired at by the Russians. Bombs might explode any moment.

I was born in the town of Jonava, Lithuania. About 4,500 people lived there, and about 3,500 of them were Jews. My father, Moshe Iwensky, had been head of the Folksbank, the nonprofit Jewish community bank in town, until the Red Army occupied Lithuania in 1940. He was then assigned to a minor position in the newly nationalized bank. He was forty-five years old and was ten years older than my mother, Mina. I was the oldest of the children and was called Shaya, or Shaike; my brother Ruvke was fifteen and my sister Nehamah thirteen.

Our family was well known in Jonava. Father had been very active in various community affairs and a leader of the local Zionist movement.

We spent the day in nervous anticipation.

By word of mouth, instructions went out to the population that bomb shelters were to be dug wherever there were no suitable cellars. We spent several hours digging trenches in the garden behind the house.

I walked outside. These were the same streets, the same people I had known all my life. Yet, everything seemed to have changed. Things that had seemed important yesterday weren't going to matter any more. We were at war.

Later in the afternoon I met the brothers Leib and Haim, and we decided to go for a swim in the Neris River behind the bridge. While walking on Kaunas Street, I sensed the increased tension around us. People stood in clusters discussing the latest rumors; conversations were agitated.

As we stood by the river next to the wooden bridge, Haim said, "I can imagine German assault troops suddenly appearing right there across the river!" This, of course, was impossible; the war had just started, and we were all aware of the power of the Red Army. German troops couldn't possibly get through so soon—if ever. With relief I remembered that long line of tanks I'd watched last year. And yet Haim's remark had a sobering effect. In my mind, I pictured helmeted, gray-clad soldiers with rolled-up sleeves astride motorcycles, their machine guns blazing away—a scene so frequently seen in newsreels.

We undressed and jumped into the water. Suddenly, we noticed two solitary planes fighting it out in the distance. They were too far away for us to hear sounds, but we clearly saw the twisting and turning of the planes, and could easily imagine the frantic rat-a-tat-tat of machine guns. How odd—to be swimming in the river as usual and watching war! But the absence of battle sounds made the dogfight seem unrealistic, like a silent movie. Finally, one of the combatants went down. We hoped it was the German plane.

Monday, June 23, 1941: The second day

Sunday night, expecting to be bombed, we did not undress and slept very little. Jonava was only ten kilometers from a huge military camp, and what with that and our strategic bridges over the Neris River, the railroad, and the highway—our town must have been a tempting target. But, as it happened, we heard no hum of approaching planes, only the loud grinding clank of tanks, crossing the Neris on the Highway bridge. The clatter of the big monsters could be heard for hours without interruption. Were they moving to the front, or were they retreating? After a while we became convinced that they were retreating, and we were concerned.

The first refugees appeared early in the morning. Initially there were only a few. Tired looking, carrying small bundles, they would stop for a snack and a short rest, then they would push on toward Ukmerge.

For a while we weren't sure what to make of it all. Perhaps these people were needlessly frightened. We couldn't believe that danger was really so close. But as the day wore on, more and more people appeared. The trickle soon became a torrent. Some took the highway bypassing the town, but enough of them came through Jonava to make it appear that most of the Jewish population of Kaunas was on the run.

We heard all kind of rumors, but the reports we heard about Kaunas were most alarming: "It's been bombed . . . it's burning!" "The Germans are very close to the city . . . even high Party officials have left." And later we heard that here in Jonava the authorities were distributing food and that whatever could not be given away would be destroyed.

With every passing minute our apprehension increased. What should we do? But by early afternoon there no longer was any doubt. Most of the Jewish population was on the move. My parents finally decided that we would have to leave as well, and we started to get ready.

Some of my friends wanted to volunteer to fight the Nazis, and I decided to join them. After spending quite a bit of time looking for information, we finally found a Russian officer who told us that there was a military headquarters a couple of kilometers behind the town, right next to the highway. "They will tell you what to do," he said. My brother Ruvke insisted on coming along with me. Mother and Father were very much against our going, but in the end grudgingly gave in. "We will be on the highway to Ukmerge," Father said. "Headquarters is on the same road, so we'll meet later. I don't think anything will come out of your idea anyway."

A relative and his family stopped at our house on their way to the highway, and we loaded food and a few valuables on his horse-drawn wagon. My family left shortly afterward on foot, planning to meet the wagon later on the road to Ukmerge, a town about thirty-five kilometers northeast of Jonava.

There were about a dozen of us young fellows eager to fight the Germans. When we finally left Jonava around five o'clock in the afternoon, the town seemed deserted. Most families had left; those who did not, stayed inside their homes. Settling over Jonava was an air of uncertainty, underscored by an ominous stillness.

As soon as we reached the highway, the full impact of what was happening hit us with brutal force. Before our eyes stretched an endless panorama of utter confusion. Civilians and soldiers all mixed together, and using all kinds of vehicles, were moving in an unbroken line. For a while we were walking next to a horse-drawn wagon, laden high with boxes, household belongings, and children, wedged between a huge tractor and a Kaunas city bus. The tractor was top-heavy with resigned-looking Red Army soldiers; the large bus was crammed with civilians, mostly women and children. So it went as far as the eye could see. The notion of finding any military staff here seemed quite absurd, and our intention to volunteer was quickly forgotten. Within minutes we became part of the mass.

Most of us had only one means of transportation, our feet. We crowded the road, a frantic populace pushing ahead in disarray. Adding to the general confusion were the disorganized Red Army soldiers, many unarmed, the insignia torn off their uniforms. They appeared to be entirely on their own, with no commanding officer in sight. They all looked exhausted, at the end of their rope.

We had covered only a few kilometers when we began to sense an uneasiness in the moving column, a wavering. Soon two fast-approaching planes appeared in the distance. "Are they friendly or German?" I wondered aloud. Some refugees immediately left the highway and hid among the sparse trees on either side of the road. The planes veered sharply, heading directly toward us.

Not a moment too soon, we dashed off the highway and threw ourselves behind a small tree. One plane seemed to be diving directly at us
emitting a shrill, blood-curdling shriek. I pressed my face hard against
the grass, hugging the ground harder and harder as the crescendo of the
scream increased, and then the plane's machine guns opened up: rat-a-
tat-tat-tat-tat-tat-tat-tat . . . . Like vicious predatory birds, the planes
wheeled and came back again and again, diving, whining, strafing while
I waited to be mowed down like hay.

Suddenly, the planes were gone. A strange silence followed. Dazed
and stunned, the people straggled back onto the highway, and resumed
their desperate journey. I was amazed that so many of us were still alive.

Similar terrifying attacks were repeated until I lost count. Always the
same routine: the ungainly procession, moving along the road as if
guided by one collective brain; picking up speed as it passed empty
fields; relaxing its pace in protected, wooded areas. Then when the
planes began their inevitable, deadly mission, we all scrambled as far as
possible from the road.

The planes came in various types and numbers. But no matter how
many or how few swooped down, they always froze us with terror. The
most frightening, the Stukas, emitted a bone-chilling wail as they dived
into the attack. We never saw Russian planes. Each attack filled me with
the same overwhelming panic. I pressed my face hard against the floor
of pine needles in the woods or unripe rye in the fields or the damp
ground in the roadside ditches, as though I'd somehow find a special in-
visibility that way. Then at last, stillness again. The planes were gone.
People straggled back onto the road, and the column— minus those who
were hit and the disabled vehicles—proceeded on its torturous way.

When I left home, I wore my holiday suit and calfskin boots. After
less than ten kilometers, I developed a blister on my heel. Walking became painful, my expensive boots a serious hindrance. At last, with
regret, I threw them away and walked barefoot from then on. Others, I
noticed, were also discarding the belongings that impeded their
progress.

I kept thinking about my family and hoping to meet up with them
soon. Our original group of would-be volunteers, had broken up, absorbed into the uncontrolled mass of humanity. At one point I saw Leib
and Haim passing by on our town's fire engine, with a lot of other
people hanging on for dear life—like clusters of grapes clinging
precariously to a vine.

In spite of the plane attacks, Ruvke and I made good progress. We boys had taken part in a marathon arranged by the sport club less than a month ago. It was held on this same road, and my thoughts returned to that time as I tried to walk as fast as I did then. The fact that we had nothing to carry helped, and we were able to overtake many of our townspeople. One of them told us that an uncle, my mother's brother, was hit in one of the air attacks. I wondered whether my other uncle got away from Kaunas; my father's brother and his family and my grandmother lived there.

It was almost dark when, at last, we caught up with the rest of the family; with great relief we continued on together.

Without stopping to rest, we reached Ukmerge, a town larger than Jonava. It was late at night, the town was quiet, and the streets were deserted. We pushed on, thinking it would be safer to stay clear of towns. At last, around midnight, a few kilometers beyond the town, we felt safe enough to stop in a wooded area. By now we became aware of our hunger and exhaustion.

I went with Father to try to get some food from the farmhouses near-by, but the farmers had little sympathy for the hardships of Jews. After repeated refusals, we were finally given a piece of bread by an old farmer. We devoured the bread and immediately fell asleep on the grassy forest floor.

Tuesday, June 24, 1941: The third day

June nights are short, daylight comes very early. But when Father woke us, it was still dark—we'd slept less than two hours. "We'd better start out while it's dark," he said, "before the planes come."

His advice proved sound. There were few people on the highway at that hour, and it was cool. Walking steadily, we managed to cover quite a distance before the planes appeared, harassing us with as much ferocity as the day before. Same pattern, too: planes strafing and bombing; people running and hiding; vehicles burning. We were marching, marching, marching—the sun beating down mercilessly. We tried to get a ride from passing trucks, civilian or military, but had no luck. One truck loaded with soldiers stopped for water, because its radiator was overheating. It was immediately surrounded with people clamoring to be taken along. "Orders, can't take anybody!" an officer called out. One soldier standing apart from the others said to me, "The Germans are only fifteen kilometers away."

Exhausted, we forced ourselves to keep going. The highway became even more crowded with retreating Red Army soldiers, mingled with civilians and vehicles of every description. The soldiers' condition was shocking—many of them barefoot. They had run all the way from the border, and their disorderly condition increased our panic. But worst of all were the plane attacks. Several times we passed a line of bodies on one side of the road— people who in their rush to take cover, had hugged the wrong side of the drainage ditch and been raked by machine gun fire in one fell swoop.

Father reminded us that this highway was leading from East Prussia through Kaunas, Ukmerge, Daugavpils, Pskov, and all the way on to Leningrad and that the Germans were making a special effort to disrupt northbound movement on this major thoroughfare. Last year they had strafed civilians in France, Belgium, and the Netherlands in the same way and for the same reason.

Around midday we found ourselves close to a small bridge that was under bombardment. We ran into a wooded area close by, crouched down, and waited. The trees shook with the vibrations of exploding bombs: phow . . . phow . . . phow . . . . It quieted down after a while, but we could still hear explosions fade off into the distance.

Father turned to Ruvke and me. "You two go ahead. After it calms down and we get a chance to rest some, we'll follow."

At first I refused to hear of it. We had just caught up with them the night before—how could we separate again?

But he insisted: "You're young and must not fall into German hands. Alone you have a chance . . . . We'll . . . meet you a little later."

He pushed some bills into my hand and said, "I kept it for you—the money you gave me every week." I'd been working as an assistant bookkeeper this past year and—aware of how short of cash we were at home—I'd turned most of my wages over to Father. Seeing my astonishment, he said hastily, "Of course I would not use the money you earned! I saved it for you. Now you must go—hurry!"

We ducked out of the woods and ran across the highway bridge. We'd no sooner left than I deeply regretted letting Father persuade us to leave them. I kept hoping that somebody would give them a ride, but the chances of that were slim. The rest of the day, whenever we met people from Jonava, I asked whether they had seen my family. No one had.

We were desperately tired. It was a mistake to have thrown away my boots, because walking barefoot made it harder, and the infrequent rests helped very little. It was sheer agony to get up and start walking again. I just put one foot in front of the other automatically, step by painful step.

The next big town would be Utena, about seventy kilometers beyond Ukmerge. Could I last that long?

Later in the day, our situation became even more threatening. The highway suddenly emptied out, leaving only small groups of refugees pushing ahead. Behind us, we saw few people—a sign that the German troops were close on our heels. I overheard four nearby soldiers speak of "parachutists."

I approached them. "Have you heard any news?" The oldest one, apparently a sergeant, said, "We heard that German airborne troops have landed nearby." He motioned to his group. "Come, let's get off the highway!"

Ruvke and I followed them up a hill into a little clump of trees, and when they all sat down in a circle, we joined them. They seemed to accept us as part of their group, and that made me feel good.

"Even if it's true that there are Germans ahead on the highway," the sergeant said, "we can still get out of here by going cross-country." His confident manner had a calming effect on all of us. "First let's see what arms we have among us," he continued. It turned out there were two rifles and two grenades among the four soldiers. "Better than nothing," he commented.

But when we checked the highway again, we found that the immediate crisis had passed, and the road was once more filled with people. Ruvke and I left the soldiers, merged with the crowd, and continued as before.

Every once in a while we found food in an overturned truck. Many of the trucks had been destroyed or damaged in the air attacks, but others were simply abandoned—lack of fuel apparently, since nothing seemed to be wrong with them.

At times someone would fall into step beside us, often a friend from Jonava or fellows from other Jewish towns. We heard frightening tales of attacks on Jewish refugees by Lithuanian guerrillas, German sympathizers. Sometimes I would meet one of our original group that had left Jonava together, and quite often we seemed to fall in with a gentile fellow from our town who was Russian. Generally, though, the great majority of the people on the road were Jewish.

I am not sure when I first heard people talk about the city of Daugavpils as a refuge. But by evening more and more people were saying that we could reach safety only in that place. Daugavpils—or as it is known in Russian, Dvinsk, was in Latvia, a large city on the Daugava (Dvina) river, only a short distance from the Lithuanian border. All I had known about it earlier was that, in the early months of the Great War, the German army had advanced rapidly through Lithuania, but was held back for more than a year at Daugavpils. Surely now, too, the Germans would be unable to cross that wide river easily. But it was 130 kilometers or more from where we were. How could we ever make it?

Wednesday, June 25, 1941: The fourth day

Sometime during the night between Tuesday and Wednesday we reached Utena, another well-known town. There must have been looting—many windows were broken, and I had to step carefully around the splintered glass.

We stopped a few kilometers beyond the town and slept for an hour or two among some trees. We left while it was still dark.

Zarasai, about fifty kilometers away, was the next large town and very close to the Latvian border.

The highway was less crowded than yesterday, and we marched very fast, in spite of a constant pain in our legs and our increasing exhaustion. Most of the time I yearned overwhelmingly to throw myself on the grass at the side of the road and just forget everything. But behind us, like a relentless beast, was the German army. So strong was our fear of the Germans that sometimes, when the danger seemed particularly acute, I almost forgot my exhaustion.

So on and on we marched, stopping infrequently, with one determined thought: to reach Daugavpils—or Dvinsk as most people were now calling it. Daugavpils became the beacon of our deliverance, pulling us forward, giving us hope. We counted each kilometer—seventy, sixty, fifty—coming ever closer to our destination, to safety.

We made repeated attempts to find a ride, but were never successful. Once Ruvke and I came alongside a tractor pulling several open trailers. It was moving slowly, bearing scores of refugees, among them some from Jonava. We jumped on one of the trailers, relieved and overjoyed at our good luck. But our joy was short-lived. After only a kilometer, the tractor turned back to "pick up something," the driver said. As it moved in the opposite direction, we jumped off, gaining nothing.

Around midday there came a glimmer of hope. Some of the army vehicles turned about and started to move back to the front. Approaching a small forest, we were stopped by Red Army officers, ordered into the woods, and told there was a counterattack in progress. "We will stop those Nazis!" one of them said. A political commissar explained that the Red Army was advancing on other fronts, but "here we were sold out by traitors. But there are armies coming to our rescue." All of the passing soldiers were being mustered back into makeshift units in an attempt to organize a defense against the German advance, and we civilians were to wait.

Our hopeful mood didn't last. In less than half an hour we saw the same vehicles which had been heading south return at high speed, apparently in more disarray than before.

We were back on the highway, and again, like the previous day, the traffic suddenly thinned out. The few retreating military vehicles, racing like mad, added a new urgency and panic. Obviously, the Germans were close behind. We began to march faster and faster, until we were actually running, overtaking even some horse-drawn carts. Some strange force was animating our weary legs.

The soldiers on foot were in no better position than we were—and not treated any better by their luckier comrades passing them in trucks. In their frenzied effort to get away from the fast-approaching enemy, some Red Army men tried to hitch rides by forcing trucks to stop. They would stand in the direct path of an approaching truck until the last possible moment; then, when the truck did not stop—or even slow down— they'd have to leap for their lives. I saw one soldier waiting at a spot where the highway went up a steep hill, and when an oncoming truck was forced to slow down, he grasped the tail gate and tried to hoist himself in. The soldiers inside smashed at his knuckles with their rifle butts, until he fell onto the highway like a sack of potatoes.

The sun was setting when we passed Zarasai. It looked much the same as the other towns we had passed earlier—few people, a lot of broken windows.

As we passed a large lake, the setting sun lay low on the water, and the lake seemed on fire—all aglow, gleaming and vast. Beautiful and foreboding at the same time.

It was almost dark when, a few kilometers later, we crossed into Latvia. Daugavpils now was less than thirty kilometers away. But nearer at hand was exhaustion. Oh, for the freedom to collapse on the side of the road! But we had to go on. Each kilometer marker was like a landmark: 20 km . . .19 km . . .18 km . . . How could our bodies endure so much abuse? 12 km . . . Mind and body sluggish with fatigue. Only one clear thought: Must reach Daugavpils.

And then, like an answer to a prayer, a wagon came along filled with Jonaver whom we knew well: Sheinale Polan and her parents and Shmulke Palec and some of his relatives. I could imagine how pitiful we must have looked. The wagon was crammed and overflowing with people, but even so, one of them called out, "Sit on the pole at the end of the wagon."

It was late at night when at last our objective was in sight: the Daugava River. Only soldiers were allowed to cross the bridge; civilian traffic had to wait. But across the water we could make out the city of Daugavpils.

My brother Ruvke said, "It is hard to believe: two hundred kilometers, in a little over two days."

Thursday, June 26, 1941: The fifth day

In the morning we were allowed to cross the long steel bridge, but only as pedestrians. The horse and wagon were left behind, and we continued on. The bridge was crowded with civilians and soldiers, and we all tried to get across the fastest possible way. We assumed the bridge was a tempting target for German planes, and the sound of explosions added to our nervousness.

But finally we were in the city of Daugavpils behind the wide Daugava River, the symbol (in our minds) of safety. But this place didn't feel safe at all. We continued hearing explosions, and from time to time a column of dirt and debris could be seen spewing into the air. Shmulke's uncle said, "Artillery, that's what it is. The Germans are shelling the city. They must be very close."

The streets farther away from the bridge seemed abandoned, with only an occasional person hurrying by. Fear seemed to hang in the air like a smell, and the danger was still as real as it had ever been.

Shmulke's uncle said, "We must go on. We can't stay here."

"But how can we?" objected one of the women. "We are all completely exhausted."

"Let's go to the station. Maybe trains are still leaving."

Ruvke and I remained with the people from the wagon and continued on to the station. Perhaps we could get on a train. But as we reached the railroad station, a shell exploded in front of us, and when we dived inside the station, we found panic and pandemonium.

Military and civilians were all shoving and pushing to get on board any train available. I was struck by the fact that there were still Soviet NKVD [secret service] men among them. Whenever word of a train passed around, everyone surged toward it, kicking, elbowing, anything to inch forward. These were not passenger trains, of course, but no one objected to boxcars, anything that moved. Even so, it seemed impossible to get aboard.

Finally, at about eleven o'clock, Ruvke, I, and all our friends managed to wedge ourselves into a freight car. Inside were platforms of wooden planks, a place for us to lie down.

The relief I felt when the train finally left the station was indescribable. We were moving. We were safe. The swaying of the car and clatter of the wheels was music to our ears, and overcome by exhaustion, some people fell asleep immediately.

We had traveled only a few kilometers when the train came to a sudden halt. We stiffened with apprehension, and Ruvke said, "After so little time!" Someone said stoutly, "We'll get moving again in a few minutes."

Outside we could hear sounds of rapid fire and explosions. When I was able to glance through a small makeshift window, I could see that we were in open country; fires were burning in the distance, and people—civilians or soldiers—were running across the open field.

"Probably German planes," someone said. I thought hopefully, perhaps the shooting is Russian antiaircraft fire. Our train was an easy target, but we were too worn out to get out and look for shelter.

The shooting became more intense. Still no one left the car. I was now so accustomed to noise and danger that I dozed off; most of us did.

Perhaps an hour or so passed. Then suddenly there was pounding on the freight car door. In seconds, it slid open, and facing us were soldiers in gray uniforms. They were Germans. We froze in terror.

In their steel helmets and heavy boots, their guns pointing at us, they looked as menacing as I had pictured them in my imagination. "Heraus, raus!" [out] they yelled. We scrambled out of our boxcar. A few of us were searched for arms, and we were ordered to lie on the ground. We had no idea what to expect next. Some people, confused and afraid, tore up their Russian money and documents. I didn't tear up mine.

Other soldiers came, and those who had captured us left. A few seemed quite decent and even offered some bread. Hours passed. The sound of battle continued the whole afternoon. When it was nearly dark, a German, pointing to the distance, ordered: "Go back to the city!"

The direction we were to follow was clear enough: The city of Daugavpils was on fire, and the entire horizon seemed to be ablaze. I thought it looked like a painting—a painting of a city in flames.

On our way back, we passed some German soldiers marching in the opposite direction; others crouched behind machine-guns, and fired occasional bursts; artillery shells exploded close by. "The front line must be right around here," I said to Ruvke. "If only we had left the rail car when the train stopped and kept going on foot, we might have escaped." (Later I learned that this guess was fairly accurate, for the German advance stopped for some days just north of Daugavpils.)

Besides those who arrived with us on the wagon, two more from our town attached themselves to our group—a Jewish boy, Peisale, and the Russian fellow we had got to know on the road.

The fire hadn't yet reached the part of town where we now found ourselves. But where were we to go? A man who looked Jewish peeked out of a doorway. When we asked him where we could find shelter, he pointed to a building across the street and said, "Go to the basement there."

Our group was lucky; the basement was deserted but well stocked with pillows, a few blankets, even a little food. But after a few hours the fire seemed to be getting closer. We all left, found a place in the open where many refugees had gathered, and stayed until morning.

Friday, June 27, 1941: The sixth day

Early morning. The fire was almost out, and our group went back to the basement we had discovered yesterday. Luckily, the building had escaped the flames, and the basement was still deserted.

After resting some, we all felt much better, and Ruvke and I went out to look around. Sporadic artillery bombardment was still going on. I said wistfully, "The Russians must not be far from the city." We hoped there would be a counterattack that would push the Germans back.

Out in the streets, looting was going on. From one store, with a Jewish name above the door, someone was throwing coats through the broken windows to civilians assembled in front of it. People passed by clutching food and clothing, a man and a woman carrying a table with boxes on top. The street was strewn with various articles. Ruvke found a pair of shoes that someone must have dropped. I put them on immediately, and though they were a little too big, I was happy to have them. We hurried back to our basement, spending little time outside. No one bothered us—neither Ruvke nor I looked Jewish.

Saturday, June 28, 1941: The seventh day

A loud disturbance woke us. Someone was shouting, *"Halt!"* Then shots. In the alley, a few feet from our door, we found a middle-aged woman lying on the ground, clutching a paper bag of candy; some pieces were strewn around her. She'd been shot dead.

Intermittent shelling was still going on, sometimes quite heavy. Once, while I was using the outhouse across the alley, all hell seemed to break loose. Shells burst nearby with a deafening crash, and the ground shook. I thought, if I have to die, at least not like this—not with my pants down.

I got back to our basement safely, but at the end of the day, the dead woman's body still had not been removed.

Sunday, June 29, 1941 : The eighth day

The first sights to greet us as we walked out into the street were large posters plastered all over, announcing that Jewish male adults up to age sixty must report to the big marketplace this morning without fail. Ignore this order, they threatened, and you would get the maximum penalty. They were printed in German, Russian, and Latvian, so there could be no mistake about understanding the message. We expected to be assigned to forced labor.

As we men were about to depart, the Russian fellow, who had been with us the last several days, motioned me aside and said, "Look, the Germans will take your wristwatch anyway, so you might as well give it to me before you go." My watch was a handsome Bar Mitzvah gift and I answered with a firm *No!* For the past two days, I had detected a subtle change in his behavior. We were Jews, he was not. Now we belonged to completely different categories—the Germans were still our mutual enemy but no longer to the same degree, no longer in quite the same way.

When we arrived at the marketplace, thousands of people were already there, many of them also refugees from Lithuania. I talked to some from Jonava, but no one had seen my family after I had left them. People were milling around, nervously awaiting orders. Most expected that we'd be sent to work.

After some time, a German soldier came looking for workers. Ruvke and I were assigned to a group of twenty men and quickly marched away under the command of a German guard.

We spent the rest of the day burying Russian soldiers and civilians killed in the fighting, whose corpses were still lying in alleys and doorways. There hadn't been much fighting in the city, so there were few dead Russians, except in the post office where they had put up a dogged defense. We had to carry the bodies down from the upper floors. Laboring under their dead weight, I couldn't help but think how bravely they had died: Trapped and without apparent hope, they had nevertheless kept on fighting. We buried them in the garden.

Our route back led us along the Dombe, the embankment parallel to the river, which also served as one of the main thoroughfares of the city.

Suddenly our guard stopped us near a large group of people, many of them soldiers, who were staring down at a large red-brick building. I realized that it was a prison and that the yard around it was filled with people. After some hesitation the guard took us down too.

What I saw was bizarre and frightening: long columns of Jewish men, thousands of them, young and old, well-dressed and in work clothes, of various shapes and demeanors, all mixed together. They were being systematically terrorized and humiliated—forced to jump like frogs, make distorted faces, perform all kinds of ridiculous gestures with their heads, hands, and feet. The Germans were enjoying themselves immensely, shouting orders and shooting over the heads of the Jews.

Our guard informed us that, since we had worked hard the whole day, we wouldn't have to take part in "sport." We could just sit on the side and wait while the terrorizing went on.

I noticed that some of the young teenagers were allowed to go free and asked our guard if he would let Ruvke go, since he was only fifteen. The guard went to the German officer who seemed to be in charge, and spoke to him briefly. Returning, he said to Ruvke:

"You have permission to go home."

But Ruvke refused to leave. "I want to stay with my brother. Wherever he goes, I want to go too."

I begged him to go, but he would not listen. I told him that his staying would be of no help to me. Still he argued, and our guard must have been touched by this scene. He said, "Wait, I'll go back to the officer and ask him to let both of you go."

Off he went, coming back shortly with word that the officer wanted to see documents proving we were both really that young.

"Come with me," he said.

The German we were facing was tall, with a beefy, brutal face. The uniform, the SS deaths head insignia on his cap, and the submachine gun hanging from his neck made him look terribly menacing. Standing near-by were more armed soldiers as well as Latvian collaborators in civilian clothing with armbands on their sleeves.

Ruvke's birth certificate was at school, but I had mine, giving my age as seventeen. Unable to read Lithuanian, the officer handed over the paper to a Latvian collaborator. The Latvian looked at the paper, tried to read it, and asked me something in Latvian. I tried to explain that the certificate was in the Lithuanian language. At the word, "Lithuanian," he pointed at me angri-ly, saying in broken German "escaped from Lithuania . . . must be a com-munist." At that, the German went into a rage, shouting and cursing, he ordered Ruvke, "Get out of here. Run fast!" Turning back to me, he barked, "You, go with the others doing exercises."

Ruvke didn't move. The German shouted: "Go! . . . Go home!"

Still Ruvke refused. "I want to stay with my brother . . . I don't want to go without him," he said quietly.

The German grabbed his submachine gun, pointed it at Ruvke, and sneeringly said, "Either you go home right now, or I'll shoot you."

He aimed the gun at Ruvke's head, and only then, with tears in his eyes, did Ruvke start walking dejectedly toward the gate. I joined the mass of people doing "sport."

At nightfall, all of us were marched into the prison and ordered into cells. In our cell, meant to hold three people, eighteen were jammed in.

Overwhelmed by the sudden deluge of violence and brutality, we sat motionless, paralyzed by fear and uncertainty, unable to communicate with each other. We were enveloped by a sense of terror that seemed al-most tangible. Silently, we sat until it became pitch dark, then found our-selves places on the floor. Three cots were attached to the wall, meant to be pulled down at night. We didn't use them.

Monday, June 30, 1941: The ninth day

Nothing much happened. We were allowed to leave the cell to go to the toilet only once and received no food all day. It was hot, and I was very thirsty.

From the people in my cell, I found out what had taken place yesterday, before I got to the prison. After waiting many hours in the square, all the men were marched off to the prison, where the tormenting had begun. At one point the people were given three minutes to live, followed by shooting, but the bullets were aimed above their heads. Then a demand was made for ten volunteers for execution "so that the rest might live." Hundreds volunteered, and an officer said: "Because so many volunteered, you will be spared for now." Later, a disjointed speech by an officer vilified the Jews. Among many other things, he accused the Jews of setting fire to the city of Daugavpils and concluded by shouting, "We must get rid of the Jews!" Then the people were made to shout, "Heil Hitler" and to sing "*Deutschland, Deutschland Ueber Alles.*" And so it went, on and on.

The Daugavpils prison was a large, red-brick building, with three floors and a basement. One of the most frustrating things about being there was that the windows, besides having iron bars across them, also had wooden covers attached several inches from the glass, limiting our range of vision to a small strip of sky. It was a severe deprivation not to be able to look outside. From my cell on the third floor, I would have been able to see the constant traffic and the activity on the embankment, but with the windows covered, I was hemmed in. The one place free of the enclosures was the washroom; those windows had only the steel bars. The entire compound was surrounded with a high, thick wall of concrete and brick which was topped by barbed wire and guard towers equipped with machine guns.

Tuesday, July 1, 1941: The tenth day

In the morning we were marched outside into the prison yard and formed into columns, three to a row. German soldiers were waiting there to take prisoners off to work. Once again, I was in a group of twenty. Our job was to bury dead horses found on the roads and in ditches outside town, five of us to a horse. The animals had been dead for days; they were swollen to abnormal proportions, foul-smelling, and extremely heavy. We used ropes to pull them out, but toward the end of the day, we found a huge horse in a ditch and simply couldn't budge the carcass. The guard shouted and cursed to no avail. Then he became quiet and said very calmly, "You have three minutes. If this horse isn't pulled out of the ditch by that time, one of you will be buried with it." Somehow, with one last desperate effort, we got the job done.

Late in the afternoon, we returned to the prison. For the first time since our arrival, we got some food: small salted fish and watery soup with *suchari*, a dried-out slice of bread, which must have been left by the retreating Red Army.

In the evening lying on the floor in my corner, I was thinking about the one long nightmare I'd become trapped in, and suddenly it came to me: Just ten days ago, I was enjoying myself at the Saturday night dance at the Firemen's Hall.

If only it *were* just a terrible dream! I would wake up, and it would be Sunday morning. There would be fresh rolls for breakfast, and later I'd meet the fellows. We might go for a hike with the girls and in the evening to the movies. And this prison, the Nazis and the fear of what tomorrow might bring—it would be nothing but a newsreel.

Wednesday, July 2, 1941: The eleventh day

Though it was crowded in my cell, we got along well. I was the youngest there and the only refugee from Lithuania. Two men were especially friendly. One was in his thirties, one of three brothers, an accountant, mild-mannered and softspoken. The other was very different, probably fifty or so, tall, lean, and muscular, a drayman and also a volunteer fireman. He talked loudly, with a touch of excitement. When I told him of my long flight, he exclaimed, "Shaike, to have come so far, by foot in a couple of days and without shoes—you are a hero!" He reminded me of the characters in the book *Pandre*, by Zalman Schneuer. I had just finished the first volume when the war started. Schneuer describes the folk people as a strong, hardworking lot with a sense of pride in themselves and the courage to face life's vicissitudes. In the foreword to the novel, he talks wistfully of the Jews of years gone by: Where are you now, you Jews of Oak . . . draymen . . . butchers . . . wood-choppers . . . In your childlike eyes played the power of life. . . .

Thursday, July 3, 1941: The twelfth day

The hallway of every floor was divided in half by a barred partition, the door of which was always locked. But our cells were sometimes open, so we could move around in our half of the hallway.

Today I had a pleasant surprise—I met a man from Kaunas who knew my father well. His cell was right across from mine. He and my father had been on the board governing the Jewish community banks in Lithuania. Both were members for years and would often meet at meetings. "Ah," he exclaimed, "Iwensky's son! Your father is the only person I knew who foresaw this disaster. What an intelligent man! He used to say, 'If war comes, we Jews are lost'."

I heard that some of the older people were released from prison.

Friday, July 4, 1941: The thirteenth day

There was a daily routine: We rose very early in the morning (around four o'clock) and received ersatz black coffee. Then they ordered us down to the large yard, where we stood three in a row in long columns. Eventually German soldiers appeared and selected groups for work—a method similar to slave auction or work-animal selection. They preferred those who looked strong and competent. There was a variety of hard jobs, including loading and unloading cement, food, and war materials, digging, cleaning, and so on. Just plain luck determined where one would get assigned.

Most of the Germans guarding and supervising us at work were brutal and constantly urged us to work faster. "Los, schneller! [Get going! Faster]!" they shouted, at times hitting us with their rifle butts. But once in a while there would be a decent one. One day, on our way back from work, we passed the Daugava, and the guard stopped and allowed us to wash ourselves in the river. We even got a chance to swim a little.

Sometimes we got a little food thrown our way at lunchtime; other times, no food until we got back to our cells in the evening when we received watery soup and *suchari*. Either way we were always hungry.

A prisoner was shot dead by a guard, because he did not sing when his column was ordered to do so. I heard of cases of casual brutality every day.

Saturday, July 5, 1941: The fourteenth day

As we formed our usual columns in the morning, I heard two gunshots from the other side of the yard. Later I found out that when the prisoners were told to form columns, an older person got confused. Somehow, every row he found himself in seemed to have three men already, and no matter where he tried to stand, he became the fourth. The guard shouted at him, pointed his gun, and got the man even more confused. Then the guard said something like, "Well, since there seems to be no place for this man, I will take care of the problem!" And he shot him on the spot.I worked most of the day unloading bags of cement from railroad cars. Using a chain system, we stood in a row and transferred a bag from one to another all the way down the line from the car. The bags were heavy, it was hard labor, hour after hour. I had to work for some time inside the car picking up bags from the stacked rows; some were torn, and the cement dust made breathing very difficult.

I often thought of Ruvke, wondering where he was and what had happened to him. How brave he was and how he argued with that Nazi! At least he was not here in this hell.

Sunday, July 6, 1941: The fifteenth Day

The man from Kaunas, who had known my father, was dead. We heard shots and ran out into the hallway. We found him lying on the floor of the washroom, bleeding from his head, his face still twitching. He died a few minutes later. Apparently, he tried to look through the barred window of the washroom, the only place where there were no wooden obstructions, and was shot by a guard from the outside.

Monday, July 7, 1941: The sixteenth day

New prisoners were brought in, mostly people over sixty. Strange, they were not required to report on the First Sunday, and only a few days before some people were released.

We had now been in prison for nine days—no documents had been checked, none requested, none issued to us. I was surprised that we'd experienced none of the expected bureaucratic procedures.

Every day I noticed more Latvian auxiliary police around the prison.

Tuesday, July 8, 1941: The seventeenth day

When we returned from work, we weren't allowed to go to our cells. Instead, about a hundred of us had to form a column and were marched away.

Right from the start, I sensed a change for the worse in our guards, an extraordinary meanness. They rushed us to a lumberyard, where we had to pick up heavy pieces of timber, three persons per board. These were very heavy, and when we first started, I thought I wouldn't be able to carry them more than a hundred feet. Not only did we carry those heavy planks several kilometers, but we had to march fast, almost at a run. All the time the guards were hurrying us with curses and beatings. Several times I thought I was at the end of my endurance and would collapse, but eventually we crossed the partially damaged railway bridge over the Daugava and were at our destination. But our hope that now at last we could catch our breath disappeared fast; now our real torment began.

In my worst fears, I could not have conjured up the kind of hell in which I now found myself. We were on a slope. It was nighttime, and the area was lighted by floodlights illuminating some spots brightly while leaving other areas in semidarkness. There was the high, hysterical *rrrrrrrr* of power drills breaking up a wall of concrete and rocks, part of a fortress. Our job was to roll up the huge broken-off chunks to the top of the hill, again with no more than three men per rock. With great effort we inched those rocks up the hill, but the pieces kept sliding back, and all around us were what seemed like crazed Germans, hitting us without mercy and threatening us with shooting. And the rocks kept rolling back, and we pushed and pulled, while our tormentors, looking like demons in that strange light, struck us with whips and waved their guns in our faces, shouting, "Move faster, faster!"

All day we had worked unloading rail cars, then we carried the timbers, now this hell. Prisoners cried out as they were whipped, and next to me a man collapsed. As I turned to look at the prone figure on the ground, I was lashed on my back: "Move, you dirty dog!" And so it went on, the shouting, the cursing of the demons, and the muffled cries of the victims. I heard shots and I wondered, "Do they actually kill some people or just scare them?"

It was late at night when another group of Jewish prisoners replaced us, and we were, at last, marched back.

As we reached the prison, I saw another column returning from the Railroad Park adjacent to the prison yard. They too had worked very hard, digging huge ditches. When I reached my cell, someone told me that the freshly dug ditches in the park had been covered with chlorine. Everything seemed strange, disturbing. What could be the purpose of the chlorine?

Wednesday, July 9, 1941: The eighteenth day

As always, we were up early and waited to be marched out to the prison yard, but time passed, and there was no command to leave our cells.

After a while, we could hear something that sounded like the back-firing of trucks on the embankment highway. The traffic was always heavy there, but there couldn't be that much backfiring, and I was worried, we were all worried, knowing full well that something was very wrong. We soon realized that what we heard was the sound of rifle shots.

"Maybe there's a shooting range nearby, soldiers might be practicing," someone said hopefully.

"Those ditches they dug last night . . . and the chlorine . . ." the accountant said quietly. "But that can't be . . . ."

No one said anything for a while.

It was hard to believe that people were being shot, but I could find no other explanation. I kept hoping the shooting would stop and we'd be allowed to go to work, but it went on. A series of shots . . . a short interruption and again shots . . . and again . . . .

It wasn't long before we got confirmation of what we'd been suspecting all along. One of the men of a neighboring cell stuck his head in the doorway, and said, "They are killing Jews. From the washroom window someone saw people lined up in the yard. They are from the first floor."

There was little talk. We all sat quietly, overcome by shock. The morning dragged on, and the shooting continued hour after hour. The sound of people being moved from the lower floors came closer and louder, closer and louder. Around ten o'clock I could hear people being ordered out from cells of the first half of our hallway, and shortly afterward they were in our half. And then a German rushed in to our cell, shouting, "Everyone out, take along everything you have!"

We were marched down to the basement. As we passed through the corridor in single file, we were ordered to empty our pockets and throw everything we had on the piled up heaps of personal belongings of the people who had just passed before us. We walked between two long, knee-deep rows of wallets, documents, pictures, watches, trinkets worthless to anyone else. . . . I kept my handkerchief and threw away everything else including my Bar Mitzvah watch. We were then marched out into the yard, formed into groups of twenty, and ordered to stand at the end of a long column of men.

We were guarded by many Germans pointing their rifles at us. Every few minutes the people in front moved ahead, and then we did also. By now any small doubt, I might have had that not everyone was to be killed vanished completely. We are waiting in line to be executed, went through my mind again and again.

I could not yet see it, but I knew there was an iron gate on the other side of the building, opening into the small Railroad Park where the ditches were dug yesterday. The column of men—thousands of them— wound itself around the prison like a vast, coiling serpent, going first north to the corner, then west lengthwise, then back again south around the wall of the building. Eventually it must enter the park through that gate. Since our group had been housed at the end of the third floor, we were toward the tail of the serpent, only a few hundred men behind us. The multitude was silent. The only sounds we heard were the sharp reports of the rifle shots and the occasional threatening bark of a guard.

When we got to the corner and started to move west, I could see above us, on the embankment, German soldiers and their sweethearts looking down at the scene below as if we were in an amphitheater.

When they had first herded us down from our cells, we third-floor Jonaver gravitated together. I was with Shmulke Palec, Froike Milner and a few other old acquaintances. It seemed a little easier to die in the company of people one knew.

The tall drayman and volunteer fireman from my cell told me that he didn't drop his pocket watch on that pile; instead he hid it in his cap. He muttered defiantly, "If they kill me, at least the murderers won't get my watch." I wondered why he said "if."

The blue sky was almost clear, with only here and there a wisp of cloud. I looked up, and the thought hit me hard: I will never see the sky again . . . . I felt a great sadness.

It is said that, when a person faces death, his whole life flashes before him. But my thoughts were disjointed, disorderly; they tumbled through my mind rather like the flimsy clouds above, forming, changing shape, disappearing and reappearing . . . . Catching myself picking at a hangnail, I thought, How silly. In a few minutes it will make no difference at all . . . . And then: Is it possible—do the Germans really believe that the Jews set fire to the city—is that why they are killing us? No. They couldn't believe that.

I was following the movement of traffic on the embankment, and it occurred to me that many of the trucks were returning from the front line. I turned to Shmulke and whispered, "The Germans must be retreating. If only we could have lasted another day or two, we would have been liberated." Illogical assumptions kept going through my head.

We had always been under heavy guard at work, but now, *unreasonably*, I thought of that time as one of missed opportunities. If only I had run away . . . at the unloading of cars . . . even when we were in the water . . . I should have started to swim away real fast . . . if only . . .

But I didn't, and now I'm going to be killed.

But then the comforting thought: At least Ruvke is in town and alive, and Father, Mother, and Nehamah must be somewhere too. God, how thankful I am that they are not here with me. How could I have faced it, knowing that they have to die with me? They are alive. And I felt lucky for it.

It occurred to me that reality was often quite unlike what we expect it to be. People standing in line to be killed didn't look very different from those waiting to buy bread. Their faces, their eyes betray nothing of what is going on in their minds. People stand in line under the hot sun, they move ahead, then their time comes to die, and it is over.

The SS guard closest to us, usually only a few yards away, was of short stature and had a sullen face. Like the rest, he was pointing his rifle directly at us, as if daring us to make a move. Not that it didn't occur to us. One of our group muttered, "If we all jump a few of the guards, we might kill at least one before they kill us." But another man retorted, "Just think what the Germans would do to the women and children in town."

It was noon by then and getting very hot. After standing in the sun for hours, we were all sweating profusely. I was glad I did not throw away my handkerchief. At least I could wipe the sweat from my face and eyes.

The column advanced slowly—waiting, moving ahead every few minutes. From the moment we turned the corner and started advancing southward, I could see the iron gate ahead. I gazed at it—at the entrance to death . . . the end. As we got closer, I could see that, when the gate opened, a group of twenty passed through it, and the whole line moved ahead; then there would be rifle shots, clear and sharp, and in a few minutes, another group was swallowed up. The routine went on and on.

The few of us from Jonava were not really close friends at home;

the others were older than I. But now I felt a strong bond with each one, and they apparently with me. We embraced, kissed each other, and said good-bye in undertones. It was hard to speak. I tried to say something to Shmulke Palec but there was a lump in my throat, and uttering any sound was difficult. Again I thought, It is easier to die among friends.

I was struck by how quiet everyone was. There was no crying or wailing or hysteria. Just stillness. Stillness, shots and groups moving ahead . . .

That I should have to die now, I thought, and I have seen so little of life. . . .

Time passed. Finally there were only a few groups ahead of us. I could see now that some people were given shovels as they were about to pass the gate of death. Tension increased even more. I was intensely aware that I would be dead in a matter of minutes. I thought, What we are going through—if only it could be related to someone in the future. But there will be no one left to tell. The group ahead of us was given shovels and marched through the gate. We were next. The sky, the sun. I would never again be aware of it . . . . Shots. Yes, those who stood just here, a few feet away, were now dead. Next the gate will open for us.

Minutes ticked away . . . . Is it really taking them longer, I wondered, or does it only seem that way? More minutes passed. Then at last the gate opened.

A German and a Latvian came through, but instead of ordering us to enter, there were some discussions among our executioners. Then the unexpected happened. We were ordered to turn around and march back into the prison, followed by the rest of the serpent's tail. All told, a couple of hundred of us were still alive.

We were herded into several large cells and locked up. What could it mean? Everybody was as bewildered as I was. But there was little talk and no lessening of apprehension. This was not a reprieve, only a delay.

I was not surprised when, about five in the afternoon, we were ordered out, marched across the yard, and taken through the dreaded iron gate.

So this was the killing ground. A fence surrounded the small park, and ahead of us were ditches, freshly covered with yellowish ground. Obviously the pit graves. At one corner stood a cart full of still unburied bodies. We were divided into two groups. One group, including Shmulke Palec, was ordered to shovel more earth over the filled ditches and then run over them, stamping and packing down the bodies with their feet; our group was given shovels and ordered to dig fresh pits nearby.

So that was the reason for the delay. They had run out of ditches. We were digging our own graves. Later, probably, other Jews would be forced to run over us and pack us down with their feet.

Like drowning men grasping at straws, a few tried to save themselves. A middle-aged man tried to explain to the guard that he was a decorated German veteran of the last 1914—1918 war, and Shmulke Palec insisted he was actually a Russian prisoner of war, but it was all quite useless. Each of them received the same answer: "You are a Jew!" and a blow.

It was hard to dig in the stony ground with its entanglements of roots, but the Latvian guards forced us to work faster and faster, using their rifle butts or heavy clubs to rain blows over our heads and bodies. Our tormentors spoke and cursed mostly in Latvian, but that language is related to Lithuanian, so I had a vague idea of what they were saying. One or another of them jeered at us steadily. "Katiusha," a Russian popular song, was mentioned laughingly. "You don't feel like singing it now, do you?" (implying that the Jews were communist sympathizers).One guard, recognizing a Jew he had known, hit him until the man was covered with blood, the guard laughing and taunting him all the time. Another, his face set in a permanent snarl, like what one would imagine a murderer's face to be, was especially cruel. He hit people indiscriminately.

But those in charge who supervised the operation were German, and of them all, the one I dreaded most was actually a pleasant-faced young man. Blond, of slight build, dressed only in tan- colored shorts and sneakers, he was the picture of cheerfulness as he skipped around among us, whistling the popular song "Rosamunde" (the tune of "Roll out the Barrel"). But a heavy pistol was thrust in his belt, and every now and then he stopped next to someone who seemed to slow down in his digging, and in a rather benevolent tone of voice, observed, "Looks like you are too tired . . . ." and, aiming his pistol, shot him from behind through the head, continuing with his whistling after a moment's interruption. In this playful manner, he finished off quite a few prisoners.

He stopped not far from me, next to Froike Milner. Froike begged for his life, at the same time digging feverishly, as if to justify his existence.

Oddly enough, he left Froike alone and went on to mete out death to someone else who seemed to be slowing down.

Running and stamping on the graves was just as hard as digging, if not harder, because the people assigned to that task were also not allowed to stop for even a moment.

All this time, townspeople watched curiously from behind a wire fence.

When we finished digging the ditches, it was almost dark. We were ordered to form a column. Without thinking, I walked back a few feet and bent down to pick up the jacket I had taken off when I began digging. Immediately the guard with the murderous face started hitting me with his club. "You stupid Jew!" he bellowed. "You don't need a jacket anymore!"

Once more, we were led back into the prison but not to our previous cells. Instead we were directed to the basement. The cells were left unlocked, and we could move around through half of the hallway.

We all knew that this was our last night, and we would be shot the next morning. People were calm and talked quietly to each other—no hysterics, no lamentations. Again I was in a cell with my friend the accountant, his two brothers and their elderly father, who was brought to prison just the day before. They looked calm and composed, but my heart ached for them. How terrible to see your close ones die!

Those who were religious kept saying the evening prayers and repeating the Vidui, the prayer before death. I lay down on the floor. After the long day of intense dread while "waiting in line," and the terror at digging the pits, I now felt almost serene. I heard the soft murmur of the people praying. I kept thinking, Tomorrow morning, at daybreak, I will die. But the hours until then seemed like a great abundance of time— tomorrow was far ahead. . . . I was deeply grateful for these hours. . . . I will think everything through carefully, I told myself. I will review my life and try to understand things. . . . There was even something comforting about anticipating this large amount of time—a whole night—still available to me.

My reverie was suddenly interrupted by Shmulke. He whispered, "Shaike, I was just talking to a fellow from Utena—he has an idea about a hiding place. . . ."

Where could one hide in a prison cell? I was skeptical, even slightly annoyed at being torn from my thoughts. But I walked into the hallway to meet Haim Kuritzky, who was a few years older than I. His idea was to crawl into the apertures of the hallway, which were there for the purpose of metal heating stoves for the individual cells.

"These are the first places the guards will check," I objected. "And then they'll beat us before they shoot us."

"I guess you're right. . . " Haim admitted.

"But this room—no one seems to be here. . . ." We were standing next to an unlighted cell that looked unoccupied. "Let's have a look."

The room was crammed with odds and ends, and in the half-darkness we could make out a small pile of blankets and boxes in one corner.

"Maybe under the blankets . . . it's worth a try."

It wasn't very promising, but what could we lose? We decided to hide here and to get Froike Milner too.

As I returned to my cell for Froike, the accountant pushed a piece of *suchari* in my pocket, saying quietly, "It looks like you are planning something—it might come in handy. . . ." The chance for our plan to succeed was so remote that food seemed irrelevant, but I couldn't refuse his gesture. I thanked him, and we said our farewells.

The four of us slipped into the room, burrowed under the blankets, and hoped for the best. The chance of our not being discovered was very slim. There weren't many blankets above us, and any one of the prison guards could notice that the small pile had grown overnight into a small mountain, but still. . . .

We had just got settled in when we heard a man cough. He must have followed us in, wanting to hide too. He kept coughing. We whispered to him to get out, but we still heard him cough. "Listen," one of us said, "there is no chance for any of us as long as you're there!" The coughing went on for a while, but finally he must have left for it was quiet the rest of the night.

Thursday, July 10, 1941: The nineteenth day

As expected, there was commotion at daylight—people being driven from their cells. We were only a few feet away and could hear everything very clearly: the shouting of the guards . . . the beating . . . the screams . . . and only minutes later, shooting. . . . I knew our friends were now being killed at the pits we had dug yesterday. Then we heard the guards return. They were searching the cells; doors were opened and then slammed shut with the distinct *clang!* of an empty room. Some people were found and pulled out. (From under a bunk? There was nothing else in the cells.) We heard the outcries of pain as they were beaten. Then they started searching our room. . . .

I hardly dared breathe. The beating of my heart sounded to me like the firing of a machine gun. Boxes were turned over . . . something heavy was moved . . . they were inches from our heads. . . .

But they passed us by and left the room. We could hear the few who had tried to hide being driven out, then the shots. . . .

We could still hear guards in the hallway, and every once in a while one came into our room looking for something. When that happened, we froze. Once, while rummaging through the boxes, a guard actually stepped on me—on the blankets with which we were covered—but we were not discovered.

A few more hours passed. Shmulke whispered, "Of all the thousands, only we four are still alive."

"If they catch us now, we'll still have lived that extra time anyway,"Haim replied.

"Yes . . ."I agreed. "It's at least three hours."Every minute of life we could grasp onto was something gained, even if every second of it was filled with the extreme of dread and horror. The prospect of getting caught now seemed somewhat less frightening. If we were shot now, at least we'd have cheated death by a few hours. There was some satisfaction in that.

As more hours passed, we began to worry about what to do next. How were we to get out? We exchanged some of our ideas in whispers: If no new prisoners were brought in, could we get out of here at night?

But toward evening, we suddenly heard many voices in the hallway. "You hear?"Froike whispered. "I think they're speaking Yiddish. I'll go and see who they are."

Carefully, Froike slipped out from under our blankets and went to reconnoiter. After a short time he returned. The men were all Jewish, he said, had all been recently arrested and were being held here in the basement. We took for granted that they would all be killed in the morning. We remained in our hiding place for a second night. There was no way for us to escape.

Friday, July 11, 1941: The twentieth day

The morning passed quietly, and no shots were heard. This offered little relief. Obviously, sooner or later the new prisoners would be murdered too.

Like the day before, we heard guards come into our room several times to look for things. And then around midmorning, while we heard them rummaging around, there was sudden shouting— "Out! Get out!"The blankets were pulled away. One of us must have made a slight movement, and it must have been noticed. This is the end! flashed through my mind.

We jumped up. Facing us were two Latvian guards, each holding a heavy iron wrench. We just took off, running as if possessed, without thought or plan. The hallways were wide open. We ran from floor to floor, guards tearing after us, shouting, cursing. I lost sight of my friends but kept running like mad. Up and down the stairways I flew, through the hallways. . . . In front of me was a closed door with a nailed-on panel. I crashed through it with my shoulder and kept on.

In the end I was cornered in the basement. Haim and Froike were there already. The three of us were lined up at the wall, and two of the guards commenced beating us in deliberate fashion with heavy lengths of rope. The blows came down mostly on our backs and shoulders. The guards were cursing and shouting as they swung their ropes.

When they finally thrust us into a cell, we found out from the people there that the guards had been yelling at us in Latvian: "Why did you hide? Why did you run?"I realized then that they thought we were brought here last night; they were unaware that we were survivors of the massacre.

Shmulke was not with us when we were caught; he'd run up to an upper-floor cell, by now occupied by Russian POWs and had claimed to be one of them. Shortly afterward, they discovered he was Jewish and threw him back in with us.

My whole body ached from the beating, but some of my new cellmates had to endure much more. They had been wounded by German planes while trying to cross the Russian border, and the injuries had gone untended and were festering. One young man, part of whose hand had been blown off, kept moaning most of the time.

In the evening we were able to move around freely in the hallway, and I was surprised to meet more people from Jonava. Hershyankale Stein and Shmerke Namjot were both classmates of mine. Shmerke's brother Eli and his father, as well as Hershale Lukman and his uncle Manishewitz, were also here. They, and many others, had left Jonava either by truck or bicycle and had made it to the Soviet border pretty fast, but they had been prevented from crossing by Russian border guards. "If you are a friend, stay and fight the enemy,"they were told. If not, then we don't want you—there may be spies among you!"

Hershale, who was only fourteen, told me that while waiting at the border, they were constantly attacked by German planes; his parents were both killed, and his brother Shmerke was wounded and left at some hospital.

After waiting for days, exposed to the strafing and bombing of German planes, many turned back, only to end up here. (Eventually people were allowed to cross the border into Russia, but too late to save most Jewish refugees.)

Most of these newcomers didn't believe us when we told them of the slaughter of all the men.

We received no food all day.

Saturday, July 12, 1941: The twenty-first day

It was quiet again this morning. Was it possible that they would let us live? My body was covered with welts. The pain and the thought that they would probably shoot us at daybreak had kept me awake most of the night.

Some people thought we were spreading crazy rumors about the mass killings. Someone said, "I'm sure that solid, upstanding citizens are in no danger of death. It will be rough, yes, but killing? I cannot believe it."

We received only a little thin soup.

Sunday, July 13, 1941: The twenty-second day

In the afternoon ten men were sent to do some work outside the prison. Among the ten who left were some of my friends, Hershyankale Stein, Eli, Shmerke, and Froike Milner.

This evening we were all lined up and asked our professions. This had never happened before, and it gave us hope. I said I was a carpenter. All craftsmen were separated from white-collar workers and professionals and placed in separate cells.

The ten men taken to work earlier in the day did not return.

Monday, July 14, 1941: The twenty-third day

We woke up to loud voices—prisoners were being beaten, forced from their cells. Then the sound of shooting. Was this finally the end for all of us? At every minute we expected to hear our door being unlocked. But no. After a while, it became quiet. Our cell was one of those spared.

In the evening we were lined up again in the hallway and again questioned about our profession or trade. We took it for granted that having a trade was an advantage, so all of us from Jonava claimed to be carpenters or cabinetmakers—Jonava was famous for its furniture factories. Carpenters, shoemakers, locksmiths, whatever—each was assigned to a particular cell. In ours there were fifteen men, and on our door a sign was fastened: Carpenters. A list of our names was compiled by Magaram, the prisoner foreman in our room. It was said that he used to own a small factory and was well known in Daugavpils.

After the big massacre, I saw few Germans in our area of the prison. The Latvian collaborators seemed to be in full control.

Tuesday, July 15, 1941: The twenty-fourth day

We each received a small piece of bread and were still very hungry.
The ten men taken to work two days ago still did not come back.

Wednesday, July 16, 1941: The twenty-fifth day

More killing today. Same pattern. It was sheer agony to listen intently to the sounds of approaching guards. Will the steps stop at our door? They came closer and closer . . . they passed our door and stopped at the next one; the door was unlocked . . . shouting . . . later shots. The guards came back; more people were taken out . . . We sat terror-ridden, helpless, locked in the cell . . . .

New people were brought into the prison every day. Since Jews were kept in basement cells only, the shootings must be to make space for new arrivals.

In the killings so far, our cell had been skipped. At first I assumed it was because we were listed as carpenters, and the Germans needed craftsmen. But some artisans were killed, while the people wounded at the border and kept in a separate cell were still alive.

Thursday, July 17, 1941: The twenty-sixth day

A repeat performance. We sat and waited. The shouting of the guards and the screams of the victims was worse today and harder for us to bear.

While these early morning routines were taking place, we usually perched on the two benches in our cell, tensely waiting. Our cell was long and narrow—at one end the door to the dreaded hallway, at the other a barred and boarded-up window. Next to the window was a small table and along the side walls two benches. That was where we sat, listening with dread to the sounds, sharing the suffering of the victims outside. Something stronger than reason prompted us to sit as far from the hallway, and as close to the window, as possible—to separate ourselves from the death right there behind the door.

Today, Hershale Lukman and his uncle Manishewitz sat right next to the window. There was a tacit understanding that he, the youngest, was entitled to the farthest spot. Because the table at the window was so small, only the first few—two on a side—had it between them. Most of us sat facing each other with nothing in between. There was enough room on the benches for everyone, but instinctively we pushed our bodies as close to the window as possible, leaving half the benches empty. Every inch that we distanced ourselves from the hallway was important.

Noise, tumult in the hallway. . . . Locks were unlocked, people driven out. . . . Steps sounded as guards came closer to our cell . . . and then a key turned in our lock. . . . This was it. . . .

The door opened, and two Latvian guards, red-faced, inflamed by liquor and the excitement of the kill, appeared in the doorway, armed with heavy clubs. "Two people, get out!"

They shouted but no one moved. One second . . . two seconds . . . We were paralyzed. One guard turned on the two people closest to the door and hit them on the head. "Out!"he yelled, but they did not budge.

Finally the guards started striking the two victims with abandon, battering them insanely, chasing them out of the cell. The door was locked again, and we could hear them still being beaten outside. One of the prisoners was Israel Namjot, the other from Daugavpils.

A few minutes later, the door was unlocked again. The same two guards ordered: "Five men out!"Again no one moved. Again, indicating those closest to the door, they struck each one brutally: "You . . . you . . . you . . . you . . . you . . . "The five were forced out of the cell. The next time they come, I told myself, it will be me . . . .

But within seconds another Latvian, apparently in charge, burst into the cell and started talking to Magaram; they seemed to know each other. The official hurried out and within minutes brought back the five men.

"Another two were removed earlier,"Magaram said, but the Latvian answered matter-of-factly: "Too late."

After the official left, Magaram told us, "We won't be shot—I was promised. They need us as carpenters."

The five returned men were all badly beaten, one with a large gash on his forehead. The guards were using clubs roughly four or five feet long. But in the afternoon another guard came in and said in a friendly manner that we'd get bread that evening. I had noticed that, when there was a killing in the morning, some of the guards showed a bit of humanity in the afternoon.

Friday, July 18, 1941: The twenty-seventh day

Today we worked fixing up some wooden barracks several kilometers from town. This must be what the Nazis needed carpenters for. We constructed a fence around the compound and wooden bunks inside.

It was said that this will be a ghetto for the Jews. But how could they fit a whole population into a few flimsy buildings?

Monday, July 21, 1941: The thirtieth day

Among those shot today were the wounded, those who had been kept in a special cell without medical attention. Obviously the wounded people had been allowed to stay alive this long so that their agony could be prolonged. That was the rhyme and reason of the Nazis and their friends. Was there no limit to their barbarous cruelty?

My brother Ruvke had been on my mind all this time, and our separation was constantly before my eyes: the prison yard . . . the Nazi officer forcing him to leave . . . Ruvke's tear-stained face as he slowly walked toward the gate.

Tuesday, July 22, 1941

This morning, while waiting in the yard to go to work, I saw Shmulke, who'd been in a different cell lately. My smile of recognition enraged one of the guards. He struck me with his club several times, shouting, "You feel like laughing, do you—you goddam Jew? I will show you!"

We were still fixing up the barracks. We got very little food.

It was exactly one month since the Nazi invasion.

Wednesday, July 23, 1941

While at the barracks, we were suddenly ordered to stop work and were marched to a half-destroyed fortress, where we spent the rest of the day cleaning and making small repairs to some rooms. We saw Jews standing nearby and thought that this might be the ghetto. This was confirmed at the end of the day. The rooms we worked on would be occupied by the guards. We were told to stay with the other Jews. I could hardly believe it. We were in the Daugavpils Ghetto and did not have to go back to the prison! I had gotten out of there alive!

Thursday, July 24 1941

I'd been watching the people who entered the ghetto, hoping to find Ruvke among them. But many people were arriving, and he might have come in unnoticed. Or he might arrive tomorrow . . . or something might have happened to him . . . or . . . But suddenly:

"Shaike!"

"Ruvke!"

There, just a few feet away, stood my brother. We hugged and kissed each other, and there were tears of joy. We were together again!

He looked just fine and seemed to have grown, and changed in the time we had been separated. He'd managed pretty well, too. Together with Peisale, the boy who'd been with us in the basement, he had found work in a military field kitchen, and the German soldiers had been good to them. They liked Ruvke and fed him well. My brother had always been very engaging: tall for his age, slim, blond hair. When he smiled, he had dimples in his cheeks. Besides, he was very bright—nobody could help but like him.

Despite his good experience at work, Ruvke had also experienced an assortment of Nazi brutalities, but when I told him about my prison experience, about the "waiting in line,"he was shaken. "How could this have happened—to shoot everyone, every single person . . . ?"

Friday, July 25, 1941

An unbroken stream of humanity passed into the ghetto the entire day. An order had been posted that all Jews were to be inside the ghetto by tomorrow.

Our ghetto was actually the old fortress, on the "other"(western) side of the Daugava. It was several kilometers northwest of the city, next to the steel railroad bridge and the newly built wooden bridge. A massive semicircular structure of concrete and stone, it touched the river at one end, completed a half circle and reached the river again at the other end. The building was very long, more than half a kilometer, and actually consisted of a series of two-story structures, all connected but with separate entrances. The walls of the buildings were thick and had no windows facing out, except for a few in the hallways. The windows faced the interior yard. There was no other wall surrounding the fortress.

The half-moon-shaped area between the river and the building was elevated ground, about fifteen to twenty feet in height. And the space between that elevation and the building was in effect a narrow, submerged court running parallel to the whole length of the building. Latvian guards were stationed on the high ground, and we were confined to the building and court only. A wide moat, now dry, surrounded the building, and some guards were also stationed on that side.

The buildings were very old and decrepit, and because in the past the Latvian army had stationed cavalry units there, many of them had been used as stables. Large parts of the building had been heavily damaged, whether from shelling or fire, I didn't know. The galvanized iron roof, smashed in many places, looked like the top of a clumsily opened can of sardines. Least damaged was the area near the gate, which was occupied by the Latvian guards. A road passed by our ghetto.

Saturday, July 26, 1941

People poured into the ghetto, saying that any Jew caught outside after today would be shot. It was a sad picture—throngs of men, women, children, elderly and invalids. People carried what they could, some using small carts or even baby buggies.

Among them were many who, like us, tried to flee at the beginning of the war and were either turned back at the Russian border or overtaken by the attacking Germans.

Besides the Jews from Daugavpils, many were from the surrounding towns and from Lithuania. Those from the provinces had marched long distances, some for fifty kilometers or more. We heard gruesome stories of the suffering on the roads, how they had discarded most of their possessions as they went because of heat and exhaustion. I also heard of people shot by guards when they were unable to keep up.

The place was soon very crowded, the rooms filled up, and even the stables were all occupied. People were stretched out in the hallways and even in the yard, bewildered, their children crying. Many women had to cope with their children and aged parents all by themselves, for their men had been killed in the prison massacre.

I met quite a few from my hometown, among them Shmerke Lukman, Hershale's brother, who'd been wounded at the Russian border. His wounds were healed, but he limped. We used to be in the same grade at school, and were happy to see each other.

Some people, when I told them about what happened in prison, still didn't believe me. Many of the women whose husbands were arrested that First Sunday thought that their men were sent to some work camp and would return soon. By now everyone here had experienced or witnessed various brutal, violent acts. But the kind of methodical, wholesale slaughter I had witnessed seemed beyond what most people were able to believe.

Sunday, July 27, 1941

So far we received no food. Those from Daugavpils brought some provisions along with them, but we refugees had nothing. I was luckier than most. Ruvke brought me a piece of bread every day from work. We were also lucky to have a place to sleep; as one of the early arrivals, I was able to get us into a decent room on the second floor. I talk about "rooms."Actually, they were more like dormitories, at least forty people in each one.

This evening I heard people yelling out: "*Kipyatok*, they are giving *kipyatok*."What was that? I wondered (I understood some Russian but not this word.) I found that it meant "hot water"in Russian—we were getting hot water! People stood in line with excitement at the prospect of getting a cup of plain hot water.

Monday, July 28, 1941

I worked today. Some people, like my brother, had been working for German military units for some time and continued to do so after they were moved into the ghetto. They had permits that allowed them to leave in the morning and return at night. We were all eager to work, so as to get some food.

About my work: This morning a German airman took me along to help dig a gun emplacement. He was quite friendly to me, although he didn't say much. He was manning an antiaircraft gun, just a couple of hundred yards away, and I had to help him dig a dugout for it. It was there for the protection of the bridge in case of attack by Russian planes. He shared some of his food and later brought me back to the ghetto, promising to come back for me again the next day.

Being outside the ghetto, I was able to take a good look at the area. A huge railroad bridge spanned the river. A section of it had been blown up, but the damage must not have been too serious, for it was being used. Next to it was a wooden bridge. With surprise I recognized this as the same place where we went through that evening of torture. The heavy lumber we had carried was for the wooden bridge then being built, and the rocks we had to roll up the hill were from the wall of the fortress, blown up in order to extend the highway toward the new bridge.

We received food today—a piece of bread and watery soup.

Tuesday, July 29, 1941

The same airman came back for me. On the way to work, we walked through part of the ghetto yard, and he was shocked by what he saw. As we maneuvered our way through the masses of people, he muttered to me, "All of these thousands, all these babies, and I saw only one faucet for water!"And later, "If I describe it to my friends in Berlin, they won't believe me."

I had been so happy to have gotten out of the prison and to have found Ruvke that until now I hadn't quite noticed the great suffering all around me. Only now was I made fully conscious of it—and by this German soldier: people all over . . . the dirt . . . the infants crying for food . . . the mothers trying to care for their families under impossible conditions. And the lines! A line to get a little cold water, a line for a slice of bread, a line for soup, a line for the latrine.

The soldier kept me most of the day. There was little left for me to do, but he kept me with him anyway, gave me some food and even offered a cigarette. Without thinking I told him I didn't smoke—and was instantly sorry. I should have taken the cigarette and given it to someone in the ghetto who did smoke. Some people there were desperate for something to smoke.

Wednesday, July 30, 1941

The night before, another column was brought in from small towns and villages. The place was bursting at the seams. I heard that, according to the *komitet*, there were more than 14,000 people here.

Yes, there was a *komitet*, a committee of about a dozen inmates, mostly of the professions and well-known in the community, who were responsible for the internal affairs of the ghetto, such as keeping order, food distribution, "housing," and so on. This committee was led by Misha Mowshenzon, an engineer.

What had happened to the rest of our family? Here, too, we asked every Jonaver we met about them, but no one had seen them.

Friday, August 1, 1941

It was announced today that a brand new camp had been prepared not far from the ghetto, with more space and food. The people in the ghetto who were not residents of the city of Daugavpils were to be moved there. Jewish ghetto police went from room to room and informed the people of the decree. We were urged to take our belongings and form a column in the yard.

Slowly the column grew and grew until there were about 2,000 people. The whole process was conducted in a leisurely voluntary fashion, and I saw no one forced to leave. The order, of course, applied to us Lithuanian Jews too, but Ruvke and I did not go. Many other Lithuanians, including a few Jonaver, did join the column. After some hours they all moved out under the guard of a few Latvian auxiliaries. The column was long and contained many young men and women. After they left, I felt a sense of relief not to have joined them.

Saturday, August 2, 1941

There were rumors that the people who left yesterday for the new camp were all killed.

Sunday, August 3, 1941

The ghetto was rigid with shock. All the people from the provinces, led out two days ago, were taken to a wood around Pogulianka, a resort area, six kilometers northwest of here, and murdered. The details were described to several ghetto inmates by gentile friends. After marching some distance from the ghetto, the column was suddenly surrounded by many Germans and Latvian auxiliaries. The people were beaten and driven to previously prepared ditches, and then were butchered. It is said, that the Nazis did not even bother to shoot babies but hurled them into the ditches while still alive. Later, some of the populace, like vultures, threw themselves upon the belongings left by the victims.

I also found out today that as early as July 28, hundreds of old and sick people were removed from the ghetto—supposedly taken to a special camp, but, of course, never heard from again.

Even I, with my prison experience, had almost believed that there might be "another camp." It had seemed logical, this ghetto being so overcrowded. I had no illusions anymore.

Monday, August 4, 1941

Fear hung over the ghetto. People were eager to be picked for any kind of work, for regular employment seemed to provide some security. Every morning there were a lot of people at the gate, trying to catch the attention of the Germans who came to select workers. I'd had no luck so far.

For some time now, many new laws had been in force regarding our behavior. Among them, we were to wear yellow, six-pointed stars on front and back, never to walk on sidewalks, never to speak to gentiles, and on and on. But all that seemed not very important in comparison to the reality that any minute our lives might be snuffed out.

Tuesday, August 5, 1941

I got work for one day—unloading boxes from railroad cars next to a military field kitchen. After working hard the whole day, we received a little vegetable soup and were allowed to rest. The cook, very fat, was sprawling comfortably in his unbuttoned tunic, reading a newspaper. With a self-satisfied grin, he turned to us and said, "In two weeks Leningrad *kaput*, Russkies kaput!"

Wednesday, August 6, 1941

This evening terror reigned supreme.

Late in the afternoon, when most work commandos had returned, we were ordered to go down to the yard and form lines—no exceptions— everyone to stand together with his family. Assembled, our column stretched from one end of the ghetto to the other. We were surrounded by Latvian guards, who swarmed all over the place, and we waited a long time. Then word was passed along the column that a selection was in progress. Workers with *Schein*, certificates issued by German military units, and their families were separated from those who had no magic documents. Ruvke had a *Schein*, but would it be good enough? A group of three German SD (Security Service) officers was moving along the line, stopping at each family group, checking certificates, and sending people to one side or the other—here to live, there to die. As the uniformed, jackbooted officers approached closer, and closer, I could see the drama being played out in all the details. If a man possessed a certificate, his family would be allowed to go to the side of "life"— usually. But there was no certainty. Except for an occasional scream of anguish and a few pleading words, the performance went on in silence. The SD officer in charge was icily polite—if a Jew didn't move fast enough, the Latvian guards would do the beating. As the trio neared us, the tension mounted, our hearts pounded . . . And then they were before us.

"Are you working?"

"Yes," Ruvke answered, showing his certificate.

"Who is he?" The German pointed to me.

"My brother."

"Go there."

We passed, we were to live. The exchange took only seconds.

The SD men moved on. I felt a moment of cool relief, but the agony in the waiting column continued. I could see that it all depended on the officer. Certificate or no certificate, if he was annoyed with someone for some reason, that person was sent to his death.

The selection ended but, still we all had to wait. Our rooms were being searched, and it took them a long time. A fine rain started coming down steadily—an autumn kind of rain, although it was August. We, the reprieved ones, were separated from the column destined for death. They stood just a few yards away surrounded by guards. Meanwhile guards returned with people pulled from hiding places and, of course, beaten, and forced them to join the condemned line. Still we waited. The searching went on, and the rain came down.

Many of the condemned were women and children. About five or six young women with infants huddled next to a small wooden building. The babies, wet from the rain, hungry and tired, nevertheless must have sensed the terror of the moment; they didn't dare cry aloud, but whimpered quietly. And the mothers, holding them protectively in their arms or over their shoulders tried to comfort them, talking softly and rocking them. I was facing the woman standing closest to me, a young mother, dark- haired, probably in her twenties. Her light brown blouse was wet, and she was trying to shield her baby from the rain; at times she caressed its head tenderly. All I could think was: Can there be anything more terrible than this—to know that your baby will soon die with you? And meanwhile to have to wait in the rain . . . .

It was late evening when an announcement was made: A gun had been found in one of the rooms. The room's occupants were beaten and pushed in among the condemned. At last their column was ordered to move. The sad procession started out slowly, but took on speed as the guards, running around like enraged dogs, cursed and clubbed the people, forcing them to go faster.

When we were at last back in our rooms, I could sense a general feeling of relief. We were suddenly free of the incredible tensions of the past hours. Thousands of people had been taken away to die, but those of us who had no relatives among them could think only of our own close brush with death and our good fortune in surviving. We had made it. There was a touch of hysteria in the air. Whoever had food was eating. I could even hear a few high-pitched voices, bragging that they had managed to get through without a *Schein* and how they had fooled the SD.

Thursday, August 7, 1941

There was a change of mood over night. The first flush of excitement over surviving had worn off. Now we were sad, and dispirited. Between two and three thousand people were taken out yesterday. Now the ghetto was less crowded, but that only reminded me of our vanished fellow Jews—people who had been here yesterday and now were most likely dead.

There was a tremendous drive to find work. Like many others I was at the gate hoping to be picked for work. You had to be working on a regular basis to get a *Schein*, this stamped piece of paper seemed to offer one's only chance of not being taken out in the next *Aktion*. But again I had no luck.

Friday, August 8, 1941

The latest news: Two boys who were among those taken out in the last Aktion survived the massacre. There were no surprises in the story they told. The people were all shot, again in the Pogulianka woods, where ditches had already been prepared for them. The boys were only slightly wounded, but had been left for dead. Later they were able to crawl out of the ditch, which was covered only with a thin layer of soil. After hiding in the forest, they managed to get back to the ghetto; there was no place else for them to go to.

I heard someone say, "The ghetto is just a slaughterhouse." It was quite true. We expected another *Aktion* any day—*Aktion*, "procedure," we had learned, was the cynical Nazi euphemism for one of these weeding-outs.

Wednesday, August 13, 1941

Today I was with a group of men doing cleanup work in a synagogue. I'd heard about this synagogue before: On Saturday, June 28, just two days after the fall of Daugavpils—it was the day the candy-carrying woman was shot outside the basement where Ruvke and I had taken shelter—Jews were rounded up, brought here, and, after a day, were taken away and shot.

Today was a very hot day. Our job was to collect the material the murdered people had left behind, a shattering task. Scattered all over the synagogue were personal belongings and articles the victims had tried to hide away in the desperation of the moment, silent witnesses to their last hours. One person even found an American twenty-dollar bill. I wondered about those doomed people. Our own situation wasn't that much different—except that we knew what to expect.

It was evening by the time we got back to the ghetto, dejected and full of foreboding. I stopped at the small building, where the *Komitet* was located, because a noisy crowd had gathered at the doorway. People were begging for advice, clamoring for answers, and, I could hear Mowshenzon, the head of the *Komitet*, repeat several times, "I don't know any more than you do. A *Schein* is the only thing that can help."

Saturday, August 16, 1941

Bad news. The German unit for whom Ruvke and his friend had worked for almost six weeks was leaving for the front. Now neither one of us had regular work and no *Schein*.

Monday, August 18, 1941: The fifty-eighth day

Both of us were in the yard near the gate early in the morning, along with hundreds of men and women, all desperate for work. As soon as a German appeared, people ran up to him, vying for his attention, pleading for any kind of labor to get out of the ghetto. After a while, Ruvke was able to get some work for the day only—better than nothing.

The morning went by, and I was ready to give up. Just then, I noticed a soldier accompanied by Magaram, whom I had known from the prison, walking in my direction. Workers were being selected, and Magaram immediately included me in his list of construction workers.

Within a few minutes our group of twelve men was ready, and we left for our new job in the post office. This was the same place where we had buried those dead Red Army soldiers on June 29. Now we were to remodel the badly damaged garage. There were among us a real carpenter and locksmith, and a few who were handy with tools, but most of us were not really skilled. Of course, we had to pretend that we were all experienced craftsmen.

At noon we received half a pail of hot soup from the German kitchen and, later in the day, a fair-sized portion of bread. Best of all, we got certificates stating that we were employed by this unit, that our work was important and that we must report daily!

We left for home in a very happy mood, only to find out from Jews coming in the opposite direction that an *Aktion* was in progress. They hoped to delay their return to the ghetto long enough to avoid the new purge, but we hastened on back. Each of us had somebody close to him, and with the new *Schein* in our possession, our arrival on time would mean the difference between life and death for them. Naturally I was thinking of Ruvke.

I came not a minute too early. The *Aktion* was in full swing, and the selection going on, but the SD officer hadn't quite reached my brother yet. I located him just in time, and we passed. In general, this *Aktion* was conducted in the same manner as the previous one—people were separated to the right and to the left. But the sieve had smaller holes now, and it was harder to fall through to safety. Older people and parents of workers had less chance to pass the selection.

Tuesday, August 19, 1941

"Oh, God, again?" Our group was just returning from work, and as we entered the ghetto, we were faced with the by-now-familiar horror—an *Aktion* in progress. Didn't they get enough victims yesterday?

People were standing in long lines, and I could see that some were already penned up in an enclosed area. Ruvke. I ran to the room, but he was not there. I had to join the line. I looked for him throughout the column but could not find him. Someone said that the *Aktion* had started much earlier than yesterday's, about three o'clock, and that people who weren't working had already been taken away. I hoped desperately that Ruvke had found work after I'd left this morning and that he hadn't returned yet.

Not much time to think. As the selection went on, a girl I had seen before but knew only slightly, ran over to me, begging me to save her by claiming her as my wife. I was seventeen, she was about my age, and if we were suspected of lying, it would be the end for us both. But I agreed. She was a refugee from Poland who had come to Lithuania in 1939, had escaped from Lithuania, and was now caught in Daugavpils. She was dark-haired and had huge dark eyes.

Many people had no certificates at all. But even the best certificate was no guarantee of safety. The decision of the SD officer, always final, was often arbitrary as well. A direct stare interpreted as impudence, could be enough to land one on the side of the doomed. Often someone begging for the rest of his family was told: "You want to stay together? Good, go to that side." And the whole family was pushed to the column of the condemned. We were all of us, the whole column, pervaded by a dread that one could almost touch.

Like a small frightened bird, the girl stood close to me, trembling. The group of SD officers was like Death in Person advancing toward us. Left, right, left, right . . . closer and closer . . . And suddenly the Angel of Death was looming over me.

"*Schein!*"

I handed over the certificate without looking at him directly.

"What do you do?"

"I am a carpenter."

"Who is she?" He pointed to the girl.

"My wife."

He hesitated for a fraction, then waved us over to the side of life.

As soon as we were allowed to leave, I ran to my room. My brother was not there. I kept inventing plausible explanations: He might have returned from work later and could be standing at the other end of the yard. Any minute he might pop in. Time passed. I became more anxious. I tried to hold on to the slim hope that Ruvke might have been detained at work. After all, I was once or twice forced to do extra work after a full day's labor.

All around were people who felt they had just escaped death. In the room there was the familiar release of tension. People were eating. Realizing that I myself was chewing on a piece of bread, I stopped with a shudder. How could I? Ruvke was no longer here. I sat in my corner and repeated to myself, My God, they took Ruvke away . . . they took Ruvke away . . . . My mind was numb with grief. He was gone, I would never see him again.

Wednesday, August 20, 1941

When our group formed to go to work, three men were missing. Although we'd all had the same certificates, they didn't make it last night. They all had families, too. Magaram chose three replacements.

There was a deep sadness in the ghetto. In the last two days how many people were taken away? Who could count? Belongings and empty spaces were scattered here and there, but I heard no wailing. For family members, the pain was felt inside. In any case, it was only a question of time before we'd all join them . . . .

Thursday, August 21, 1941

This evening Haim Kuritzky and Shmulke Palec, the two friends with whom I hid in prison, came to see me. Haim handed me a 100-ruble note and said:

"Ruvke asked me to give it to you."

I grabbed at him.

"What do you mean? When did you see him?"

"The day of the *Aktion*, in the morning," Haim explained. "We were all at the gate hoping to get work. Ruvke was picked for a work commando, and just as they were leaving, he pushed the money into my hand and said, 'In case of something, give this to my brother.' That's all I know."

My poor brother. I just couldn't understand it. Had he had some kind of premonition of what was to come? How could he have guessed? We'd never had *Aktionen* on two consecutive days. And yet he was worrying about me!

Shmulke, with a good job in town, had had no trouble passing the selection, but Haim was not working; he'd lost his mother and just barely made it himself. On Monday he was with a group of about thirty people who were saved by two German soldiers. Aware of the impending *Aktion*, the soldiers pretended they needed the Jews for work and kept them until the danger had passed. The next day he was saved by a young woman who claimed him as her brother.

Saturday, August 23, 1941

Rumors about the latest double *Aktion*: On Tuesday, while being led to be shot, a large group of young people managed to escape and were expected in the ghetto. I knew it was probably untrue, but maybe—just maybe. But if escape attempts were made, my brother would be among the first to try. I had a glimmer of hope.

As in the previous *Aktionen*, the hospital patients were not liquidated. On the other hand, people consigned some weeks before to help farmers with the harvest were all returned on Tuesday, the day of the *Aktion*, and taken away with the rest of the condemned.

Tuesday, August 26, 1941

Shmerke Namjot was here in the ghetto! He was one of the ten men taken for work from the prison six weeks before and not heard of again till now. This is what he told me: They were taken from prison to a cemetery—a real cemetery—and ordered to dig graves. After they buried ten German soldiers who had died of wounds, the German in charge said: "Now it's your turn—you'll pay for their deaths." When Hershyankale Stein started begging for his life, explaining that he was not really Jewish but a Karaite (a small sect who circumcise their males), Shmerke and some of the others began to run. The guards opened fire, and Shmerke was hit, but he kept running and escaped. Severely wounded, he reached a hospital, and remained there until his wounds healed. Being circumcised, I didn't know how he'd managed to conceal the fact that he was Jewish. Shmerke said that one other man, also wounded, was able to get away too. The others were all killed, including Hershyankale, Shmerke's brother Eli, and Froike who had hidden with us in prison.

Nothing more was heard about the supposed escape from the last massacre—I was giving up hope of ever seeing Ruvke. Of course, my own days were probably numbered as well.

There's been talk for some time that the killing of Jews is going on throughout all of Latvia and Lithuania. I imagine that the Jews of the other German occupied countries must also be facing the same fate.

Thursday, August 28, 1941

Our work at the post office consisted of rebuilding the garage. We mixed cement with gravel and poured the concrete; we put up timber supports, repaired ceilings, and made all the other necessary repairs. A German corporal, Goerbel, was in charge, responsible for all necessary repairs, and had complete authority over us. We promptly fulfilled his every wish. He was not especially fond of Jews, but we were "his Jews," so he felt a certain sense of proprietorship and treated us fairly well.

Month of September 1941

Magaram was more or less in charge of our work group. He was competent at every task, in general a fair person, and attempted to help us all whenever he could. Corporal Goerbel trusted him and talked to him a lot. Before the war Goerbel had attended an engineering school, but never finished. In the army, he was only a corporal but now he had an opportunity to do pretty much as he pleased. I could tell he was enjoying his situation. He had a dozen people under his complete control, eager to satisfy his every whim. But we had it nice, too. We got some food at work, while people in the ghetto were starving.

One day Goerbel drove us by truck to the forest to get timber needed for our construction. We spent the whole day there. Although only twenty or thirty kilometers away, it seemed like a different world, so calm and serene among the trees. We cut and trimmed small trees and loaded them on the truck. While we worked, Goerbel and a friend, another German soldier, spent the time at a farmer's house, eating and drinking. We could hear merry sounds from the house, including the laughter of women. He didn't bother us at all, and even let us go to the neighboring farmers to buy food, after first telling a farmer to feed us. The rubles we had weren't worth much—the official rate of exchange was ten rubles to one Ostmark—still, we were able to purchase food we never got in the ghetto or from Germans. It was pleasant to have the whole day in the country. For a while, the ghetto seemed farther away.

A few weeks had passed since the last *Aktion*, and some people were getting slightly optimistic. After all, most of us were working, performing useful tasks. We kept hearing a variety of rumors to justify both the optimists and pessimists.

I found a few Jewish books, left by people who had been taken away. I put them under my cot. I was amazed that, at the time of banishment to the ghetto, when people could bring along only a very limited amount of belongings, some still insisted on bringing their books.

Manishewitz gave me a handsome pair of light gray breeches that had belonged to Hershyankale Stein. I could remember Hershyankale dressed in them with his high leather boots and Betar uniform—the militant Zionist organization. For a short time I had belonged to it too. I could close my eyes and still see a double line of Betarim on parade, each one standing tall and proud. Were any of them still alive?

Besides me, there were still five people in the ghetto from my hometown. I saw them quite often. What happened to my other friends from home? I wondered about Leib. I last saw him on the highway, riding on the fire engine. He must have made it to Russia. But my parents, Nehamah—I had little hope for them. With what the Nazis had been doing to Jews here, what chance could they have had in Lithuania? Still, there was always a possibility; maybe by some miracle they had managed to get a ride on the highway.

We were, of course, forbidden to read newspapers or listen to the radio, but news filtered through to the ghetto. We heard that Leningrad was surrounded by the German Army, and, that the city might fall any day. Also, down in the Ukraine, the important city of Kiev had been captured by the Germans. We knew they were advancing deeper and deeper into Russia. But for some time now, I'd been hearing the name "Velikie Luki," a Soviet city about 250 kilometers away. A big battle was being fought there, and the Russians were apparently putting up a good fight. I was still convinced that the Germans couldn't win the war. Russia was so huge; surely in the end the Nazis would be defeated. But when? Next week we might all be dead. There were still about 6,000-7000 people in the ghetto.

Every week or so we made a trip to the forest to get logs, and we always looked forward to it. It gave us a chance to acquire food from farmers, and being in the country was always a treat. One time, though, an unpleasant incident occurred. As usual, we were cutting down trees, while Goerber and his buddy were enjoying themselves at the farm some distance away. We heard the sound of shots and assumed they'd had quite a lot to drink and were target-practicing. Suddenly Goerber's friend ran over to where we were and ordered us to follow. The problem became apparent in a few minutes: Smoke was pouring out of the barn next to the house. The Germans had apparently been shooting into the wall of the barn, and the hay inside had caught fire. Now they were in a panic. As the smoke increased, Goerbel yelled to us: "Fast, fast, remove all the hay! If we don't get the fire out, I'll shoot you and say you Jews set it!" We worked feverishly. Some of us emptied the barn, while others brought pails of water. Finally, we put out the fire

I'd been working at the post office for over a month. I wondered, how long it would go on; few repairs were left to be made. The past few days we'd been moving furniture, and a few of our people had built an elaborate rabbit hutch for Goerbel. He, too, was trying to stretch things out. It was quite clear that he'd like us to continue on with him, but eventually it would have to end. Meanwhile we still received food every day and continued making trips to the country quite often.

Tuesday, September 30, 1941

Tonight was Yom Kippur. Shmerke Namjot and I went to Kol Nidre services in one of the blocks. The room was packed with people praying devoutly, some crying. On Yom Kippur eve, as a child, I'd always experienced a sense of awe unlike any other time. But I hadn't been observant the past few years and had little faith right now.

How could one be inspired with religious belief—Ruvke was dead, most likely my parents and sister were too, and any day now we would all die, too. I thought of the Aktion of early August, the mothers huddling in the rain with their babies waiting to be taken to the pits. Surely, if one had faith, one had to believe that there was some reason for all this to happen. But no one in the world could possibly convince me that there was some divine purpose for what was being done to us. And as I looked at the people swaying back and forth in the fervor of their blind faith, I felt like an outsider. I left shortly after.

Month of October 1941

We knew it was coming, yet we couldn't help feeling bad. This was our last day of work at the post office. Everyone except Magaram and one other man was told not to return tomorrow. Goerber would probably hang on to the two men as long as he could.

These last days I had smuggled a lot of potatoes into the ghetto, which I had bought from farmers on our trips to the country. At least I would not starve for a while yet.

Without work, I was faced with the dark, miserable surroundings all day long. The weather was cloudy and rainy, night came much too soon. No electricity. In some blocks our people ingeniously improvised kerosene lamps, "organizing" kerosene from God knows where. But it was a gloomy place, and people were starving. I felt lucky to have my potatoes, and I baked some every day; it helped a lot. Above all else, there was the constant fear that at any moment the ax would drop on our necks. In our bitterness we criticized our so-called leaders, blaming our komitet and the Jewish ghetto police. They got better jobs or extra food for their friends and relatives.

The last couple of days I'd been reading one of the books I had found earlier, called *The Weavers of Kolomyya*. It's about Jewish workers in the south of Poland, their struggle with the bosses, and a bitter strike that goes on for many months. I got quite engrossed in their plight. But the present was never too far from my mind, and now and then it flashed through my head: God, how insignificant was their plight in comparison to what we're experiencing right now.

I was getting to know more people in my block, and talked often to two men, probably in their twenties, Bentzke Kotzin and David Weksler, both from Panevezys, Lithuania. Bentzke was sharp-witted and had a shrewd look in his eyes. Weksler was older, a violinist. In the ghetto he gave haircuts, for which he sometimes got a little food. Both were smart and worldly-wise.

There was a lot of talk of a small town, Braslav, in White Russia, about fifty kilometers from here. They had never had an *Aktion* there, no Jews were killed. That was the story. Shmulke told me he had heard that some Jews even had their own cows.

I'd been trying to get regular work for the past couple of weeks, but instead wound up with an occasional day's work, which was usually hard labor with no chance of a work certificate. At least I still had potatoes to eat. Last time I fell into the so- called lion's den. In the morning waiting to be picked for work, a group of us were marched away to the SD Headquarters. These were the people who conducted the

Aktionen in ghetto—no telling what they might do to us. In fact, it was quite bad.

Our work consisted of removing a mound of earth, shoveling it into wheelbarrows, and rolling it away to dump in a different spot. Several of the SD kept hurrying us ("Schneller . . . schneller . . . ") with curses, foul language, and threats of shooting us. During the whole day we could not stop to catch our breath and, of course, got nothing to eat. At last the mound was all gone, but since it was still daylight, they made us remove ground from one pile to another and then back again until it got dark. I found out that four Jews, two men and two women, worked regularly for the SD as handymen and charwomen. In the perverse way these Nazis had, they admired and even liked these Jews. I was told they made remarks like "Don't worry, you'll be the very last ones to be shot," followed by a hearty laugh.

One man, captured on the outside, was being held in the ghetto "jail" (a small, one-room wooden structure, in the middle of the yard). I got a glimpse of him through the small barred window. He had a reddish beard and looked very sad. There were all kinds of rumors about him. Some said he was a Jewish Red Army man, who had escaped from a POW camp.

Next day Haim Kuritzky came with surprising news. The "bearded man" was a first cousin of his, Max Kuritzky, from the town of Anyksciai in Lithuania. A few days later, he was released from jail, and I heard from Haim that this cousin of his had been wounded before and that a bullet was removed from his wrist. This was done at our hospital, but now he was in a barracks like every one else and was starving. When I got to the fellow's room with four cooked potatoes, I found him asleep. I left the potatoes on a bench next to his bunk, asking a neighbor to give them to him when he woke up.

There's been more and more talk about Braslav. Bentzke Kotzin told me that word was received from someone who had escaped there last week. It was true; Jews were not being shot, and in comparison to Daugavpils the situation was very good. Some peasants arrived regularly from there and usually stopped close to a certain German unit in town, where Jews were working. For money or valuables, they were ready to take anyone back to Braslav. I had neither money nor valuables. I talked about it with Shmerke Namjot, who was very eager to run away. Two days later, I heard from Manishewitz that both Smerke and his cousin had escaped to Braslav.

I saw Max Kuritzky. He was very grateful for the potatoes. He couldn't quite get over the fact that I'd brought him food, although I had so little myself and didn't even know him. With his strong face and erect bearing, he looked very different from the sad man with the beard whom I first saw through the jail window. He was a few years older than I, with brown wavy hair and dark eyes.

He told me a little of his experiences before his arrival in Daugavpils. The Jews were being killed in all the Lithuanian towns the same as here, he said. In his hometown, Anyksciai, he had run away from certain death many times. In the end, he and a group of men were taken by the Lithuanian auxiliaries to a previously prepared pit and machine-gunned. He was left for dead but was only wounded. In the darkness he pulled himself out from among the dead bodies and ran away. With the help of a gentile girl, he'd been hiding out in the vicinity until his wounds healed and then had headed in the direction of the front line. He spent a couple of months wandering through forests and fields until he was caught around Daugavpils by German soldiers. At first they took him for a Russian spy and were going to shoot him, but in the last minute determined that he was a Jew and brought him to the ghetto.

We heard that the German army was marching deeper and deeper into Russia. Kharkov, Odessa, and almost all of Crimea had fallen. Leningrad had been surrounded for more than a month, barely holding out. But our "military experts" in the ghetto didn't give up hope. I heard someone say, "The next thirty days will be decisive, one way or the other." But the favorite saying, one I had heard repeated by several people and usually with a knowing smile, was, "The Russians have a new general, General Winter." No one really knows anything. It was true, though, that as winter approached, we were more hopeful of a German reversal. Everyone remembered what had happened to Napoleon in 1812 and never got tired of reminding each other of the well-known facts: how the French cut through Russia and they reached Moscow only to be done in by the Russian winter and the perseverance of the Russian people. Back home I'd spent many an evening engrossed in Tolstoy's War and Peace.

I had run out of potatoes and was always hungry. Once in a while, Shmulke helped out. Last time, watching me eat the piece of bread he'd just given me, he remarked, "You eat it as if it were the tastiest confection." I chewed it slowly, carefully, savoring every bite and making sure that no crumb was lost.

Shmulke hoped to get a Red Schein, something new. Actually it is a pink card issued to those who have regular work, confirming that they are engaged in useful labor. These certificates were different from the earlier *Scheine*. They were uniform for all the work commandos, and all certificates issued previously were void. It gave a feeling of security to the people who got one, but made those who could not get work even more insecure and helpless. I said to Shmulke, "Whatever happens, we have already lived three and a half extra months." We often referred to that day, July 10, when we were supposed to have been shot—the date had become a point of reference for us. We felt that if we were to die now, at least we had cheated death of that extra amount of time. There was comfort in that.

It was the end of October. Ten weeks had passed without an Aktion, but we had not relaxed. As always, plenty of rumors were flying around, some encouraging ("Electricity will be installed"), some frightening ("The Latvians are pressing the Germans for permission to kill all the Jews.") Any little scrap of good news was clutched at—people were so eager to believe that we had a chance to survive.

Lately, in the evening, we sometimes played cards, usually twenty-one. It helped to relieve the tension that we always felt.

Wednesday, November 5, 1941

Nothing unusual most of the day. Typical fall weather—chilly, cloudy, with the threat of rain. It was quiet during the day, but it would soon be dark, and then the ghetto would become alive as the work commandos returned from the city.

I was sitting with David Weksler on his cot, talking about the latest events and trying to interpret their meaning. A few days ago there had been another order that all valuables—gold, silver, diamonds, furs— were to be turned over to the authorities. There had been orders like that before; I couldn't imagine there being much of value left in the ghetto. More disturbing was the new rule about providing each worker with a Red *Schein*; it effectively separated the workers from nonworkers, and the meaning of it was clear enough. Then, there was a new development: Some people were being *kaserniert* ("barracked"); certain German units had *"their* Jews," people working for them, billeted on their own premises. These people were lucky, they didn't have to stay in the ghetto.

"If only I had the money,' Weksler said, "I'd escape to Braslav right now!"

We all had a very strong urge to flee, but I felt there was another side to this:

"Life in Braslav may be all right now, but sooner or later, they'll kill the Jews there too. If only there was a way to get to the front line and cross it . . . " But I knew this was just a dream. The fighting was taking place hundreds of kilometers away. "Daugavpils is doomed," Weksler insisted. "We have no chance here at all."

"That's true," I had to admit. "And if I had the money, I'd escape too. Still, Braslav is probably no safer than Daugavpils."

Abruptly our conversation was interrupted as Bentzke Kotzin and another fellow rushed in from the outside.

"Did you hear what's happening?" And he answered his own question: "A fence is being built across the yard. People with red certificates will be on one side and all the rest on the other. Listen . . ."

The staccato sound of nails hammered into wood could be heard distinctly, and in my mind I could see a coffin being nailed together, a coffin for me. We knew that it meant the end for those without certificates, and none of us four had one.

"Let's go," Bentzke said.

Sometime ago he'd told me he had a plan and that I should stick with him in case of an emergency. Now we all followed him to a spot where there was an unused, nailed-up wooden gate in the outer wall. I could see that some boards were loose, and I felt some hope. We hardly ever saw guards on this side of the ghetto, because the building here was built solid with no windows. Since the moat was dry, we should be able to squeeze through the opening, get across the moat, and escape. But like the rest, I looked through a crack, and what I saw sent a cold shiver through me: guards were stationed on the road at short intervals. We were completely surrounded and trapped.

We turned back. It was now completely dark and starting to snow large wet flakes. The workers had been returning from the city, and the yard was crowded with people milling around in agitation and fear. The fence was nearing completion, symbolizing our approaching doom, like a scaffold for a man sentenced to die.

I noticed Bentzke was hanging back. Pretty soon the other two fellows were gone. Bentzke started walking very fast. I asked him if he knew of a *molina* (hiding place), but he just mumbled. He must have something in mind; it was now my only hope, and I made sure not to lose him in the crowd. Pretty soon he slipped into a doorway and emerged in a few minutes carrying a small loaf of bread under his arm. Again we walked fast. He made another stop and came out with a fellow I'd never met before, both walking briskly through the throng. I followed close behind. We walked up a stairway and were on the landing. To the right and left were doors to rooms, and facing us was a window with broken windowpanes. We waited awhile. As soon as there were no other people around, Bentzke leaped through the window; I was right behind, and the other fellow followed me. We landed on a tin roof. Quickly Bentzke removed a loose section, and we slid in one after another, covering the opening again from the inside with the same piece of tin.

Complete darkness. But I knew we were in some kind of loft. I crawled after Bentzke until he stopped; then we all lay down close to each other. In the cold, we tried to gain a little heat from the closeness of our bodies. We were all dressed lightly; I had only a jacket on.

Later that night, there was a slight disturbance, someone getting in through the hole. Then a heated discussion in muted tones between two women about a child they were trying to save. I couldn't make out the details. After a while it was quiet.

Thursday, November 6, 1941

The two women left before daylight, and we never saw them at all. We could hear the voices of people passing on the landing just outside, and therefore knew the expected *Aktion* had not started yet.

Later in the morning we decided to leave our hiding place in order to get warmer clothing and, if possible, food. As we got out or in, we had to be very careful not to be noticed by anyone, for the landing was used by many people.

Although the fence was in place, people could still move around from one end of the ghetto to the other. I could see quite a few Latvian police or auxiliaries inside the ghetto yard—they usually stayed outside.

The next day, November 7, was a big Soviet holiday, the anniversary of the Bolshevik Revolution; whatever the Nazis were preparing for us must be their way of "celebrating" that day. I could see that people were aware of what was to come but could do nothing about it. It was painful to witness total helplessness.

We got a little food and some clothing and went back to our *molina*. Bentzke had told two friends, who had certificates, where to find us. They were to let us know when it was safe to emerge.

This hiding place—it really was not a bad one—was located in the space between the roof and ceiling of a small building that extended toward the moat. It was lower than the main building and when we slid out through the broken window, we had to jump down about three or four feet to the roof. The place, a sort of attic, was about twenty to thirty feet long and had no opening at all. The piece of tin was loosened up purposely and was the only entrance.

Bentzke Kotzin's buddy, the third member of our group, was Borekh Fixer. He was in his early twenties and seemed to be a resourceful kind of person. Even though I barged in, not quite invited, I was treated as an equal by both of these older fellows.

Friday, November 7, 1941

Apparently no change yet outside. We could still hear normal sounds on the landing; we decided to go back out and see what was happening.

Everything seemed be the same as yesterday; the ghetto was surrounded, and Latvians were in the yard. Snow mixed with rain was coming down and it was wet and dismal. Our hiding place was in the part of the ghetto assigned to those without certificates. I knew what the others were going through, living since Wednesday night with terrible certainty. As time passed, the quiet tension increased and the waiting continued.

As I walked, a Latvian auxiliary approached me from the opposite direction. When he came close, he looked at me in a strange way. Did he see me the way one sees a calf ready for slaughter?

We spent very little time out in the yard and wanted to rush back to our hiding place, certain that the ax would fall any minute. We passed an open doorway, and Bentzke saw someone he knew. We all walked into the room. In a corner I noticed a young woman with two little children. She was very attractive, dark curly hair, dark eyes, full red lips, and a sensuous figure. Even now, her whole bearing exuded a sense of vitality.

Realizing we had some scheme in mind, she was glad for us. "I have no chance," she said, gazing at her babies. "But you . . . do what you can . . . life is so wonderful!"

We spent only about an hour outside; it was a relief to be back in the *molina*.

I kept thinking of the thousands of people waiting, waiting, waiting. We could hear them moving around, going in and out of the rooms. I knew that some, especially those with children were sitting in their rooms; others were milling around the yard continuously, as if they might still find a way out. In my mind I could see the Latvians roaming around the ghetto, and I thought of the look on the face of that Latvian I'd met in the yard. That kind of cruelty—to give every indication to people that they are going to be murdered and then hour after hour, for days, do nothing, just watch them endure the waiting—that seemed worse than murder.

The day passed without incident. We spent a lot of time telling each other our experiences and how we each had lost our families. When I talked about the separation from my parents, Borekh Fixer wanted to know more details. I described Father's appearance—so distinctive with his fine beard and walking stick (hardly anyone had been using a walking stick in recent years). "I saw him on the way to the Russian border," Borekh assured me. "And they could have gotten through." I doubted very much that he'd seen Father, but it was kind of him to try making me feel better.

Saturday, November 8, 1941

We were awakened by a commotion outside and then the angry shouts in Latvian: "*Arah, Arah*! (Out . . . Outside!)." The inevitable was happening.

The din outside increased, the sounds vividly describing the events to us: the Latvians surge into the rooms, reeking of liquor and waving clubs. . . . Yelling, cursing, they hit the people, most of whom were women and children. . . . The panic . . . the stampede down the stairs . . . babies wailing . . . mothers frantically trying not to become separated from their children. . . .

I had that familiar, terrifying feeling: Only a few yards and a piece of tin separated me from the ultimate horror outside.

Slowly the noise subsided. I could hear a few shots, and after a while there was complete silence. We heard no sound the rest of the day. We wondered why our friends did not come to give us the all-clear signal. Wasn't the danger over yet? Or had everybody been killed? The total silence was unnerving.

Sunday, November 9, 1941

Outside it was sunny, but inside it was bitterly cold. We dared not move around for fear of giving ourselves away. We wondered what to do next.

Suddenly we heard the distinct sound of someone walking over tin. What we saw through the cracks struck terror in us. About half a dozen Latvian guards, spread out over the whole width of the roof, were walking toward us, checking for people who might have hidden under the loose and crumpled sections. They approached our small building. We knew they could easily notice the loose piece of tin. Their loud, jocular voices grew more distinct, and the sound that their steps made on the metal roof seemed terribly loud. Then they were on our roof, walking directly over our heads. And then they passed. We began to breathe again. Slowly the sound of their walking and of their voices faded.

There was no sound of anything at all the rest of the day.

We considered the possibility that the whole ghetto had been liquidated. Should we try to escape by climbing down from the other side of the building and crossing the moat? If no Jews were left, there should be no guards left either. We decided to wait until tomorrow.

Nothing to eat all day.

Monday, November 10, 1941

Early in the morning we got the all-clear signal from one of the friends and climbed out of our *molina*.

The scene before us was lonely and sad. It was said that 4,000 people or more were killed. Most of the ghetto was now empty, and the survivors, a little over a thousand, were all living in one corner far from the gate and from where we had hidden. The place was just a shadow of what it had been only a few days ago, and the people too moved around like shadows, keeping even their voices low when talking.

From our friends we found out that the *Aktion* started Friday, on the anniversary of the Bolshevik Revolution, and continued for three days.

Already on Friday afternoon, a great many German SD and Latvian auxiliaries had appeared in the ghetto and had taken away many people. The area where we had hidden was not yet affected. On Saturday, the *Aktion* started early in the morning. None of the workers was allowed to leave the ghetto, and the rooms were thoroughly searched. Only people with red certificates and their families were allowed to remain; the rest were taken away. On Sunday, all those still alive were assembled. Workers were ordered to go to their working places. They felt quite confident, because their wives had also been furnished with certificates, but when they returned later, their wives and children had been taken away too. Their grief was shattering.

But again there was a screening. Everyone had to pass between two lines of Latvians, who picked out people from the slowly moving column. At the same time the whole ghetto was thoroughly searched, and more people were found. I was told that this *Aktion* was conducted in an even more inhuman manner than the earlier ones. Joining together, Germans and Latvians beat the people, and some were shot on the spot. Most Latvians were drunk. It was in this latest selection that the other friend, who knew of our *molina* was taken, even though he had a certificate.

There were, perhaps another dozen who, like the three of us, slipped through the net. Max Kuritzky and David Weksler were among those. Max hid on the roof under bent pieces of tin the first two days. Sunday, when that area was searched, he hid in a latrine with seven other people, who jumped into the sea of excrement, and stayed there for hours with waste up to their necks. One woman who was not tall enough was held up by the rest. Although the place was searched, they were not discovered.

Oddly enough, although some patients were taken away, there were still some sick people left in the hospital.

Tuesday, November 11, 1941

My feet were quite painful, probably because of the cold we had suffered in the attic. But lots of things had been left behind by those who were killed. I found an old overcoat with a sheepskin lining and also a pair of *voliki* (felt boots)—clumsy but comfortably warm. That helped.

All the people now had certificates, except us. How could we legalize our existence?

Wednesday, November 12, 1941

Something encouraging. A German unit needed craftsmen, and there were still places for painters. I gave my name. The work was to start the next day.

There was much talk about the big *Aktion* as we now called the latest massacre. There are rumors that the Latvians had formed a special army unit to aid the Germans, and the murder of the Jews was what they had demanded in return. It was also said the Latvians were pressing the Germans for the total liquidation of the ghetto.

Thursday, November 13, 1941

In the morning, a German soldier took our group of twenty to the citadel, just across the river. Quite a few of my friends were here with me: Bentzke Kotzin, Max Kuritzky, Borekh Fixer, and Magaram. None of them was registered as a painter.

Maybe things would work out, but this first day of work was a complete fiasco. The different "craftsmen" were sent to various locations, and we, the five "painters," went to a small building where we were to paint two empty rooms. None of us knew anything about painting, but it seemed simple enough. The German gave us brushes and pails, told us where there was a ditch filled with liquid lime, and left. Two of the fellows brought the white stuff, and we mixed it with water. Small particles in the mixture refused to dissolve, but we applied it to the walls. Our eyes kept watering from its sharp smell, our fingers and hands burned from touching it, nevertheless we struggled on most of the day, smearing the stuff all over the walls. At last the soldier came back in the afternoon. As soon as he saw what we were doing, he said, "You are not really painters, are you?" It turned out the two fellows had picked up chlorine instead of lime. I didn't know what would come of this.

Saturday, November 15, 1941

Not much was said about the paint episode, but none of us was painting. We were all assigned to do different work.

The German unit for which we worked was called Heresbaudienststelle (Army Construction Service Department) 100. It had to do with renovating and repairing buildings in the citadel. So far there was a lot of confusion.

The citadel, where the unit was stationed, was a huge fortress located right across the river from the ghetto, on the same side (eastern) as the city. At one time it must have all been a single series of fortifications, with the wide river running between the large citadel where we worked and the smaller outwork where the ghetto was located.

The citadel was at least one and a half kilometers in length and one kilometer wide, maybe more. It was surrounded by huge walls, massive ramparts, and a moat which was now dry. There were four large gates, one for each major point of the compass. Inside the walls was a complete town, consisting of various buildings—barracks, hospitals, warehouses, workshops and horse stables. Some of these buildings were very old and had massive, walls. Others were modern three-story, brick structures. It was crisscrossed by streets and even contained a small park. Russian, Latvian, and Soviet army units must have been stationed here for many years, and now it was jammed with German soldiers.

So far there seemed to be only one German in charge of us—Rudy, the man who picked us up the first day. We called him, among ourselves, the *Blondinger*, because he was very fair-haired, slim and boyish-looking. He said nothing about the painting fiasco; he couldn't be too bad.

Monday, November 17, 1941

Bentzke Kotzin escaped to Braslav today, and I heard that Shmulke Palec also escaped directly from his workplace a few days ago. We who remained talked a lot about Braslav, but I still felt it was like jumping out of the frying pan into the fire. Yet, if the opportunity presented itself, I would run too.

Many people I knew were taken away in the Big *Aktion*, including the girl I'd saved in August. Of course, that lovely, dark-haired woman with the two children I'd met just before the *Aktion*, was gone too.

It was very cold in the unheated buildings. Whenever possible, we scrounged potatoes; we'd discovered some in a basement.

Wednesday, November 19, 1941

Good news! We had been *kaserniert* and from now on would live in the citadel. We were told to build wooden bunks for ourselves.

Our living quarters were in one of the large buildings, a block long, with many separate entrances, facing a large square with a few trees. Across the square was the large military hospital. Sometimes we could see a few soldiers, recuperating from their wounds, moving around slowly or sitting on benches. Our building was quite modern, occupied mainly by an air force unit. When you walked into the small hall from the outside, there was a stairway to the second floor, used by soldiers who were billeted upstairs. We lived downstairs. First, there was a room for storing wood and another we used as a carpentry shop. Most of us, thirteen in all, lived in a nice, bright room, with a wood floor painted red and a large white-tiled stove in one corner. Our bunks lined the walls, and three windows provided enough light to make our room pleasantly bright. Another six people lived in one of the smaller rooms. No guards watched us.

There were also four women working for our unit. They and a child of one of them lived in a room on the first floor of a building whose upper floors were used as offices by our unit.

Most people now worked at construction. What used to be an old bathhouse was being completely rebuilt into an *Entlausung* (delousing bath), while five worked in the carpentry shop. Strangely enough, I was the only one working again as a painter; I assisted a German soldier, who was painting an apartment in the city. Massey Stein, who actually was a professional painter, worked as a glazier.

I'd been "eating together"—sharing food—with Simke. He was my age, and since we started working, he'd been seeking my companionship. Almost none of us here had any family left; there was a great need for friendship.

My feet still hurt, but not as much as before.

Sunday, November 23, 1941

I went to the ghetto to visit Manishewitz and his nephew, Hershale, who were the only Jonaver still in Daugavpils.

A few days ago I saw a dead Russian POW on my way to the city. His body, lying on the side of the road, looked strangely small and wax-like. In the citadel, I saw a lot of POWs. They looked like scarecrows and at every opportunity swarmed over garbage cans trying to find scraps of food. Often columns of POWs passed by on the road, with guards urging stragglers on with their guns. This Russian must have been shot when he became too weak to keep up. In late afternoon, on our way back to the citadel, the Russian's body was still in the same spot.

Simke told me that, before they came to the ghetto, his family, which used to be wealthy, buried a lot of gold, silver, and other valuables in the yard where they lived. With just one tiny fraction of that wealth, we could escape to Braslav. But how could we get to it?

Saturday, November 29, 1941

In the morning we were awakened by screams: "My money, they stole my money!" Kantor, an old man in our room, had a large number of rubles, and when he got up, he discovered that the thick wad of bank notes was missing. The man was beside himself, crying and making shrill noises. We immediately began to search, turning everything in our room upside down, and thoroughly examining the front rooms and washroom. No money. We decided that no one was to leave the premises until the money turned up, because it had to be here.

But after some time, we all became worried. Kantor kept carrying on, and we had to report for work soon. Finally, when someone checked the washroom for the umpteenth time, there it was. I guess whoever took it decided that it had better be found. Who the culprit could be, I couldn't even start guessing. It was hard to imagine anyone in our room doing it. Could it be someone from the other room? I just didn't know. Someone must have thought: This old man has no chance anyway, while with all that money, I could escape to Braslav and possibly survive.

When we finished painting in the city, my new job became that of a woodchopper. I cut logs with a saw, then split them with an ax. My main duty was to see that there was always enough wood for the heating stoves. I carried armfuls of wood to the second and third floors of the building, where the offices of our German unit were located. Borekh Fixer, who worked at the *Entlausung* building site, just a few hundred feet away, usually helped me with the sawing. I did my work in a shed at the entrance of the building. When fresh logs were needed for sawing, I'd get a cart and about half a dozen POWs to help me bring it from the other end of the citadel. Every once in a while I was allowed to carry a cartful of logs to our living quarters for our own use.

We were all supposed to be skilled craftsmen, and most of us worked as glaziers, carpenters, locksmiths, and tinsmiths. At the *Entlausung* site, besides our people, there were also many POWs and some civilians from the city. The POWs did the hard unskilled, labor. The supervisors were Wehrmacht soldiers.

Although we lived in the citadel, officially we were under the jurisdiction of the ghetto authorities, and we still got our bread ration, a slice a day, from the ghetto.

Max Kuritzky worked as a glazier right around the corner and was able to slip away occasionally to visit me at my woodshed. As long as I had enough wood on hand for the stoves, I didn't have to worry much and could even duck into the kitchen to get warm now and then. There were usually one or more of our women there, including Sonia, our cook. The only ingredient she had available for cooking was red beets, of which there was a pile in the corner of the room.

Another small group of Jews was *kaserniert* in the citadel, working for a different German unit. Once I saw two Jewish girls pass by our building site.

Even though it was almost winter, the Wehrmacht still seemed to be advancing deeper and deeper into Russia. According to the Germans, they would enter Moscow any day now, and on the other fronts they also kept moving ahead. We heard that Rostov had fallen.

We had a nice surprise in the evening. A Russian POW who worked for the German air force unit upstairs, brought us half a pail of leftover soup from the German kitchen. It was dangerous for him to do this, and we were grateful. He looked very different from most Russian prisoners—well fed and neatly dressed. He told us he was an air force officer.

I kept thinking about Ruvke and reliving the details of that day when they took him away. Often I could not fall asleep for thinking about him.

Sunday, November 30, 1941

Today was Sunday. In the afternoon I went to the ghetto with some bread for the two Jonavers.

The ghetto was a picture of gloom. The few people still there lived in the least damaged part of the building, but even so, what a miserable place it was! The Latvian guards on the high ground were always in view; their presence and the many empty blocks were a constant reminder of the many thousands who had lived here and now were only a memory. The room where we sat was cold and half-dark. Outside the wind was blowing, and the yard was wet and dirty.

We talked some, mostly of my father who was so well known and respected. Manishewitz said. "I can see him before my eyes. Everyone used to say he looked just like Theodor Herzl. . . ."

I did not stay long, but promised to come back next Sunday.

As I hurried away from that place and passed the gate, I stopped and looked back at the familiar massive walls—the Ghetto of Daugavpils. Twilight was descending, and the wind was lashing out with increased force. I felt a slight shudder go through my body. How much pain, and terror those grim walls contained! Thirteen thousand ghosts, and a handful of the living, starving and waiting in the cold to share the fate of their fellows. . . .

In less than a quarter of an hour, I was back in our room in the citadel. What a difference! In the stove a fire was going with the comforting sound of crackling wood; the electric bulb gave out a bright light, and the other men were playing cards. It was my good luck to be here, but the whole evening I kept thinking of the ghetto, of the people I knew there.

Tuesday, December 2, 1941

On Monday Simke got sick; Kantor also didn't feel well. Both were taken back to the ghetto.

By contrast with that bad news, I met a very lovely girl today. Around noon Max came over to the woodshed, but it was very cold, so we went to the kitchen to warm up. The two girls I'd once had a fleeting view of were there talking with Sonia.

She introduced them to us: "This is Golda Gutterman and Jenny Berger. They live across from the work site."

Both were nice looking, but the one called Golda, who was about my age, made my heart beat a little faster. What an attractive girl! I was always awkward with girls, especially attractive ones, so I just stood there dumbly, not saying much. It turned out that Max had met Golda's sister, who was also living in the citadel.

"Come over, and visit us," he urged them, adding, "and bring your sister."

Surprisingly, in the evening all three did come to our room, where we sat on Max's and Borekh's bunks—the only corner somewhat apart from the rest of the room—and talked. I spoke mostly with Golda, soon losing my awkwardness. She wanted to hear about life in Jonava.

"It is nothing like Daugavpils," I told her. "It's only a small place." But I went on telling her of the four Zionist clubs, the occasional camping in the summer and ice skating in winter, and, of course, the swimming in the Neris. When, the Russians marched in, many things changed, but that was also the time when the sport club started having weekly dances. "Oh, yes, I love to dance," she admitted. "But I'm really quite a serious person."

"So am I, but I used to go to dances every Saturday night."

What a charming girl she was. I'm sure, in normal times, there would have been many fellows hanging around her. I'd have had no chance to come close to her. It was a memorable evening— for once memorable for its pleasant moments.

Wednesday, December 3, 1941

Typhus had broken out in the ghetto, and it was quarantined. No one was allowed to go in or out, for fear that the disease would spread. We were all concerned about the people there.

Month of December 1941

By now, I knew the people in our room quite well, each one different. What a bunch of characters!

Sleeping next to me was Bolmat, an older man, maybe sixty or so. Before the war he used to operate some kind of travel bureau in Daugavpils. He was basically cheerful and had a ruddy face, merry eyes, and a small Vandyke beard. He was great at "organizing" food. With a slight change in his facial expression, a pull on his cap and an adjustment of his collar, he transformed himself from a cosmopolitan man of the world to someone pitiful and hungry-looking, who could sometimes elicit a tin can of soup from a German cook, without even asking for it. He lost the last member of his family, a son, in the most recent *Aktion*. He was very friendly toward me but was especially partial to Berke Kaplan, who reminded him of his dead son. All in all, he was an old rascal, and I liked him very much.

Berke was a strapping fellow about my age, who had lived all his life in Daugavpils. He exuded courage and had a streak of recklessness in him, talking frequently about avenging his family. He was a good friend.

Tall, thin Massey Stein was probably in his early forties, puffing on a cigarette whenever he could find one, inhaling the smoke hungrily. He had a long thin neck, prominent Adam's apple, darting eyes, and a habit of swiftly and suddenly turning his head. He had been an interior decorator before the war, and seemed to be a skilled and proud artisan. His most evident traits were his honesty and integrity.

Yankl was probably around sixty, short with a small moustache. Immersed in grief for his family, he was a very bitter man. He hardly ever spoke except to scold us younger ones when we were not serious and subdued.

Issar Hayet was tall, slim, around twenty; he had been active in a Zionist youth movement in Daugavpils.

Turick and his son-in-law, my neighbors to the right, were Lithuanians, and consequently there was a cordial relationship between us. Turick even knew my father's brother, who had lived in Kaunas. Aside from that, the two generally kept pretty much to themselves.

Of course I'd known Borekh Fixer and Max Kuritzky before we came here. Borekh and I had hidden together in the ghetto, and, as for Max, he had become my closest friend.

Avrom was middle-aged, short, and swarthy, another Lithuanian. There was a certain dullness in his large brown eyes, and he used a very limited vocabulary, expressing himself mostly with a few simple words—exclamatory utterances helped along by jerky movements of his hands. He was very religious, knew many prayers by heart, and prayed several times a day. His faith was striking, complete and boundless, and that made him always full of hope. He often said, "God will save us," or "God has a reason for everything." He did mason work, which, I believe, he used to do before the war. He was very good at improvising from an absolute minimum—he could put together an edible dish from just a few scraps.

The other room was not as nice as ours. The floor was of concrete and they had only two-tier bunk beds in their small space. But the six people in it were apparently willing to give up some comfort for the sake of privacy. Perhaps they knew each other from before and chose to stay together.

I'd been through a lot with Magaram, counting back to prison days, and continued to have a high regard for him. Pressma and his wife (the only woman here) mostly spoke Russian between themselves. They often walked around holding hands and seemed very devoted to each other. David Stoler was a short man in his thirties, another man, formerly a dentist, and also there was Borke, an unobtrusive boy of my age. That completes the roster of "our group."

On December 7, Japan attacked America! And then Germany too declared war on the United States. We heard the news days later and talked a lot about it in our room. I was puzzled: How could Japan dare take on the United States? Didn't these Fascist countries realize they had no chance, now that the United States would be in the war too? This was really exciting news. I was certain that it would be like in the last war: The Americans would land and help free Europe of oppression.

The other war news was not good. I saw the front page of a German newspaper, reporting huge battles in the suburbs of Moscow; the city itself was expected to fall any day. Yasnaya Poliana (Serene Globe), the estate not far from Moscow where Tolstoy used to live, had also fallen into their hands. I could not help but think of *War and Peace*, where Tolstoy describes Napoleon's capture of Moscow. That was as far as the French army advanced before retreating in disarray. If only history would repeat itself!

I came home after work one day and lay down on my bunk, feeling depressed. I'd been thinking a lot about poor Ruvke. After a while, Max got me up. The Gutterman girls had brought some German soup, enough for all of us in the room. Though the soup was much appreciated, it was more the appearance of the girls in our room, bright-eyed and friendly, that changed the whole atmosphere; we all grew cheerful and animated.

With the ghetto quarantined, we got no bread at all. We were always on the lookout for food, and today I got a small piece of bread from a German soldier and exchanged it for two potatoes. Cooking them with some bread crumbs and a little salt, I made a very tasty and filling meal. It made me think of potatoes in general. What a versatile and excellent food! Potatoes don't spoil so fast and are easy to store. They grow easily in a cold climate and are filling to eat. They can be cooked, baked, roasted, or fried, and they can be eaten with the skins or peeled, whole, cut up, or grated. What would we do without potatoes?

Trouble. The SD was here and took away Issar Hayet. It all started about a week earlier. Many civilians worked in the citadel, but none of them lived there. Sometimes we worked together with them, but any other contact was strictly forbidden. Issar got to know a gentile girl who worked in the military hospital, and he took her to our room to exchange some clothing for food. I also decided to acquire something to eat and gave her the only thing I could possibly spare—a nice red blanket. She promised to bring me a loaf of bread for it in a few days.

Now we learned that the girl had been arrested and during interrogation had confessed to her dealings with the Jews (the food she bartered might have been stolen from the hospital). I was in serious danger too. When the SD men were in our room (I was at work) they asked for the name of someone else who had dealt with her. Our people insisted they knew nothing, and the girl had never heard my name. Of course, all they had to do was to bring the girl here and make her identify me. For a couple of days, I was worried and even thought of not sleeping in my room, but where could I go in this bitter cold?

After a few days, a young *Volksdeutsche* (someone of German descent who had always lived in areas outside Germany proper), who worked for our unit as an interpreter, came with the news that Issar hadn't yet been shot, and his release from prison could be arranged for a large sum of money. We didn't consider the German dependable, and didn't have much hope of ever seeing Issar again, but even if there was the slightest chance . . . We scraped up the sum of money somehow and turned it over to the German.

A few days later, the *Volksdeutsche* disappeared. I suppose, he already knew he was going to leave the area at the time he took our money. We never saw Issar again.

I saw Russian POWs often. They looked like skeletons, many so weak that their comrades had to help them walk. I got a chance to talk to them at the work site and whenever they were assigned to help me pull the cart with logs. One I encountered quite often was Maxim, who seemed to be in better condition than most. He said that they were housed in a huge camp not far from the citadel and were treated with much cruelty.

"Hundreds die every day from starvation and hard labor."

"What happens to Jews who are in the Red Army and are captured?" I asked him.

"Most of the time they don't even reach the camps. Jews of all ranks—and political commissars, too are shot as soon as they are captured. Fellow prisoners usually point them out to the Germans."

I gave Maxim a small piece of bread. Overjoyed, he said, "If you get me another piece tomorrow, I'll bring you a knife, a good one."

The next day he gave me a clasp knife as he'd promised. It was sturdy with a smooth wooden handle and a four-inch blade. I was very glad to have it.

We heard nothing at all from the ghetto during its quarantine. It was so close to us, just across the river, that we could see it clearly from the ramparts; yet we might as well have been thousands of kilometers away. Only 800 or 900 were left there. What was going on?

As for the rest of us, roughly 150 lived outside the ghetto, about thirty-five in the citadel and the rest in the city. We had some contact with the city-dwellers, primarily through Berke Kaplan, who was a native of Daugavpils and had gentile acquaintances. He often made the dangerous trip to the city. To be caught without yellow stars meant death, but Berke went anyway. Every time he returned he brought food and news of the other Jews in the city.

It was about three weeks since we'd first met the girls, and by now they came to see us almost every evening. We usually sat in what I called, in my mind, the compartment. Our room was not large, and every bit of space was taken up by our cots, except for some lab equipment that was enclosed by a portable partition. This is how it was when we first came, and we left it that way; it was never used by anyone. The space between the partition and the other wall formed an alcove, occupied by the two bunks of Borekh Fixer and Max. Borekh somehow "organized" a piece of fabric and hung it in front of their bunks, so that it closed that corner off completely. The girls and we young fellows now had some privacy. Our corner with the drawn curtain gave the appearance of a small, closed, third-class rail car compartment, with six to eight of us sitting on the two cots facing each other.

It was not just that Golda was attractive, there was also a certain wholesomeness, a brightness about her. From the very beginning we hit it off really well, but for the last few days, she had also been nice to Borke, the fellow from the other room. I was hurt. In the evening, when we were all sitting together, I was rather quiet most of the time. When the ten o'clock curfew came around, I did not help her with her coat and hung back, letting Borke take her home, usually a privilege I coveted. I caught a puzzled look on her face as she left.

I was certainly wrong about Golda. Next day she asked me why I had not escorted her home. I said, "I thought you'd rather have Borke take you." She looked at me and said quietly, "You know better than that, Shaike."

One evening, Ella, Golda's oldest sister, came to visit us. She was in her early twenties, very attractive, with hair the color of gold, truly a striking woman. She must have heard a lot about us from the girls, and as an older sister probably thought she'd better check us out. She told us she was married the day before the war broke out, and one week later, on First Sunday, her husband as well as her father were taken away to the prison. She was friendly and warm toward us, so I suppose we passed her tests.

The Russian prisoner from upstairs still came down from time to time and brought us soup. Sometimes he sat with us in our compartment. He taught us two Russian songs about the outbreak of war: "Sinii Platochek (The Blue Kerchief)" and "The Twenty-Second of June." They were sad and wistful. He called Golda "Zolotaya," the golden girl. I didn't blame him for being nice to her; his attitude was just one of friendship.

It was not very common for the Germans to use horses. But the Guttermans worked for a horse-and-wagon transport unit. The Gutterman family consisted of the three sisters, Ella, Hinda, and Golda, a younger brother of about fourteen, Leiser, and their mother. They worked together with the Berger family—a mother and two daughters, Jennie and Bertha. Their job was to take care of the laundry and to clean officers' rooms, while Leiser helped in the German kitchen. Two tailors and a shoemaker also worked for their unit. In general, these artisans were highly valued by the Germans; in addition to making necessary repairs for the soldiers, they kept the officers in beautiful custom-made uniforms and boots. Shoemakers and tailors also worked in the city for other units.

It was six months since the war started. But at last there was good news: The Germans were being hit hard around Moscow! We were all very excited. It was not just rumors. We could piece together the facts from discarded newspapers and casual utterances of German soldiers. It seemed that early in December, when the Germans were practically in the city, the Russians opened a counteroffensive and pushed the Germans back quite a distance. The Wehrmacht may still be in retreat. It was the first time since the outbreak of war that the Germans had been forced to make a sizable retreat. And Leningrad, though surrounded, had not fallen yet. We were now convinced the Nazis would be defeated eventually. With the Americans in the war and the Russians on the offensive, it was simply a question of time. Unfortunately, we didn't have much time.

I had tried to smoke several times. The girls brought us cigarette butts which they found while cleaning officers' rooms. We emptied the tobacco into a piece of newspaper and rolled ourselves cigarettes the way Russians did. One night, when I took a few puffs, I got dizzy. I found some excuse, put on my coat, and walked out into the yard.

The air was cold and crisp, and my head cleared up fast. It felt good to inhale the fresh, clean air. The ordinarily drab yard, now covered with snow, seemed somehow special, different, and as I looked up at the bright stars, I was overcome with all kinds of feelings. Golda, I was thinking. She's waiting for me inside right now! We both wanted to be together all the time and shared a feeling of deep understanding—she'd made her feelings clear in many different ways. Life seemed full and rich with unexpected joys. If only they'd let us live . . . But I shied away from that thought, dwelling instead on my present happiness, so full of promise and hope.

Tuesday, January 1, 1942: The 194th day

We were awakened in the middle of the night by a tremendous racket—shooting, sudden light flashes, and loud excited voices. Yes, even a few Russian voices.

For a while we were puzzled, and someone said, "Maybe the Russians are back." We had all heard lately of the progress they were making on the front. Could it be that a Russian advance unit had captured the citadel? No, impossible—the front was hundreds of kilometers away. Meanwhile Avrom climbed over the partition and hid behind the equipment. Then we realized—it was New Year's Eve. The Germans were welcoming in 1942.

Month of January, 1942

When I escorted Golda home one evening, I saw a long row of antitank guns and trucks parked at the curb. They must have been on the way to the front, a reminder that battles were raging and huge armies fighting with unheard-of ferocity, locked in a life-and-death struggle. But to us, the handful in the citadel, the news came only as a muffled echo. The cold weather and the snow, made our isolation even more complete, and being cut off from the ghetto added to the strange feeling of being suspended in time and space.

Some of the older people said that this was the coldest winter they could remember. It was very cold in my woodshed, but there were always the evenings to look forward to. We were not bothered much here, and I was grateful for each day. The anti-Jewish regulations were enforced by the death penalty in the ghetto or the city, but they were not always strictly enforced here. We did not even wear the yellow stars all the time. There were no Latvian auxiliaries, and only occasionally did we see even a wounded SS soldier. We kept a low profile and thus were left alone by the regular German soldiers. Some of them felt sorry for us, and when we did some work for them, we were sometimes offered a bite to eat.

One evening, I heard a German conversation in the outside room. David Stoler was in the midst of a heated discussion with a German soldier. Probably the soldier's unit was on their way to the front and had stopped overnight in the citadel. Somehow the soldier got into a discussion with Stoler outside and accompanied him back to our quarters. I couldn't hear everything that was said but apparently—despite the fact that we were being exterminated ruthlessly—here was a German soldier to whom it seemed important to convince a Jew of some philosophical idea. What a world!

An unexpected surprise! We were taken to the bathhouse in the city. It must have been on the order of the Oberzahlmeister (chief paymaster), our boss, who seemed to be a decent person. There were no bathing facilities in our washroom.

We were all excited and in good spirits. As we passed through an open area before the city proper, I kept thinking how strange everything was. The snow squeaked as we marched—a sign of a big frost. And farther ahead the smoke from the tall factory chimneys rose in straight columns to the sky. The whistle of an engine switching rail cars echoed, and in the distance a freight train, probably loaded with war material, chugged along. The phrase "a city at war" crossed my mind—the mood seemed to fit a description I'd read somewhere of Leningrad in the winter of 1917.

In the bathhouse the other men looked at us strangely, as if unable to believe their own eyes: Jews here? I suspected that most of their homes were filled with the possessions of murdered Jews, and I wanted to throw it in their faces: Yes, damn you, a few of us are still not dead, and we sure are going to try to stay alive!

One evening Berke brought a small bottle of alcohol from the city; he was not sure what it was but thought it was used in hospitals for medicinal purposes; he was assured it was drinkable. I had hardly had any experience with liquor. Father used to have a little sometimes on a Saturday, I remembered. When I was quite small, on the way home from services, we would stop at the house of one of his friends, and together with a few cronies, he would have a jigger or two of vodka, followed by some chopped liver or gefilte fish. He would then be in an excellent mood and become even more talkative than usual, acting as if he hadn't a care in the world. (A few times he let me taste the liquor, just by touching it to my lips. I didn't like it.) Then, it was home for the *tsholent*, the Shabbes meal. The only time I actually drank alcohol was on May 1, shortly before the war, when I had a part-time job keeping records for the movie house. That evening there was a party for the employees, who were much older than I, and there was quite a lot of drinking. I drank too. Later at night I felt very sick.

Now, sitting on Max's bunk, the three of us poured the clear liquid in our cups and gulped it down. We had no food, except for two onions. Berke said: "It is good to inhale the aroma of black bread after drinking liquor, but onions are also good." I was surprised at the very good effect the stuff had on me, on all of us. We had a feeling of well-being and a devil-may-care attitude, something we hadn't felt for a long time.

I wondered how the Germans we worked for expected us to survive without food. After the ghetto was shut, we had stopped getting our small ration of bread. We received practically no rations from our workplace, just a little soup sometimes. The fact was, we had to fend for ourselves completely and were always on the lookout for something to eat. The fact that we could move around freely in the citadel did make a difference. Sometimes there was a windfall from a completely unexpected quarter. Once we learned that a group of Lithuanian peasants was here. They'd been drafted to deliver supplies out east with their horse-drawn wagons, and were staying in the citadel for the night on their way home. We, the Lithuanians, went to see them immediately after work. Naturally, our purpose was food. The peasants were surprised to see Jews still alive. One of them said matter-of-factly, "In our area, there is not one Jew left alive." Still, meeting us so far from home and conversing in their mother tongue made some of them feel sorry for us. We got a real bonanza: a lot of bread, some butter, and even smoked bacon.

Every day I looked forward to Golda's visits in the evening, when we could enjoy a few hours together. What tomorrow would be, who knew? Meanwhile I was thankful for my good fortune in having met her.

Max was usually with Hinda, Borekh with Jennie, and I with Golda. With Berke often joining in, our evenings were spent in a bittersweet mood, as we sat together in our compartment, talking of the old times, the hopes and dreams we used to have. In an undertone we sang or hummed the sad Jewish songs, the wistful Russian tunes, or the Hebrew melodies that are full of hope. Sometimes we even dreamed of what it would be like to survive. But always the heavy dark cloud hovered over us, the awareness that our days were numbered.

One Saturday, we were suddenly taken to the *Entlausung* bath. The remodeling that had been going on for months was not completely finished, but the showers were working. I was pretty sure we wouldn't be allowed to use the facilities once German soldiers began to use them, but for the moment it was still under the authority of our Baudienststelle. I guess our *Oberzahlmeister* wanted to give us a treat. Actually, he'd been taking a very personal interest in us. While we were under the showers scrubbing away, he walked around (in his uniform) inspecting and paying a lot of attention to us, the young fellows. And as we were dressing, he admired and complemented our physiques. He walked over to me, touched my arm, and smilingly asked: "Did you do some boxing before the war?" Although in his officer's uniform, he looked like the rest of them, our *Oberzahlmeister*, a middle-aged man with a twinkle in his blue eyes, was really an unusual person. It was surprising that a German should be so decent to us.

His attention made me aware of my body. No, I never boxed; nevertheless, my body was smooth and firm. (Since our arrival at the citadel, our diet had improved.) I glanced at Max and Berke, and, by God, we did look good! I remembered Mother telling me how she used to enjoy giving me a bath when I was little, "Your small body was like alabaster," she would say. I was suddenly overcome with great pity for that body of mine, almost in an objective sort of way. Amid the bustle and excitement, as we were getting dressed, I felt deep sorrow at the thought, that one of these days I will be shot. I had the clear vision of our smooth young bodies rotting in the ground. Oh, those goddamn Nazis, let them be damned a thousand times!

Month of February 1942

For the second day in a row, we had no food. Oddly, our whole room seemed to be in the same boat. Most of the time we'd manage to scrounge a scrap here or there. Lately, though, there had been a bad stretch, and we'd eaten up our little reserve. But today help came quite unexpectedly. As Max and I passed the place where the girls worked, Ella, the older sister, suddenly appeared in the doorway. "Wait for me a moment," she said. She went back in, and in a few minutes reappeared with sandwiches for each of us. We were bewildered; we'd never mentioned our lack of food to the girls. "Come on, take it," she urged us. "I know you're hungry." Someone from our room must have told them of our predicament, so here was a sardine sandwich.

Again I had been made a painter and was working with a German soldier, who was my boss. He hardly talked, except to scold me occasionally. If I seemed to spend too much time painting in one spot, he would growl: "Come, come, stop tickling the wall—it will start laughing." I worked quite hard. I actually liked painting; there was satisfaction in going into a dirty, dark room and transforming it into a clean place, bright and smelling of fresh paint.

In comparison to the terrible months in the prison and ghetto, our life now was almost tranquil. This made it easier to look back and try to understand what had been happening to us. We had been talking about it a lot lately.

In about four months, July to November, at least 15,000 Jews were killed in Daugavpils, and probably not one German was lost in the process. What they did to us was so sudden and unexpected that it left us confused and overwhelmed. I thought about my own experience in prison, especially that unspeakable day of waiting in line to be shot. Even then we could not imagine that this same massacre was being repeated in hundreds of other towns. At the time, we just assumed that it had something to do with the savagery of a local commander, a *pogrom* conveniently connected with the burning of the city. And many of the women whose husbands were taken away that First Sunday, went on believing for weeks afterward, that their husbands were alive in some work camp. The reality was unthinkable, and it took a long time before it penetrated our inner consciousness: they intended to kill us *all*. They couldn't fool us anymore; we were not going to allow them to take us away that easily.

We often discussed escaping, but in the winter, where could we go? How long could we survive in this terrible cold? If only we had weapons. What wouldn't I have given for a gun!

How was one to explain it? Here we were, living on borrowed time, and what was going on in our room? Pillows were flying through the air! In the morning, just when we were about to get up, one of the fellows threw a pillow, and soon objects were flying in all directions, with much shrieking and laughter. Pandemonium broke out and lasted for quite a while. A few of the older people voiced their disapproval, and once the din subsided, the usually cheerful Bolmat, with only slight reproach in his voice, spoke of the unseemliness of our behavior: "The morning has to be a time of silence, a time to ponder and to consider quietly one's actions for the day ahead."

We didn't often let our spirits get out of hand in this fashion, but it was not at all unusual to hear mirthful sounds and good-natured banter in our room. Despite our experiences, most of us were young, and—temporary though our reprieve might be—the joy of being alive manifested itself in many ways.

Saturday, February 21, 1942

Saturday night. Some people were playing cards. We were sitting with the girls in our corner. Suddenly Berke, who had gone to the city on one of his expeditions, rushed in with dreadful news: "The Jews *kaserniert* in the city are to be returned to the ghetto by tomorrow night."

We were quite certain that the decree applied to us in the citadel too. The news, though not unexpected, hit us like a bombshell.

Sunday, February 22, 1942

This morning, the official news: We are to be returned to the ghetto in the evening to sleep, but will continue to work in the citadel.

I hardly slept that night. Since the news came, Max, Berke, Borekh and I had been talking incessantly, trying to come to a decision. Obviously ordering us back to the ghetto meant that an *Aktion* was pending—the final liquidation of the Daugavpils Jews. No, we must not return. We would escape, even though we had no idea where to go, and it was bitter cold outside.

But in the afternoon Max came with news that made us change our minds for the moment. Rudy the *Blondinger* met him outside our quarters and told him: "I know you're all scared, and you and your friends might be planning to escape. But I know for a fact that nothing is going to happen to you now. I myself am supposed to deliver you to the ghetto and pick you up in the morning. I assure you, you are safe. You'll have to sleep in the ghetto a few nights only, and then will be back in the citadel."

I knew that Rudy was very partial to Max, but still we were not sure. However, one factor helped us decide to return—the *molina* where Borekh and I had hidden in the big November *Aktion*. If anything went wrong, we could hide there again.

That evening, when Rudy delivered us to the ghetto, there was no sign of an *Aktion*, and we all breathed a sigh of relief.

Saturday, February 28, 1942

A week passed. Every morning we were picked up for work and taken back again to the ghetto in the evening. There had been no *Aktion*, and today we were told by Rudy that we'd be allowed to stay again in the citadel very shortly.

I wouldn't have thought it possible, but the ghetto dwellers looked worse than ever. How much they must have suffered during this bitterly cold winter! One could read the effect of the quarantine—of having been sealed up for almost three months—in their faces. People looked either very emaciated, skin and bones, or their features were swollen and unnaturally puffed up.

They had had to live in unheated buildings and in constant terror of the Latvian guards. But it was starvation that caused the fiercest suffering. People had always been hungry in the ghetto, but as long as some could go out to work, a few scraps of food were smuggled in by returning workers. But during the quarantine, this trickle of food was shut off. Everyone was dependent on the official ration only—two pounds of bread per person for a week, and soup once a day, which was really nothing but water cooked with rotten sauerkraut (many got sick from it). Some people died, especially children and those who were not young and strong.

I brought some bread to my two townspeople, Manishewitz and Hershale, who had suffered like the rest. They told me of the hardships they had experienced, and Manishewitz explained:

"Even then, some barter was going on with a few of the guards—if you can call it barter: Whatever one still possessed of value, of jewelry or clothing, was given away for a piece of bread. And if you were caught . . . A woman, Mrs. Shalmon, whose husband had been killed in prison, somehow managed to save her children throughout all the *Aktionen*. She was frantic to get a little food for her children and bartered with a guard: a piece of bread for a dress. He immediately reported her, and she was executed by shooting. All the people of the ghetto were ordered to assemble outside to witness the punishment."

One day, we found some rotten potatoes in the citadel, messy and foul smelling. When we took them to the ghetto, people grabbed them and were very grateful.

All of a sudden we had become rich. Each of us received three loaves of bread! It was the ration we hadn't gotten from the ghetto during the last three months. As small as the official ration was, more than this must have been due us. Nevertheless, it felt like an abundance of food.

When, some days ago, we'd first heard of the windfall we had coming, we'd made all kinds of plans about what to do with it. But now that we had it, Max and I, as well as many of our other people, divided up most of the bread among our friends in the ghetto. Needless to say, they were overwhelmed. Manishewitz had tears in his eyes.

Max and I had been spending a lot of time together and sharing whatever food we got.

Month of March 1942

We were again allowed to live in the citadel. This was a great relief.

Many changes took place here these last few weeks. All of a sudden, a couple of hundred Jews were living in the citadel. About 150 were *kaserniert* by the *Heresunterkunft Verwaltung* (Army Barracks Administration) No. 322. They worked in warehouses and workshops unloading uniforms of wounded German soldiers. The workers had to clean, sort, and repair the uniforms and then ship them back. In *Heresunterkunft Verwaltung* No. 200, another forty women worked. There were also big changes in our own unit. At least twenty more people were brought from the ghetto and billeted in what used to be the carpentry shop; the shop had been moved to a new location. No change had been made in our room, though; I was still with the same people and glad about it—I was fond of them all. Among the new people there were some I knew, and I was especially pleased to see David Weksler. He even had a violin with him; he must have found it after the last *Aktion*.

Our unit had also changed in different ways—more German soldiers, more workshops. We worked hard, almost all of us as craftsmen. Curiously, I was still the only one working as a painter. In Golda's workplace, the Berger family, mother and two daughters, were transferred to 322. The Guttermans would have to work even harder, although they wouldn't have to clean officers' rooms anymore.

I didn't know how the people did it, but they determined that March 24 was the first night of Passover. Max and I celebrated the Seder with Golda's family. During our meal together we reminisced about past Seders, and there was a feeling of warmth, capturing, even here, something of the spirit of the holiday.

In our quarters, the holiday was not much noticed. People were happy enough having a bite of bread to eat—with one exception. How, I had no idea, but Avrom managed to get some kind of flour and baked himself a couple of dozen flat biscuits. Pointing to them, he said, "For the next eight days, I will eat only this matzo." He was the only one of us who had been keeping up his religious practices, using a lot of ingenuity in the process; he was trying to eat only kosher food and prayed every day.

With so many of us Jews working in the citadel, we were no longer as inconspicuous as we used to be in the winter. Now we had to be careful not to break any of the myriad rules that governed every minute of our existence. Nevertheless, we still didn't see any Latvian auxiliaries here, and in comparison to the ghetto our life was good. But we heard the news of the ghetto. Even though the quarantine had been lifted, the terror continued. Recently, two young women were executed by hanging. The people were all forced to assemble and witness each of the executions, and the bodies were left hanging afterward as an example for all.

I did not see the hangings, but was told the details by several forced witnesses.

The crime of Masha Schneider was clear: she was caught in the city without her yellow stars.

The other case was that of Mina Gittelson, an attractive, woman in her twenties. She was accused by her Latvian employer of breaking the racial-sexual laws. Actually—the true facts were known in the ghetto— the Latvian suspected that Mrs. Gittelson had discovered that many Jewish valuables were in his possession and decided to eliminate her. He denounced her, and she was condemned. For the people ordered to watch the proceedings, the scene was painful beyond words. Mrs. Gittelson, well-known and popular in the community, stood by the makeshift scaffold wearing obvious marks of recent physical torture, while Pasternak, head of the Jewish ghetto police, was ordered to perform the execution. He was known as a decent person and, in his position as the transmitter of Nazi orders, always tried his best to be helpful to fellow Jews, often to his own detriment. His struggle with himself was quite visible, but in the end he had no choice but to put the rope around the woman's neck.

The body of Mina Gittelson was left hanging for three days.

We had been seeing the girls almost every day. Until recently we always met in our room, but now we sometimes went to their quarters. Golda's mother was very kind; I was always made to feel welcome.

I wish I could describe Golda fully, the way she was. She was certainly what is called good-looking, and even lovely. She had a fine, light complexion, light auburn hair with a tinge of red in it, and a shapely figure. But that could be said of many other girls. I think it was her intelligence, her natural grace, and her unassuming air that made her so special. Everyone liked her.

Her father was a house decorator. From what I heard about him, he was a good man, lively and attractive. Golda's two older brothers emigrated shortly before the war, one to America and the other to Palestine.

Lately, we had been bringing our laundry to the girls for washing. As Hinda put it, "If we can wash laundry for all those Germans, we can certainly do it for you." We had little to be washed, but still it was a great help.

Month of April 1942

During the winter the Russians pushed the Germans back on many fronts. The German soldiers suffered terribly from the bitter cold winter—and, it was said, many lost limbs. During the past months we ourselves had seen many wounded apparently suffering from frostbite. Oh, they were going to lose the war, I had no doubt about that. But when? If only the Americans would land in Europe!

I'd been working with two gentile painters from the city. The older one, a Pole, was short and of dark complexion; the younger was tall, blond, and Russian. It seemed that many Russians and Poles lived in this area, probably because Daugavpils was located close to the borders of White Russia and Poland, as well as to Lithuania. As to my co-workers, this was just a regular job for them. After some awkwardness in the very beginning, we worked pretty well together, doing the same things I'd done before, painting rooms. The ceilings were usually white; the walls, except for a white margin about a foot wide, were painted in various colors. We used brushes to paint and rollers to apply patterns on the walls. The German *Meister* (supervisor) came to check on us a few times a day; mostly we were on our own.

After work, Weksler practiced conscientiously on the violin, repeating a certain fast passage over and over.

Some years before, I had read a book called *I Burn Paris,* and lately I thought of it often. In the story, a man poisons the water supply of Paris, spreading a deadly plague throughout the city. Paris is quarantined and completely isolated. As the death toll rises dramatically, it becomes clear that no one is immune; everyone will probably die. But what made such an impression on me, when I read it, was that while people were aware of death lurking in every corner, they kept going on with life's daily activities—loving, hating, being jealous, being concerned with all kinds of matters. I remembered being surprised—how could they go on with everyday concerns?—it seemed unreal. Lately, I'd marveled at our own capacity to go on with "ordinary life" in spite of our awareness of impending doom, and in my mind I called this condition "I Burn Paris." I see now that the author correctly captured an important aspect of human existence: There must be something innate within us that makes us go on.

I had been marking down dates and making notations on scraps of paper, using the Lithuanian language and some personal symbols. I wondered at myself. I had very little hope of surviving and of being able to use this information, yet I kept going on with it.

The Pole with whom I worked was an experienced painter and I learned a lot from him. He was also very friendly and talked to me often.

Weksler kept practicing the same tune. When I asked him the name of what he was playing, he said: "It's Mendelssohn's Violin Concerto."

Friday, May 1, 1942: The 314th day

The ghetto was liquidated today.

It was quite logical. May 1 was one of the two most important Soviet holidays. On the other one, November 7, the Big Aktion took place, and now the last remnant of the Daugavpils Ghetto—about 600 people— were killed.

Already in the afternoon, there was talk at the citadel that something was going on over in the ghetto. Later someone from 322 said that from the citadel wall you could actually see people being buried. It was true. From the top of the ramparts Max and I observed figures walking back and forth carrying what looked like bodies.

We got the details late in the evening when a group of about fifteen came to us from the ghetto with permission to work in our unit and live here with us. They were artisans who had worked in the city but slept in the ghetto. When they returned from work today, most ghetto inmates had already been removed, but bodies were strewn about the premises and yard. The group was put to cleanup work immediately, gathering all the corpses, carrying them to ditches, and burying them—just as we had seen from the ramparts. They also had to clean up the blood, which was splattered all over. It appeared that many of the old, sick, and small children were shot on the spot, and those who had poison took their own lives. No exceptions were made—everyone was taken away, including the ghetto police, the staff and patients of the hospital, and the whole *komitet*. Manishewitz, Hershale, and Simke were now gone too.

Month of May 1942

A few days later we heard more details about the liquidation of the ghetto. (Two people had managed to hide and survive the roundup. One was a woman and the other a young fellow.) The Latvian auxiliaries went wild, they said. They threw old and sick people through second floor windows, shot those who refused to leave their rooms, and killed some of the very small children by cracking their heads against the concrete walls of the buildings. Even when the column was assembled for departure, shots were fired into the mass of people.

Something bizarre also took place on Thursday, the day before the *Aktion*. For the first time in the history of the ghetto, all the inmates were taken to the public bathhouse in the city. To people with no bathing facilities all these months, this was a great treat, encouraging them to hope that there was to be a change in attitude towards Jews. They did not have to wait long for an answer. For some reason, the people were first taken to the prison, and only from there to Pogulianka, where they were shot.

In the wake of this latest *Aktion*, a grand total of between 430 and 450 Jews were still alive in Daugavpils, out of about 16,000 who had fallen into German hands. About 250 were in the citadel (including the fifty-five now in our unit), another 180 to 200 work in the city.

Again and again, we had slipped through the net. Now there really was nothing between us and the angel of death.

Among the people who were transferred here lately was also Haim Kuritzky. Unbelievably, there were even a couple of small children here, the only Jewish children still alive in Daugavpils.

The Russian I worked with told me that he could get me food in exchange for clothing. This was a tremendous opportunity, for very few of us worked side by side with gentiles.

The next day I gave the painter a dress, a coat, and a suit, which I had got from some of the people. He was to barter it for food, and my share of it would depend on what he brought. He said he could get, besides bread, some butter and perhaps even bacon.

As the weather improved, the Germans again seemed to be on the offensive. We heard a lot about very heavy fighting around Kharkov, which had changed hands several times.

We had been talking a lot about escape. Among the new people who arrived here during the last few months, there were some eager young fellows ready to join any plan. Finally we decided to make a definite decision. Max, Berke, Borekh, and I were joined by David Bleier, who was about seventeen, and two older fellows in their twenties, Eli Kurland and Yeshia. We were all eager to escape. The main problem: We had no arms. Eli said:

"Suppose we escape and get beyond the city. What do we do next? Where do we get food? How long would it take before we are caught—a few days, a week at the most?"

And someone else said, "Suppose we go to a farmhouse to ask for food. Even if the first farmer won't give us away, it is a sure bet that the second or third will inform the police."

"And the fact that only Jews are circumcised—if there is any doubt about who we are, it's easy for them to check."

We knew people got a special food allowance for every Jew who was turned over to the police; whereas, someone caught helping us could expect harsh punishment. (Not that the population had any love for Jews even without the inducement of food.) What chance did we have?

In the end we agreed that we would stay here until the moment of immediate danger. Since we were not shut up together in a ghetto, there was hope that we might be alerted before it was too late. In the meantime, we would make every possible effort to get arms.

Thursday, May 21, 1942

Today was my birthday. I was eighteen. Golda's mother put together a meal. The main dish was a thick soup, which Leiser brought from the German kitchen along with some sour pickles. It felt like a real party.

I remember Mother saying that I would always be lucky, because I was born with a "silk shirt" (red caul)—she'd say it half-jokingly. But I was the firstborn in our family, and according to the Jewish calendar, my birthday is on L'ag B'omer—spring festival of the trees, the most beautiful time of the year. And so my birthday always seemed to be something special. To think that I had survived until now, after all the many thousands had died, had met Golda, and had escaped being in the ghetto during this terrible winter—truly, it was easy to start thinking of oneself as someone set apart.

Even as I thought of my inevitable end here, which was always on my mind, quite often another thought flashed through my head, like a streak of lightning: lasting a bare split second. "But it can't happen to me." This was probably human nature speaking. Back in the ghetto I'd talked to other people who had also had that same feeling of inviolability. Later, they were all taken out and shot. No, I was not fooling myself. Despite that irrational undercurrent of hope, which surfaced in odd split seconds, I knew what my end would be.

Month of June 1942

The tall painter swindled me out of the clothing—that was now clear. He hadn't reported for work the last three days, and now the other painter told me that he had quit his job. The dirty rat! I hadn't expected much; if he had just brought some bread and a bit of fat, at least something. The people whose clothing it was understood and didn't blame me, but I felt very bad.

We all knew we were fair game. We could expect to be cheated and swindled anytime we tried to exchange something of value for a piece of bread; we even stood a pretty good chance of losing our lives in the process. All a gentile had to do was denounce us to the police, for just about anything—true or not—it was enough to get us shot. We were completely helpless.

A few days later, after we had finished our work, a German sergeant gave me half a loaf of German bread and a can of marmalade—most unusual. If we did get something, it was usually a piece of bread or a little soup. I gave some of it to the man who had given me the coat. He was pleasantly surprised. I told him I felt responsible and would continue to repay him. What's more, I intended to repay the other owners of the clothing as well.

A lot of anxiety lately. The latest rumor was that the Latvians were demanding that we be returned to the ghetto. If only the world would somehow become aware of what was happening to us! We talked about it in our room from time to time. People had different ideas of what the Allies could do. Some felt that the mere threat of reprisal would be enough to save us.

Monday, June 22, 1942: The 366th day

The war started a year ago, and I was still alive. For how much longer? The rumors were true—all Jews working in the city and citadel were to return to the ghetto on June 26, the anniversary of the capture of Daugavpils by the Germans. No doubt they would be celebrating by putting an end to the last handful of us.

The fellows were of one mind: We would not return to the ghetto. But there still seemed to be some hope: The Germans in charge of units employing Jews were not happy with the order and were trying to have it rescinded.

Wednesday, June 24, 1942

Two days had passed. I didn't know about the others, but six of us were determined not to return to the ghetto. We had no elaborate plan. We'd just try to run due east, in the direction of the front line (probably 600 kilometers from Daugavpils). But we were going to wait for a while; there was still some uncertainty. Magaram had been in contact with Jews of the other units, and also with our Oberzahlmeister and Rudy, who reported that every effort was being made to keep the Jews at their working places.

I talked with Golda about escaping, but she wouldn't consider leaving without the rest of her family. In any case, the captain of their unit was quite sure that we'd be allowed to stay at the citadel. We'd just have to wait until we were sure that we really were to be taken back to the ghetto before we made our move. We were all grimly aware that our chances of survival on the outside for more than a few days were very slim.

Thursday, June 25, 1942

The crisis was over. The order was rescinded, and things were to stay as they had been. Great relief.

Tuesday, June 30, 1942

The Germans protected us because our work was of use to them; it was also true that some felt sorry for us— especially for *"their* Jews," those they had gotten to know personally. Whenever Jews worked for any length of time, with ordinary German soldiers, the relationship often became quite friendly. At 322, Yasha Magid, the *Oberjude*, and Dr. Itzikowitz were much respected by their chief and so was Magaram at our place. The fact that Jews understood the German language, whereas most gentiles did not, was also helpful. But we had no illusions. Sooner or later there would be a direct order and we'd be done away with.

At Magaram's suggestion, we gave our *Oberzahlmeister* the fine riding breeches, that had belonged to my friend from Janova and which I had kept all this time.

Saturday, July 4, 1942,

Golda's birthday. She was eighteen. In the afternoon I went with her to the attic where the wash was hung out to dry. I helped her take it off the lines, and it gave us a chance to have some privacy for a while. God, how I loved her! And what was so glorious was that she seemed to love me just as much.

Month of July, 1942

I had been lent out to the air force unit that occupied the entire building where we ourselves were also billeted. I was helping a corporal paint the place. If all the rooms were to be painted, I would be working here a long time. The corporal was quite young, probably in his early twenties. He wore that light blue Luftwaffe uniform; however, I doubted that there were actual pilots here; he must have been from some ground-support unit. I was apprehensive on the first day. He was going to be my boss. Would he be a "good German" or a "bad German?" When he came for me, I overheard him telling my *Meister* that he was from the Sudeten Gebiet (in Czechoslovakia) and that a brother of his had been killed in Russia. My heart sank. He'd probably blame the Jews for his loss and take it out on me. But we worked a whole day, and he seemed decent. His name was Otto.

After a few days, at lunchtime, while I was eating the soup he had brought from the kitchen, Otto suddenly said, with a certain element of wonder in his voice, "Paulchen, you are really not different from any other guy." He'd probably never known any Jews before. He'd been calling me by that name, the affectionate diminutive of the name "Paul," though why he'd settled on this particular name for me, I had no idea.

Working as a painter, I was luckier than most: At work I sometimes got a crust of bread or some soup, and now that I was working with Otto, I received some food from him every day.

The others had to be constantly on the lookout for food, using a lot of ingenuity to acquire it. For example: Eierov, who was from Lithuania and used to be a biologist, was very good with his hands. He worked now as a carpenter, but in his free time made small shapes, figures and pendants, from flat sheets of plastic. I had no idea where he got a tiny saw and a few other simple tools, but the trinkets he made were attractive. He was able to get food from Germans in exchange for them.

A few of the people were especially good at organizing food, regardless of the conditions, even when no one else could. Yosl, around forty and a tinsmith by profession, was great at it. He was also probably the most amusing person I had ever known. He was tall, had large uneven features and long arms and legs; when he walked, he took very long strides in a particular gait that somehow expressed his joy at being alive. Always bubbling with irrepressible excitement, he talked a lot about food and sex and had his own jargon (food was pihlovka). His humor was earthy and he made us laugh very often. We'd also been using a lot of his expressions.

After work, while I was talking to David Bleier, I heard one of the fellows shouting:

"Hey, Shaike, your German is looking for you!" There was Otto, waiting for me at the window. He handed me the container of his mess kit, and said, "Here, Paulchen, pour it into something and bring me back the can." It was a thick soup with pieces of meat in it!

Max and I spent a lot of time at the Guttermans. I was accepted and approved of by the whole family, but, then, parents of my friends had always approved of me; I guess I came across as a "good boy." Max, however, had been in hot water lately. He had "a roving eye," and Hinda was very jealous and highstrung. Lately they'd been having heated arguments, and Hinda had been walking around with eyes red from crying. The whole family was upset with Max.

I lost my knife with the wooden handle and a lighter made of a shell, both bought last winter from Maxim, the Russian POW. It was very foolish of me. First I lost the lighter and realized that I had a hole in my pants pocket; however, it seemed too small for the knife to slip through, too. Later it was gone. Golda and I went to look for it, but no luck. I felt bad, especially about the knife.

We got the news that the Jews in Braslav were killed; they had by now wiped out the Jews of all the small towns in White Russia. I thought of all the people who had escaped last fall to that "haven." Did anyone manage to get away from there?

The people of 322 lived on the second floor of one building, and Russian POWs were kept on the street floor. The Russians were marched to work in the morning and brought back in late afternoon; they were kept locked up the rest of the time. Iron bars were on their windows and they had no freedom of movement, but how very happy we would have been to change places with them! In general the situation of POWs seemed to have improved since winter.

Otto never stopped surprising me. As I was getting ready to go home—we quit earlier on Saturdays—he suddenly asked, "Do you like swimming?"

"Sure," I answered.

"Then let's go to the beach!"

I was taken aback; for a Jew to be caught at a public beach could mean the end. But before I could answer, he urged me on:

"Come, Paulchen, don't worry. I'll pick you up in twenty minutes. Yes, and I'll have a pair of trunks for you."

I took off the yellow stars, and we walked to the Daugava. It was hot, and the beach was crowded with Germans. We jumped into the river, and the water was wonderfully refreshing. But for me the expedition was not fun. Only the wet swimming trunks covered my distinguishing mark of Jewishness—the fact that I had been circumcised. I worried all the time we were there. I promised myself not to do it again.

There had been some improvement in the food situation in the citadel. Some people from 322 had been swiping army shoes from the warehouse where they were being sorted, and people who had contacts with civilians exchanged the shoes for food. We were all aware of the danger; if you are hungry, you take any chance to get something to eat. I didn't know how many people were involved in this scheme, but I know that when some people got food, it usually filtered through to many more, and there was less starvation all around.

We picked up from the German soldiers the expression *organisieren*—to organize. It was mostly used to describe acquiring something, anything at all. The means of "acquiring" ranged from simple efficiency to out-and-out stealing, plus every other technique in between.

"He was taken away to prison that First Sunday." This remark was often used, especially by women when they spoke of their lost husbands and sons. The Daugavpils Prison—I thought often of that terrible place.

I was talking to Haim Kuritzky about that time. More than a year had passed, and as was often the case when we talked about the prison, we congratulated each other on the extra time that we had managed to snatch from death's jaws.

"You know, Haim," I said, "when I think of how they ran out of ditches just when it was our group's turn to pass the iron gate, it really seems unbelievable. You must have been in one of the groups behind me."

"No, I must have been just in front of you."

"Oh, no, not possible! The people who went through the gate before me were all shot."

"Except for a few in my group."

Seeing my dumbfounded expression, Haim said, "Well, I thought you knew. Let me tell you what happened." And he recounted this astonishing story:

His cell was on the third floor, and like me, he was among the last to be ordered out into the yard. They waited and waited standing in line. When their group was already at the iron gate, he took the hand of his friend Michael and told him that they should jump into the ditch at the same time, holding each other's hands, so that they could die together. Michael agreed, and then the group of twenty was marched through the iron gate.

At a long ditch ahead of them were four Latvian auxiliaries loading their rifles. A German officer yelled at the prisoners, "Four of you, march ahead!" When the men reached the ditch, the German yelled, "Fire!" Each of the Latvians fired at one man—one bullet in the head at close range—and the four fell into the ditch. "The next four!" They were shot too. (All this was being filmed by German soldiers.) But then, the remaining prisoners were given spades and ordered to cover the ditches with dirt—there was no more room. The ditches were full of dying people and blood.They struggled spasmodically like fish out of water . . . heads hanging back . . . a wet, slippery, moving mass. . . .

"Faster, work faster!" the German screamed. And then, in a hysterical tone he delivered a diatribe against the Jews, how they should all be exterminated, and that Haim's group would die tomorrow. And then whoever didn't seem to work fast enough was made to lie on top of the bodies, and the German shot him in the head with his handgun. Haim's friend Michael was one of them. The prisoners spread chlorine over the quivering bodies and then a layer of sand. The rest of them, those still alive, were taken back to the prison. " A few hours later," Haim concluded," we had to dig our own graves together with you."

I thought about what Haim had told me. So that was how it was, the reason for our long wait. I had not quite expected that each person would have been executed individually, but there would be less chance of leaving victims for dead who were only wounded, the way it had happened to Max. The four Latvians, the executioners, were probably working in teams and must have been changed frequently. July 1941—this was only the beginning of the killings. Later, procedures changed, and people were forced to undress before being killed. I kept thinking of Ruvke and imagined his suffering before they killed him. And my parents and Nehamah, where did they meet their end?

Golda told me that at one time the family tried to persuade Hinda to stop seeing Max. As she put it, "That flirting with different girls—it was driving Hinda crazy." Of course, Hinda wouldn't hear of giving him up. But Golda admitted now, "He seems to have changed. Lately he's been behaving very well."

Both Max and I spent a lot of time with the girls. Eli Kurland had become quite friendly with Ella, Golda's oldest sister. He was a serious person, spoke slowly, pronouncing every word clearly. You couldn't help but take him seriously.

We were talking about the war news we'd heard. It was very discouraging. Eli said, "The Germans are advancing on all fronts."

"In another few months it will be fall, and in the winter they'll be hit again." I was trying to be optimistic, but it wasn't easy. Even though we didn't believe everything we heard, there was no doubt that the Germans had captured some more big cities on the Eastern front, and in Africa they had taken Tobruk from the English in June.

"And where are the Americans?" Eli asked.

"Just wait another six months. They'll be in Europe by then!"

"Oh, yes," he said, "eventually they'll come, and the Germans will be defeated. But will any of us survive to see it?"

The last few days I had been running out of things to do at work and was not surprised when at last Otto said, "I am sorry, Paulchen, our work is finished, and you have to go back to your old *Meister*. I wish you good luck." He gave me half a loaf of bread and a tube of cheese, and we said good-bye.

Month of August 1942

Life went on. Though our world might collapse any minute, "Burn Paris" syndrome was in full force.

It was late Saturday afternoon. We wouldn't have to work tomorrow, and the feeling of anticipation, even of a certain excitement, was in the air. Yosl was clowning around, his loud and boisterous voice reverberating throughout the rooms; Weksler was fiddling away, still practicing the first part of the Mendelssohn Violin Concerto, and Eierov was bantering in a good-natured way with Stoler. Max and I were expecting the girls. For a while I stood in the largest room—the doors to the other rooms were open—and observed the animated atmosphere. I tried to imagine what an outsider would think, looking at us here. He would certainly find it hard to believe that the people he saw knew they were condemned to die. And later, when the girls come, he would see a group of boys and girls, spending an evening in a romantic way—humming songs, teasing, giggles, the usual behavior of young people. He could not see that inside us is the fearful knowledge. But that was the way it was: Life goes on—"Burn Paris."

It is said that opposites attract each other. Certainly Max and I were completely different people, and perhaps that was why we were so close. We spent all our free time together. We shared everything we had, whether food or money, and if one of us lit up a stub of a cigarette, we smoked it together, each taking a few puffs and handing it to the other. In his concern for me there was something of an older brother, for he was older and more experienced than I was.

From time to time, Berke had been bringing a bottle of *samogon* (moonshine) from the city. The stuff didn't taste very good, but now there was usually a bite of bread, and inhaling that fine smell of black bread helped kill the taste. Anyhow, it was the feeling one got afterward that counted.

We usually raised our cups, and I'd say: "To the one who discovered alcohol!" Every time we were about to drink, I'd make this toast as a tribute to the liquid that made us feel so good. The dark specter became remote, and what counted was the immediate joy of life.

As soon as we came to the Guttermans, Ella said: "Eli, tell them about the plan."

We knew that Eli, who had lived in Daugavpils all his life, had friends among the gentiles and was in contact with some of them. He now told us that someone he had known for a long time was working on an escape plan.

"It might take another week or two until everything is ready," he concluded, " then we'll get away. All of us!" Answering our excited questions, he explained, "The details are not yet completed. But what is involved is a truck, a closed truck in which we'll all travel with a driver in a German uniform. Once we get close to the front line, we'll cross over to the Russian side at night by foot."

The scheme sounded too good to be true, and I had my doubts about it. But there was also that tiny spark of hope. "Maybe there is something to it."

Month of September 1942

Sunday. It was only early September, but today, fall was in the air. There were dark clouds overhead, and it was chilly.

In the afternoon, when we went to the Guttermans, everyone was in the room, and right away I was struck by the cheerful atmosphere. They were preparing dinner. Hinda was peeling potatoes, while Golda grated them—Mother was going to make potato dumplings. Talking about his plan, Eli still didn't have many details but said that his friend had "good connections," and "the truck to be used will be German." I still couldn't believe that anything would come of this scheme. All of us, except for Eli, were quite skeptical. Eli had a lot of trust in that gentile friend of his. In the meantime it was nice to speculate—sort of daydream about the possibility of us getting away. Meanwhile the room was filled with warmth—the great feeling of being with people one cared about a lot, and knowing the feelings were mutual.

Outside it was getting darker and gloomier, but that only made our room seem cozier. While we ate our meal, Leiser recounted a humorous incident in the German kitchen, imitating one of the cooks; it was really funny. We continued talking in a leisurely way—nothing important, just the pleasure of communicating with people one feels close to.

I thought of how little one needs in order to feel that quiet happiness.

There was a lot of talk that, with the arrival of fall and later the cold weather, the German military success would end. Last winter their army was stopped at Moscow and thrown back many kilometers. Our "politicians" were convinced that again this year, with General Winter's help, the situation would change dramatically for the better. As they say in Yiddish, "From your mouth to God's ear." Meanwhile, though, things didn't look any too good. Today I came across the front page of a German newspaper with the news that they'd reached the outskirts of-Stalingrad on the Volga River—so deep into Russia! Stalingrad used to be called Tsaritsyn before the revolution, and the name made me think of a book I had read about the Russian Civil War. In it the turning point in the protracted Civil War came in battles around a city that, I thought now, was Tsaritsyn, where the Whites were badly defeated. But was it Tsaritsyn? The more I dwelled on it, the more I convinced myself that this was indeed the city. Yes, I told myself firmly, Tsaritsyn-Stalingrad will again be the turning point for the Soviets. They'd come awfully far, the Germans, but this would be their high-water mark. Feeling optimistic and hopeful, I decided not to share these thoughts with anyone. My talking about it might somehow prevent it from happening.

Saturday, September 12, 1942

This was Rosh Hashanah. Avrom sat on his cot, praying quietly. I could see his lips moving. At times he swayed back and forth, keeping his eyes closed in the manner of ecstatic supplication to God. I wondered, how much of the prayer he remembered. Some of the other people in the room had also taken note of the holiday, and Yankl prayed some too, but it was Avrom who put his whole heart and soul into it.

Later, I was in the small room where Eli had his cot. Weksler was there, playing the Kol Nidre melody on his violin, the beautiful music for the solemn prayer on the eve of Yom Kippur, a week from today. We sat transfixed, listening to the heart-tearing sounds. Suddenly there was the head of a German soldier in the open window. Weksler stopped. We jumped up as if out of a trance.

"Why did you stop?" the German asked. "Please, continue, it is a very beautiful melody."

Weksler began again from the beginning. The German stayed outside and together with us listened to Weksler play Kol Nidre on his violin.

The Guttermans were moved to new quarters, a couple of blocks away. We looked forward to the move with some apprehension, afraid of any change. Actually, the new place was quite satisfactory. Strangely enough, it was the same two rooms where we had our first experience as "painters" in the citadel, when we painted the walls with chlorine. The front room had a table and benches for eating; the other room was the bedroom with barely enough room for the five of them to sleep. We were all happy with the arrangement. Their quarters were the most "luxurious" of all the Jews remaining in Daugavpils. Of course, they were also the only family who still had five members alive.

Across the small hall was their laundry room, all fixed up for them. It had wash basins and a special huge kettle for boiling the laundry. There was also a small brick cooking stove—and a bathtub! Truly fantastic.

From the hall there was a staircase leading to the second floor, occupied by Germans.

The "friend" of Eli disappeared. It was no surprise to us. Actually the scheme had not been discussed much lately, but Eli felt quite bad. He gave the man a lot of clothing as part of the "expenses" for the escape—now he had lost it all. That was the way it went. We had to explore every possibility and take any chance, knowing all along that just about anyone could take advantage of us. We were ready prey for any two-legged louse.

Sunday, September 20, 1942

Tonight was Yom Kippur. It was time for Kol Nidre, the beginning of the twenty-four-hour period when a religious Jew believed that every man's fate for the next year was sealed. Avrom was praying. He stood next to his cot with his eyes closed, swaying his body in religious fervor. I could hear him recite *"Al Heth Shechotonu L'fonecho* (For the sins we have committed before Thee)." He specified the various sins as prescribed in this solemn supplication to God. Every time he said the word "sin" he hit his chest over his heart with his clenched fist with much vigor in the customary way. Oblivious to the rest of us, he was completely immersed in what he was doing. Avrom, whose whole family had been killed and who had experienced every possible hell, was begging God for forgiveness for the sins that he, Avrom, had committed this past year.

Bolmat, likable old Bolmat, was arrested and taken to prison. He was as good as dead. A Jew who gets to prison doesn't come back. I had a pretty good idea of how it happened. Every once in a while, Bolmat used to walk to the city to get food from one or another of his gentile friends. He must have been stopped and found to be without his yellow stars.

The fighting in Stalingrad continued. The city had not fallen yet, though according to the Germans it was just a question of a few days. The battle had already lasted weeks, and the Russians were still holding out. I kept hoping.

Today Berke said, "If only I could kill some Germans to repay them just a little bit! I would not mind dying!" We had been talking about how sweet it would be to take revenge for what they had done to our families. But it always came down to the fact that we had no guns. How could we get guns? It was something we all dreamed about. Berke had talked about it to the few gentiles he saw from time to time. But it didn't look promising.

There were rumors of partisans in the forests of White Russia. How much of that was true?

Month of October 1942

We kept wondering about our *Oberzahlmeister*. One of the young fellows, who was about sixteen, was now working for him, more or less, as a personal valet. The special attention he paid to us boys was very obvious, and we assumed that he was homosexual. None of us knew much about this subject, but we kept speculating about it. It was hard to imagine how it was possible not to have a sexual urge for girls, but instead to have that desire for other men. Anyhow, the *Oberzahlmeister* was a very fine person, and I wished there were many as decent as he.

As I was walking with Max, he suddenly pointed to some pigeons. "You see those birds landing on that roof? They are very special."

"How can you tell what kind they are? To me they all look the same."

"These are homing pigeons. They can find their way home, even if they are released a hundred kilometers away." He explained, "My uncle used to have a pigeon coop in the attic, and I'd spend hours there."

Max was that way. He knew all about animals and birds, getting excited about a tree, a flower, or any growing thing. He could be very gentle but also tough and forceful in his dealings with people.

Since the Guttermans moved to the new place, there had been a big change. It happened gradually, but during the last several weeks, both Max and I had become members of the family. Max's "behavior" of a few months ago had been forgotten, and we were both accepted without reservation. We spent most of our free time with them, often returning to our room only to sleep. We usually had all our meals together, running in early in the morning for breakfast; Mother gave us sandwiches to take along for lunch, and we returned for supper after work.

Food had become less of a problem. Besides what Max and I managed to bring, Leiser got some leftovers from the German kitchen, and the girls were occasionally given something by soldiers who appreciated the clean laundry.

The food situation in the citadel in general had improved, but only because stuff was swiped from the warehouse by the 322 people and bartered with civilians for food. However, many had no opportunities at all and were always hungry. I often wondered about our German bosses. They must have known that we could not possibly survive on our ration—one small piece of bread per day. No doubt, many of them would be happy to see us all die of starvation, but the few of them who do show some concern for "*their* Jews"—how do they think we survive?

I dreamed last night about my family—we were all there at home, and they seemed so real: Father and Mother, Ruvke and Nehamah. It did not feel like an ordinary dream. I had a definite sense of having been with them. For quite a while the feeling lingered on. Nehamah talked to me, telling me something. I couldn't remember what it was about.

How I wish I could have truly spoken to her! Before the war, I was the big brother, and she was the little sister with the ginger hair and freckled face. How little I really knew her! When we parted, she was not quite thirteen, just beginning to blossom.

Was any one of them still alive? Ruvke was gone, but the rest— maybe by some miracle, someone felt sorry for them there on the highway and gave them a lift, enabling them to get away. I knew there wasn't much chance, but just maybe. . . .

Whenever I passed by the 322 building, I could see Jewish girls outside the barred, first-floor windows. A kind of quiet courtship was going on between some Russian prisoners behind the bars and these young girls. I could hear at times sad Russian songs sung softly, and once in a while the sound of harmonica playing. Most of the girls were all alone and lonely.

The POWs didn't look as starved as they did last winter. I didn't know whether there had been a general change in the way POWs were being treated, or if there had been just some improvement in their situation here. The Ukrainians among them were encouraged to volunteer for special military units under German control. I doubted that they were being sent to fight the Red Army, but I saw them armed and in their special uniforms, guarding other Russian prisoners.

House-to-house fighting was still going on in Stalingrad. The city had not fallen yet! I still kept my secret thought deep inside about that city and had not given up hope.

"Do we really care what happens after we are gone? Or is it like—who said it . . . Louis the Fourteenth?" And Mrs. Pressma quoted in Russian: *"Posle menia khot' patop* [After me, the deluge!]"

A big discussion was going on when we came back to our room from the Guttermans—all about death, the fear of dying.

There were different opinions. Quite a few expressed the thought that went more or less like this: "I would not mind dying, as long as I could see the Nazis defeated first." But I thought, Most of the time, you only fool yourself when you think you wouldn't mind dying. I guess we all feel it would be *easier* to die if we could see their downfall. But life is precious, and we'd mind dying all right. We all want to live, God, how we want to live!

I thought a lot about death—in fact, it was never quite out of my mind. Before the war, death seemed unreal, scary. I could remember when I was very young, worrying about Father. He was ten years older than Mother. Perhaps because of his beard, he seemed to be getting old, and I was concerned about his having to die (he must have been then in his middle thirties). But this anxiety lasted only a short time.

Now living so closely, so intimately, with it, death was very real and I tried to understand it. Of course, I was scared of dying. I wanted to live very much, but I realized it was not so much the act of dying that bothered me—one minute you're alive, the next you're dead, perhaps feeling the momentary prick of the bullet. But the cessation of life—that was what bothered me. That life in all its splendor, exciting and interesting, would be going on without me, without my consciousness, without my awareness—the finality and irreversibility of it. I remembered reading tragic stories of the Great War, of young men losing limbs, or eyesight. When I talked about it with my friends, some would say they'd rather die than live an invalid's life. I was not so sure then. Now, I knew. I'd want to live, regardless. It was hard to believe now that, in normal times, some people took their own lives, sometimes even young persons. To think that people have killed themselves because they lost a great deal of money or were forced into bankruptcy. To die for that! With all the misery of last fall and winter, I had not heard of one person committing suicide in the Daugavpils ghetto.

The three of us, Berke, Max, and I, were having a little celebration. Last night there was an air raid warning—Russian planes were in the vicinity! The sirens sounded like music. It was the first time since the outbreak of war that this had happened here.

We were on our third or fourth drink, and I said in a boisterous voice: "Things are changing, you'll see—and Stalingrad still has not fallen!"

Max answered in a somewhat subdued tone, "The damned Germans will always find time to kill us before they're beaten."

Berke then became quite excited. He stood up and shouted, "The god-damn Germans! Get me a knife, and I will cut up a couple of those rotten bastards!"

"Sit down, Berke!" Both of us were trying to calm him.

"We've got to take revenge, kill them!" he shouted; then became quiet.

I got a piece of smoked bacon as part of a deal and brought it home with a feeling of triumph. Bacon was much sought after but very hard to get. It was nourishing, could be used in a variety of forms and combinations, was easily stored, and most important, could be saved for a long time without spoiling.

As a child, I knew that a pig was not to be touched. There was a special taboo: Pork was not only *trayf* (nonkosher) but was unique in the extreme repugnance we Jews felt for it. On market days (always on Wednesdays in Jonava) I would look with fascination at the huge pigs tied up, lying immobile in peasants' carts. I'd wonder what would happen to me if I touched that despised beast. How would God punish me for such a crime? And now, a piece of bacon . . . During the ghetto quarantine last winter, one of the fellows I knew gave his dead mother's gold ring to a guard for a small piece of bacon.

There was a great difference between the SS or SD and the regular Wehrmacht soldiers. Among the former I had so far never met one who was humane, but most of the regular soldiers, once they got to know us, were not so bad, and some were downright decent. Nonetheless, there were some vicious brutes among them, too. A certain overseer at 322 was such a man. At the slightest transgression he became enraged, kicking and hitting his victim in the stomach and face until the unfortunate was covered with blood. Bertha Berger was his latest victim. I was told the German beat her so much she could hardly move.

An air raid! How extraordinary. Bombs were dropped right here in Daugavpils.

It happened in the middle of the night. Suddenly we were awakened by the wailing of sirens. Then it became quiet for a while. It was completely dark, and we all listened tensely. Berke jumped into my cot with me. After a while we could hear the drone of airplanes. The sound became louder and louder, and Berke was overcome with emotion. "Imagine, Shaikele," he whispered loudly, "imagine, Russian planes are just above us!" The planes were now very close, and then came the deafening sound of exploding bombs. Bombs were falling on German soldiers! We were happy, excited; Berke had tears in his eyes.

In the morning we found that the bombs had hit the other end of our long building, and the glass of hundreds of windows had been shattered by the blasts. We were elated, encouraged by the penetration of Russian planes so far behind German lines. I didn't know, though, whether German soldiers were killed in the raid.

The immediate effect of the bombing was that most of our people were turned into glaziers. With the weather getting colder, people were made to work at a feverish pace.

In about a week or so, all the broken window glass had been replaced, and things were returning to normal. But now there was not enough work for the glaziers, and they were being sent to different jobs. Max talked to the *Blondinger* and asked to be assigned to work with me as a painter. The German agreed, and Max was to begin painting with me.

Stalingrad had become very important in my mind. I kept thinking of it. As the days went by and the city continued to hold out against the Germans, I became more and more optimistic .

Month of November 1942

Golda was always cheerful and understanding. Actually she, Hinda, and Ella were working very hard, doing the laundry for a whole company of soldiers. Every piece of underwear had to be first soaked, rubbed by hand on a washboard, boiled in a kettle, rinsed several times, and then hung out to dry in the attic of the building where the soldiers were billeted. Later, of course, it had to be taken off the lines and folded neatly. They really slaved away at it, especially since they did not allow Mother to help them. I knew they sometimes argued about it; she wanted to help, but the girls insisted that she do just the cooking and other housework. Max and I were going to get chlorine for them to help bleach the laundry.

The Gutterman family had been washing laundry for the same German unit for more than a year. They'd become almost like a fixture for these Germans. Among them were "good Germans" and "bad Germans," but good or bad, every single soldier benefited from being constantly supplied with clean underwear. Occasionally a "good" one would in some way express his appreciation, even sympathy. In general the girls were not bothered much as long as the work was done properly and on time. The captain in command of the unit was a middle-aged, heavyset man. When he met one of the girls, he usually smiled and occasionally made a friendly remark. A few of the soldiers were very considerate, and of all of them, Corporal Liederman was the most helpful. He was tall, probably in his thirties, very clever, and a great "organizer." He might turn up any old time with a gift of food.

It was curious that the two of us, Golda and I, spent so much time together, and yet we never got bored with each other. We talked about everything. Today we were talking about the fact that one doesn't always see the same thing the same way. Things that don't seem so bad during the day might look very different at night. I said that it reminded me of a little incident when I was about twelve maybe even younger.

Golda asked me to tell her about it, so—diffidently—I did.

It was the summer when I and my other three buddies, the twins Leib and Haim and Motke Segal, were completely under the spell of the Jules Verne books. Almost every Saturday afternoon we'd go on what we used to call expeditions. We'd prowl around the countryside, exploring or trying to discover objects that were sometimes real and sometimes imaginary. But that Saturday we had a very definite goal: We were going to locate the source of the little creek. This ten-foot wide stream was a favorite hangout of ours, and it seemed fitting to find the place where it originated (like discovering the source of the Nile). But after several hours of following the twisting current, this turned into one of our duller ventures. Our feet were wet from crossing and recrossing the little creek, and the end of it was nowhere in sight. But when we suddenly reached a road and Haim recognized it as the one leading to Seimai, our spirits rose considerably.

"See this bend?" he exclaimed. "We're at least six kilometers from home, and I bet it's only ten kilometers farther to Seimai." We all gazed wistfully at the winding dusty roadway, stretching there between green pine woods and ripe late-summer fields; with the mellow glow of the warm afternoon sun and a lazy stillness all around, it seemed very inviting. In short, we decided to walk to Seimai. Of course we knew we couldn't make it back the same day, but that's what appealed to us most: We'd sleep someplace under a tree and would return home the next day. There was a moment's hesitation—what would our parents think when we didn't come home at nightfall? But we brushed it aside lightly. In high spirits and full of plans for the night (one of us would stand watch with a wooden stick for defense), we were off.

We were close to the town when we realized that the day was slowly fading away, pretty soon it would be dark. Our gay and boastful chatter died away, and we suddenly saw the whole thing in a different light. Motke recalled having heard stories of wolves roaming the forests, and we all talked it over in subdued voices. The whole business of sleeping under a tree lost its glamour and now seemed quite impractical. And our parents—we now reminded one another of them and the effect our nonappearance would have.

By the time we reached Seimai, a small shabby place, it was dark, and we were just four very worried little boys, far from home. We were almost at the other end of the main street, desperate and at a complete loss of what to do next, when a friendly, smiling stranger stopped us and asked for our destination. It wasn't hard for him to see our predicament. He took us to the railroad station, bought tickets, and put us on a train. When we got back home, it was almost midnight. Of course, by then our parents were all sick with worry, and Motke Segal's parents, from then on, forbade him to have anything to do with the twins. . . .

"You were just kids," Golda said when I finished. "It's different when you grow up. You can anticipate things much more realistically."

"You're probably right. I haven't thought of that little escapade for a long time, but there might be a moral there somewhere, I don't know. . . ."

It was only a couple of weeks since Max started painting with me but he was catching on real fast. It was pleasant to be working together.

The Germans have just about captured the city of Stalingrad—or so Liederman's paper said. There were just a few pockets of resistance left to be cleaned out. Was it possible that this was the end for Stalingrad? The city had held out so long, so grimly. I still had some hope. The Germans were probably exaggerating the gains they had made there.

Of all of us, Hinda was best at the business of barter. Lately she had been getting stuff from 322 people and trading it with civilians. Mother kept telling her not to do it, and said many times, "I'd rather starve than see you risking your life." But Hinda wouldn't listen. She was quite fearless and had a quiet determination and a way of doing things without fuss, as if the danger were not worth talking about.

There was a brick, wood-burning range in the laundry room, and this was our favorite spot, Golda's and mine. In the evening the family was usually in the other room across the hall, quite separate from the laundry. Now that winter was almost here, we liked to sit on a bench in front of a burning fire. We decided to use the room on alternate evenings, one evening Max and Hinda, the next, Golda and I.

Tuesday, November 24, 1942

Good news at last from the Stalingrad front! A few days ago, the Russians started a strong counteroffensive in that area. Obviously, German papers didn't tell the whole story, but one could read between the lines. The Russians seemed to have had great success there.

It struck me that both of us, Max and I, in a most natural way and without us being conscious of it, had for some time been calling Golda's mother "Mother," and that she had been referring to us as "Children."

Month of December 1942

The Germans were getting hit hard in the Stalingrad area, no doubt about that! There was even talk of a Russian "breakthrough." Was it possible that it would turn out just the way I'd hoped and dreamed it would—that this would be the beginning of the end for them?

While Mother was preparing food in the laundry, Hinda said : "I want to show you something." She pulled out from under a blanket a black and velvety article of clothing. While we felt its silky softness, she explained: "This is a sealskin vest. I don't want Mother to see it." And she put it back.

The vests come from 322. They were supposed to protect the Germans from the Russian winter and were probably issued only to pilots or officers. I couldn't imagine regular soldiers getting something so valuable. Lately, in the 322 warehouse vests had been appearing and people had discovered that there was a very good market for them—Latvian ladies made fur coats and jackets from them. What happened when someone was caught with such a prize possession can well be imagined. When I said, "Don't you think it's too dangerous to handle something so hot?" she answered, "What I am thinking is that, every time I get rid of one of these, a German has to freeze in the bitter Russian cold."

The embers in the range were glowing brightly in the half-darkened room. Only the bench where we sat was illuminated by the sparse light of the fire, the only sound being the soft crackle of burning wood. It was snowing outside. For the moment we felt quite snug—only Golda and I and the love we felt for one another. Everything else was far removed. How simple life could be—what else did one need? But reality always intruded sooner or later, never allowing us to forget that death, was here in our snug room too.

I said to Golda, "I would die gladly—if I knew that my dying would somehow save you, that you would survive. . . ."

"Yes . . . I feel the same way about you. . . ."

Bertha Berger was arrested. She was a courageous and defiant person going to the city often without stars. This time she was stopped while on the way to town and found to have a sealskin vest in her possession. She was in prison now, good as dead. The people of 322 were very worried. A search of their rooms was expected, and they must get rid of anything incriminating as quickly as possible.

Friday, January 1, 1943: The 559th day

Last night we could again hear the sounds of merrymaking—the Germans' celebration of the New Year. Not much for us to be thankful for except that we were still alive. Who would have expected it? This by itself was reason to celebrate: We had something to drink last night, and Mother prepared a fine dinner.

Month of January 1943

When I came in from work, a big surprise awaited me: a note from Shmulke Palec! It was left by a young woman named Shiff. She was from Daugavpils. In the fall of 1941 she and her father escaped to Braslav. Shmulke wrote just a few lines: "Dear Shaike, I am together with Mr. Shiff in one camp. We are starving here. If you can spare any food at all, give it to Miss Shiff. She will bring it to me. Shmulke."

The package for Shmulke was picked up the next day while I was at work. One of the fellows here talked to the woman. Shmulke and her father were in a camp not far from a town in Lithuania called Dukstas. It was very bad there; they got very little food. The daughter came to Daugavpils illegally. The whole thing was baffling; how could she manage it? But Shmulke was alive, needed food, and I was glad I could help him.

I heard the news in the evening: One of the fellows got a gun from a farmer, an old and rusty one. Could it be made to work?

Yeshia worked as a locksmith and had a key for the locksmith shop. On Sunday a few of us met there. Eagerly, we crowded around him as he struggled with various tools to take the gun apart. It was a revolver completely covered with rust and dirt. It must have been buried in the ground for a long time. After a while, with an abundance of prompting and advice, the gun at last yielded—one side of the wooden butt came off, revealing a broken spring. It was doubtful that the gun could be made to work even with a new spring; the whole thing was just rusted through and through. We were disappointed, yes, but the fact that we had held a gun in our hands, even if only a broken one, put us all in an upbeat mood. I had the feeling that something important had happened today.

My friendship with Max. We were so different from each other in most things, and yet we felt very close. I found it hard to talk of my emotions and feelings; it embarrassed me. Besides, I believed that these things became apparent without words. Max was just the opposite. He talked often about how he felt about me, often saying something like, "Shaike, if I had my own brother here, I could not feel any closer to him than I do to you."

But today we were talking about dogs. A mangy, hungry-looking mongrel was scurrying across the street. Max said:

"We always had a dog in the house."

"I like dogs, too," I said. "We had a cat and at one time a dog named Rex, a light-brown mongrel. He seemed to have appeared out of nowhere and stayed with us quite a while. Then on a market day, Mother gave him away to a farmer, without our knowing about it. A few days later, Saturday morning, while we were still in bed, I heard scratching at the door. I opened it, and there was Rex! How happy we kids were to see him!A piece of rope was dangling from his neck—obviously he'd been tied up, but chewed through the rope and found his way to our house."

"What happened to the dog later?"

"He disappeared. I guess Mother gave him away again. I can still remember how I felt when I saw that poor dog, with the chewed-up rope, jumping for joy when we opened the door. Imagine, finding his way back from who knows how far away!"

"Yes, some dogs are that way," Max said.

Winter was in full swing. The cold, the ice and snow made us feel isolated, almost as if we'd been forgotten by "them," which was fine with us. The hope was that we'd be left alone as long as this cold weather held; it would be hard to dig ditches in the solidly frozen ground.

Eierov made plastic pendants for me and Max. We gave them to the girls.

Month of February 1943

Our work was running smoothly. Most of the time only Max and I were on the job, with the German stopping by here and there during the day. Usually we painted one large room a day. Sometimes we had an hour or two free, because we could not start another room late in the day. We moved around quite freely in the citadel; there was always the excuse that we needed paint or a ladder. Dressed in our dark blue work suits stained with patches of paint and holding a pail or brush in hand, we must have been a familiar sight in the citadel.

Like many others, I was wearing German infantry boots. Strange, no one questioned it here in the citadel. But, then, everyone wore an odd assortment of clothing—some of it civilian, some of it pieces of Russian and Latvian army uniforms.

Max told me of an interesting remark Rudy had made to him. "You Jews take off your caps for us, and act submissive, but I am not fooled. I know you don't mean it. I can see defiance in your eyes."

The Germans were being slaughtered around Stalingrad, and the Russians were still keeping up their advance. I was elated. It seemed miraculous—my secret hope was actually coming to pass. Now I had no doubt that Stalingrad would be the turning point in the war. Naturally we gave no indication that we were aware of anything—the Germans walked around with long noses.

As I sat with Golda in our favorite spot on the bench, there was cheerfulness even in the crackle of the wood burning in the range. Tonight I felt hopeful. "Just because the Germans took more than a year to get to Stalingrad," I said, "it doesn't mean it need take that long to chase them back. Don't forget: The Americans might land in Europe any day now."

"That may be so," Golda answered dubiously. "But the Nazis will make sure to finish *us* before they leave. A murderer doesn't leave witnesses to his crime."

"At the right time, we'll escape. In another month or so, it will be spring."

"Where could we run? And what about Mother?"

The wood in the range was turning into red embers that still emitted pleasant waves of heat. After a while we got back to the same subject. "All right, our chances of surviving the war are slim. But it is so hard to imagine life going on afterward, without us being there, without our existence."

We spoke of that certain hope, latent and irrational but always deep inside us, that we would live to see the defeat of the Nazis. We talked about that and about what life might be like afterward. It seemed so hard to visualize. Still, tonight was a time of hope, and Golda said jokingly, "Who knows, maybe a long time after the war, we'll suddenly run into each other, at some restaurant or nightclub—maybe even in America or Palestine. . . ."

I took up the story: "You will be dancing with a handsome man, and suddenly I'll recognize you. . . ."

After the last war there were many stories of "dead" people, suddenly turning up alive after many years. We had both seen many such movies with happy endings.

We were ecstatic! At last we had something that could be considered a real weapon—two grenades! We bought them from the fellows at 322. Lately, a grenade was occasionally found in a pocket, when uniforms arriving from the front were being sorted. They looked like large eggs of an olive color with smooth skin. They didn't seem like much, still these were real weapons, with a string to be pulled from the top. Pull the string, count, then throw! I wasn't sure exactly how much counting we'd have to do. Someone said count to five, another to eleven. We'd have to find out.

What was more, Berke was promised a gun by a gentile who lived in the city. We had to prepare a large sum of money. It seemed that this time something might really come out of it.

Something strange happened to me. While I was outside the room where we were working, a German soldier called to me from across the small courtyard, "You, come here!" When I walked over, he told me to follow him. I thought he wanted to give me something, maybe a piece of bread. But once inside the room, he put his hand on my fly, unbuttoned it and began to fondle my private parts. I was completely bewildered. Suddenly he jumped back—there was the sound of approaching footsteps. I ran out as fast as I could.

Eli Kurland was arrested and taken to prison. As usual there were few details. I wasn't in the room when they came for him. Someone said he was mistaken for someone else with the same family name who was supposed to have been a communist before the war. Although he was a friend of Ella Gutterman, he never quite became a member of the family the way we did, but he was a good guy. We all liked him—now suddenly he was gone.

Outside it was pitch dark and cold; the wind howled. We talked about Palestine. Golda said wistfully, "It never gets cold there."A picture of the Mediterranean shoreline, which I had seen a long time ago, was before my eyes: People in swimsuits frolicking on a golden beach, waves lapping at the shore, and the whole scene bathed in sunlight. One of Golda's older brothers went to Palestine to be a pioneer, to work the land. I told her of the time when as kids a bunch of us talked of running away from home and marching all the way there. We'd get together, make plans, and come up with all kinds of schemes. Palestine—it had always been a dream for us.

After a while we became less serious and began to talk in a lighthearted way. I told Golda about Sheinale Polan, with whom I'd been pretty taken at one time. We were in the same class at school, but no one noticed her much. Then at about sixteen or so, she suddenly blossomed into a shapely, attractive girl becoming wildly popular. That year—just before the war— I'd go to dances, and we'd kid around with girls, but Sheinale was the only one I'd had a really serious conversation with. She was about a year older than I, so our meetings were on her initiative, of course.

As I was telling Golda about Sheinale, it sounded funny, and we both laughed a little. "Sheinale told me that she liked me a lot, but she wanted to be honest, so she admitted that there was a boy in Kaunas, a couple of years older than she, and that if she had her choice, she would have preferred him. Since he was in Kaunas, she actually encouraged my interest in her. On the back of a small photograph she had given me, she wrote, 'To Shaike with love'."

"I certainly would like to see that picture. . . ."

"Gone," I said. "You remember I had to discard everything, when we were in prison waiting to be shot."

"Just don't you dare throw away *my* picture," Golda said with mock severity—referring to the small photograph, she had given me some time ago.

Of course, we were not always deep in conversation. Our arrangement for using the laundry room on certain evenings, was working out very well. When I was there with Golda, no one ever entered and we had complete privacy.

We still heard good news from the fronts: The Russians were advancing, retaking many cities, even Kharkov. Here, however, everything continued the same way; the Germans acted as if they would stay in Daugavpils forever.

Month of March 1943

Tonight we celebrated properly and for much reason—we had a revolver! It was a Nagan (A revolver used in Russia). It was in perfect condition and looked like new. What was more, Berke was promised two more in a week or so—we'd each have one.

It was very unusual for a German officer to engage any one of us in conversation. But this was what happened at my temporary job, where I'd been helping a soldier paint a few rooms. The German captain (apparently not a combat officer) started talking to me, while I was in a shed mixing paint. It turned out that he was looking for gold coins and was willing to pay for them in genuine French three-star cognac. I told him none of us had any gold. But later it struck me that it was worth checking on. In the evening I talked to Bentzl Shafir, who, I knew, had been a prosperous person before the war. Yes, he had a ten-ruble gold coin, and, yes, he would be interested. As he put it, "If I have to die, I'd like to get nicely drunk at least once on French cognac." Such a coincidence! That the one person with a gold coin would also be ready to give it up for liquor; I didn't think anyone else of our people would have done it. But that Shafir sure had a zest for life, one could see it when talking with him. He still had his wife and a little boy of about seven with him. His wife was very attractive and was said to have won a beauty contest some years back. As to the danger in dealing with an officer—A German didn't need an elaborate scheme to trap a Jew—he could do whatever he wanted with me anyway.

Two days later I brought three beautiful bottles of cognac to Shafir, getting my compensation in the form of German marks. I was no wheeler-dealer but I did learn a thing or two.

The same people in our room had been jammed together for almost a year and a half without any privacy, yet we hardly ever had any arguments and generally got along very well. Maybe the people here were more decent than most. Golda thought that the fact that none of us had any family might have something to do with it.

Berke brought two automatics! He bought them again from the same person. They were TT pistols of large caliber and looked like new. I could remember Russian officers wearing the same kind of guns before the war. They were beautiful. They cost us a great deal of money, but we were overjoyed. At last we were armed. Berke and Max would each have a pistol and I the revolver. The pistols were much better weapons, however, there were only twenty bullets for the two of them, while I had more than a 100, and Berke was promised even more revolver ammunition.

"You know," I said, "if we could only get a compass and a map of the area east of us, of White Russia, we'd really be all set."

Month of April 1943

Early spring. The sun was warm. As I passed an open window of some officer's quarters, soft strains of dance music came from a radio. It was the first time since the war that I had heard this kind of sentimental music, and for a moment there, I was carried away by it to a different world and time. . . . An evening in May . . . the balmy air, the starry sky and the smell of lilacs . . . a feeling of restlessness with an expectation of something that was not easily definable. The main street of Jonava was crowded with young people marching back and forth, back and forth with nervous energy. The girls promenaded in twos or threes. Clearly, we were all enveloped by the same restlessness, by a certain yearning. Countless times I passed Eva walking with her girlfriend and every time, returning my gaze, she looked intently at me. How could one go to sleep on a night such as this? . . .

But now, it was escape that was constantly on our minds. We had heard rumors of Russian partisans (guerrillas) fighting in the forests of White Russia. But even if that was true, how could we find them? We must fight the Germans, take revenge; we were determined not to sell our lives cheaply. We talked about it constantly, and our state of mind was altogether different. Spring was here, we had weapons, and news from the fronts was still good, although the big city of Kharkov had been recaptured by the Germans. But there was always the awareness that we must use extreme caution. We could take only one chance; there would be no second one.

We heard of an escape from the city that failed. I didn't have all the details, but six Jews were involved, four men and two women. They had an arrangement with a German to take them to the forest, but the driver drove them only a small distance, then dropped them off. Some of the group returned to the city, and their absence was never discovered. The others continued to the forest and were captured shortly afterward.

As we went on from day to day with our strange kind of existence, life before the war seemed farther and farther away, almost unreal. But how was one to understand our existence here in the citadel? The Nazis had been exterminating us without mercy, and though most of the actual killing had been done by Latvians, it was the Germans who had given the orders, who conducted the *Aktionen*. Yet, the few of us here in temporary reprieve lived among Germans, sometimes in the same building, using the same entrance. And I thought of Liederman, Otto, the *Oberzahlmeister*, and a few others I had come across, certainly decent human beings. Here too, however, there was a strangeness. Regardless of how friendly a German became with a Jew, awareness that one had absolute power over the other made such an association seem unnatural.

In general, the mood, in the citadel seemed feverish, with a nightmarish, unreal quality about it. Added to the bizarre atmosphere were the constantly marching columns of Ukrainian soldiers, now collaborators of the Germans. Some of the Russian marching songs, which they sang at the top of their voices, were tunes that had been adapted to Zionist lyrics; before the war we had sung them in Hebrew in our Zionist youth organizations. How eerie to hear them, as if our enemies were singing Zionist songs.

It was only about six weeks since we first acquired our first gun, and I could not help thinking of how strangely things happen. For such a long time we had yearned for arms, ached for weapons, dreamed and hoped for a hard metallic something in the hand to defend ourselves with. They had seemed utterly unattainable. Now, all of a sudden we had weapons—not only the three of us, but quite a few friends from our unit and others from 322. Our own arsenal had also increased. We'd bought an additional two grenades, now totaling four. We also received even more bullets for my gun, though, so far, there was no more ammunition for the pistols. The unattainable was slowly being attained.

News about Shmulke Palec. He was here in Daugavpils, and this was what happened to him. He escaped from Dukst, but when he came here with Mr. Shiff (whose daughter had taken my package to him a few months ago) and asked to work for 322, they were both promptly arrested. We were all of us certain that this had to be the end for them, but after a few days they were released from prison, and it was a happy reunion for us. I could hardly believe it. Shmulke himself didn't expect to leave that place alive. "You know," he said, "after what happened to us there, you can imagine how I felt when I faced the inside of the prison again." He assumed that Shiff's daughter must have found a way of bribing somebody important.

It took Shmulke several hours to tell me about all that had happened to him. In that year and a half, since his escape to Braslav, he spent a lot of time on the run. Starting in the spring of 1942 and throughout that year, the Jews of all those western White Russian towns were wiped out, except for one or two cities, where, Shmulke thought, there still might have been a ghetto. Eventually, he wound up in a work camp around the town of Dukst and, learning of an impending *Aktion*, he escaped with Shiff to Daugavpils.

He doubted that anyone—of those who had escaped from Daugavpils to Braslav in the fall of 1941—was still alive. He too had heard that there were partisans in the forests.

Max and I were on a new job, working in Pogulianka, a resort area. We were painting the rooms in luxurious villas, apparently being prepared for German officers. Everything was lovely here: the houses, the forest, the clear country air. But we could not forget that nearby was the place where most of the Jews from Daugavpils, including my brother Ruvke, were killed.

Our working conditions were satisfactory. We were transported by truck to and from work. I guess we were "leased" to a private German concern. Our overseer was a German civilian, partly handicapped with some speech impairment. The other Germans also seemed to be either old or in some way disabled, and that was why they were not in the army.

Berke bought more guns. Shmulke got a Nagan like mine and David Bleier an automatic pistol of small caliber. There were only three bullets for the pistol, but more were promised.

We were waiting for an opportunity to escape. Berke, Max, and I were constantly making plans. Actually we wanted to plan our future actions with the other fellows, but didn't spend much time in our room. We were with our family, the Guttermans so much. Most of the young men were ready to fight, talking of resistance and revenge. I often talked with David Bleier, who was an active member of a Zionist youth organization.

Sunday. Two of Golda's friends who'd been working in the city came to visit us. The girls were attractive and pleasant, and we spent an enjoyable afternoon. It was nice to hear them reminisce about old times; it made me wish to have known Daugavpils the way it used to be: the young people full of life and active in the various organizations and, judging from the few who were still alive, so many attractive girls.

Month of May 1943

We finished our work in Pogulianka and were now back to painting rooms in the citadel.

Most of the time we referred to someone who was not alive anymore as having been *aroisgefirt*, ("led away" or "taken away" in Yiddish) but very often we abandoned such euphemisms and said straight out "he was shot" in this or that *Aktion*. We all talked often and bluntly about death. A year had passed since the last *Aktion*, but, except for Avrom, no one seemed to be optimistic about our chances for survival. We were not fooled and in one way or another, we tried to prepare for the next one. Many Jews like us were trying to acquire arms; others, especially women, were making every effort to provide themselves with poison to be taken at the last minute.

Now that it was warmer outside, Golda and I often sat on a bench at the side of the building, an out-of-the-way spot somewhat obscured by a wall. Our mood was bittersweet. Our impending separation hung over us, for we'd accepted the fact that I would escape and Golda would stay with her family. The Guttermans understood that Max and I had to escape to fight.

Shiff's daughter had been arrested and was in prison. There was no hope for her. There had been something mysterious about that woman. Shmulke said that she was an unusual person, very courageous and resourceful, able to live as an Aryan for a long time. Even while she'd lived as a non-Jew, she always remained close to her father, watching over and protecting him. Lately, since her father had been living in the citadel, she had been working here too, now as a Jew. While at work here, she was recognized by a German, who must have known her as a non-Jew, and was promptly arrested.

It was the middle of May. This should have been the right time to get away, but we were all aware of what we'd have to face the moment we left.

In the evening the three of us talked it over once more. Our situation was different from what it was last year. We now had guns, and although none of us had ever fired one, we didn't feel so defenseless. But we still had to face most of the same problems, and the front line was still as far away as ever. Our worst problem, though, was the hostility of the native population. How long before we would be given away? Sooner or later, we'd have to get food from farmers. There were a lot of Russian POWs in the citadel and it seemed logical that our chances for survival would be much better if we were to escape together. They were experienced soldiers, and just as important, the populace east of here was mostly Russian and would naturally be much more sympathetic to other Russians.

We all agreed to wait and watch for any opportunity that might come our way. I reminded Berke again about getting a compass and map from his friend.

We were all stirred up by the news: Gutke Yachnin escaped together with some POWs. It happened on Saturday and the Germans never found out about it. He was one of four boys working for the 200 unit in the stable as cart drivers; they took care of the horses and also delivered various stuff.

But Yachnin was back Monday morning. Actually few people knew he'd been missing, since he lived in the stables. He didn't talk much about the escapade, but we pieced together the details. He escaped with several Russian prisoners he'd gotten to know. After receiving a gun and other necessary supplies from him—and using his guidance to find their way out of town—the Russians abandoned him. Fortunately he was able to return to the city, then to the citadel without being caught.

The few Jews in the citadel who had some authority were intelligent and educated people who tried to help the rest. They had no illusions, knowing that when the moment came, their fate would be the same as Klal Israel (all the Jews).

In *Heresunterkunft Verwaltung 322*, they were Dr. Itzikowitz from Kaunas and Yasha Magid. At 200, it was Dr. Grisha Goldman. At our *Herresbaudienstelle 100*, there was no one in charge—Magaram often acted as our spokesman, but was working the same as anyone else.

The buying of guns, the talk of escape and of fighting was done mostly by the young fellows. Living so close together, they had few secrets. It was well known that the Germans would hold the community responsible for whatever a few of us might do. Some of the older ones looked at us askance, but mostly people, including those in charge, understood and gave us little trouble about it.

Month of June 1943

Another escape, and this time it was much more serious. Three girls from 322 ran away together with three POWs.

In the morning the bars of a window in the prison compound below 322 were found bent, forced apart, and three Russian prisoners were missing. The girls, all sixteen or seventeen were: Sarah Ziv, Sarah Pressma, and Sonia Levin. It was clear the girls had furnished tools or whatever else was necessary for the escape.

The people of 322 were all lined up in the yard and subjected to a harangue by the head of the outfit as he threatened them with reprisals, fulminating at the top of his voice.

For the next several days we talked of almost nothing but the escape. The Germans were outraged and we wondered what the repercussions would be.

And then, after about five days, the girls were back. It was said that the Russian prisoners had abandoned them once they were no longer needed. Left alone, and defenseless, they came back to the citadel and were immediately arrested and taken to the prison. About a week later, the three girls were shot, together with some other Jews who'd been in prison for some time.

It amazed me how fast we became aware of news that had to do with us and that the news we got was usually correct. Apparently someone of our people must be in contact with a Latvian bigwig.

The incident with the girls left us very bitter and sad but not particularly surprised. For some time now we'd realized that even the enemies of the Nazis were not necessarily our friends. Was the whole world against us? From all the betrayals and disappointments that we had experienced, we had learned our lesson: We cannot trust anyone and must be most careful in our plans.

As a result of the girls' attempted escape, there was a big change for the worse. The POWs were transferred to a different place, and we of the *Baudienstelle* were moved into their place. The Jews in the citadel would all be kept in one place from now on. We didn't like it at all.

The whole compound could be effectively surrounded and sealed by just a few Germans. The building was rectangular and had steel bars on the first-floor windows. The space between it and another building formed a courtyard with a gate at one end. At the other end, where there used to be an opening to the street, a high brick wall, rising seven or eight feet, had been freshly constructed. Jagged glass fragments had been cemented into the top, a constant reminder of the certainty that sooner or later they would come for us. I could see myself trying desperately to escape over the wall and my hands bleeding without stop. We should have some heavy clothing ready to throw over the glass, we told ourselves matter-of-factly, but still the vision of the sharp edges cutting through my hands remained with me.

The Guttermans were assigned the small structure, actually more like a shed, which was part of the border of our yard. There was very little space, only room for a cooking range, table, a few benches, plus, behind a makeshift curtain, two double and one single-tier bunks. They still had their laundry room in the building where they'd lived till now. We felt lucky, there would still be privacy, a luxury that no one else had.

While Max and I were walking one day, we noticed two baby birds not far from our building. How did they get out of their nest? There they were, fluttering around helplessly in the dust, so very vulnerable. We felt sorry for them, and fretted trying to figure out how to save them. We just could not see their nest, so at last we put them up on the branch of a tree hoping for the best.

Golda and I were listening to Weksler playing something very beautiful on the violin. He said it was by Tchaikovsky. "It reminds me of Father," I said to Golda, "He liked music a lot, but it was violin music that he loved best."

"You mention your father much more often than your mother. . ."

"I guess it's true, but I love them both. They were both always ready to do anything for us children; we meant so much to them. . . . But Father, he spent so much time teaching us and telling us about things. Mother was only seventeen when they got married, Father was ten years older. He was in the Great War and witnessed the Bolshevik Revolution, so he knew a lot of things. . . ." Once started talking about Father, I couldn't seem to stop; the words just tumbled out of my mouth. I talked about how Father would always impart knowledge to us, making things seem exciting and interesting. When we were very young, he started telling us the history of the world. He started from the very beginning and continued with the story at least once a week. We looked forward to it. Saturday mornings, we'd crawl into our parents' bed and listen attentively to the exploits of Alexander the great . . . Julius Caesar . . . or the tragic endings of Hannibal or Spartacus. . . . The very first book, I bought for myself was a Lithuanian book about Hannibal. And Napoleon. I guess father was fascinated by him. In Jonava, they once had a tribunal, a sort of a mock trial of Napoleon. The Jewish community organized things like that—debates really—every once in a while. People would come to them as they would to the theater, to listen to the arguments about whether a certain historical figure was guilty of doing more harm than good for humanity. Father was Napoleon's defender, sort of defense attorney (although he may have had his reservations about Bonaparte), and he must have put up a good argument in his favor, because the verdict was Not Guilty.

"And he would always take us places," I rushed on. "To the countryside, to one of the few plants in town, or anywhere . . . and would always explain things. Sometimes, on a summer evening, the children of the neighborhood would gather together in our yard, and Father would teach us anthems of various countries, or tell us about Palestine or just about anything. . . ."

Tuesday, June 22, 1943: The 731st day

Before the war people used to say, "If war comes, it can't go on for very long. With all the modern weapons and with the poison gas they can use against whole cities, at the most it could last six months."

It was two years since the war began. And for some people it's been almost four years. Who would have thought it could last so long?

Sunday, July 4, 1943

It was Golda's birthday. She was nineteen. She was wearing a green dress of silkish material, which fit her perfectly and emphasized the loveliness of her figure in a most seductive way. I'd never seen the dress before; we paid very little attention to clothing, in our circumstances. Golda usually wore a skirt and blouse. In this green frock, she was stunning.

In the afternoon, a little celebration; we even danced a few steps while humming a tango melody. I gave Golda a watch I'd obtained from someone at 322 through a complicated deal.

Month of July 1943

Our preparations for escape continued. At last Berke got a compass and a map. The map seemed quite detailed, but I didn't have a good look at it—to spread it out would draw too much attention—and I didn't even know what area it covered. The Russian army compass had a leather strap, to be worn on the wrist; the needle and indicators were luminous making it possible to read it even in total darkness. We also had army bandages and iodine. The man who supplied all this was Polish, doing it not just for money but in order to help us.

We saw Misha, one of the Ukrainian collaborators, quite often. We'd met him some time ago and had had a friendly relationship with him. Before he was captured by the Germans, he used to be a senior lieutenant in the Red Army. Lately he'd been talking of our escaping together with him and a few of his friends. We told him that we had arms, and believed that he was sincere in wanting to escape. (I could well imagine what would happen to him and his friends if they fell into the hands of the Red Army here in the citadel. These Ukrainians, who a short time ago had been prisoners themselves, were now the armed guards of the Russian POWs.) But I didn't know if anything would come of it.

What could be nicer than to go swimming on a nice summer day!

This had never happened before, but Saturday afternoon, we received permission to go to a lake, provided we were accompanied by a German guard. The lake was some kilometers away, not used much by the general populace. The girls had bathing suits, also trunks for Max and me, and Liederman was our guard.

It was fun right from the very beginning. We all had our swimming stuff on under our clothing. As we got closer to the lake, we started undressing as we walked, to enjoy the hot sun on our bodies—just the way we used to do as kids back home in Jonava, going to the Neris River. For a while Golda was ahead of me. She was wearing a two-piece swimsuit, and as I watched her slightly swaying walk, I was overcome with a feeling of pride mixed with a touch of wonder that she'd chosen me. I thought, This is really my Golda.

We all enjoyed the swimming hugely. I just hoped that we'd get permission to do it again.

American and English armies had landed in Sicily, and huge battles were going on around Kursk. Surely, everyone could see that the Germans must lose the war sooner or later. I kept wondering about the German soldiers. Couldn't they see it was only a question of time?

Misha kept talking escape. We told him we were ready any time. We were convinced that he was indeed eager to escape, since he must have known that the tide of war had turned against the Germans. But that didn't mean that he might not try to take advantage of us in some fashion. We'd seen too much of that.

When Misha asked for money, one day, we were not at all surprised. "You know," he said, "we have to buy necessary supplies for escape." We were doubtful that he would buy the "necessary supplies," but we gave him some anyway. A few days later Misha again asked for money and again we gave it to him. Later in the evening we met him, and he was quite drunk. We decided to give him no more cash.

Berke fell very ill, and Dr. Goldman said it was typhus. We kept that diagnosis from the Germans for there was no telling what they would do with all of us if they found out.

Month of August 1943

Summer was slipping by. We'd been talking a lot about what to do next. One thing was certain: we were not going to allow anyone to take advantage of us anymore. We were looking for an opportunity to get away. Meanwhile, in case the Germans decided to finish us off, we established a warning system, to give us enough time to get away. We were not guarded and we did keep getting information. At the slightest rumor or uncertainty we would have our own guard posted at night, and would make our break at the first hint of danger. If in spite of all our precautions, we were unable to get away, then we'd die fighting right here—and take a few Germans with us.

Misha again requested money. We told him that we didn't have any more, but we still kept up friendly relations. One never knew, and the Ukrainian continued to talk of escape.

I often tried to visualize the end. I'd daydream of fighting off the Germans as they tried to take us away from here. I could see us crouching at the upstairs windows, firing away with our guns, lobbing grenades. It wouldn't be very easy for them to take us. All the buildings around were filled with Germans, so they would have to be careful not to hit their own people. I was glad to have so many bullets for my gun, I should be able to keep on firing for a long time. I realized I was only daydreaming; still, the prospect of making the Nazis pay for our lives was comforting. And to die while fighting it out to the very end, surrounded by my close ones, had its attractions. Most of the time, though, the daydream included a scene where, at the very last minute, we managed to escape.

Max and I had a new job: spray-painting all the roofs in the citadel an olive-greenish color, obviously meant as camouflage against enemy planes. It was another indication that things were not going too well for the Germans. The work we did was hard. One of us held the nozzle directing the spray, while the other pumped the large cylindrical container of paint. The roofs here were of galvanized iron and quite steep. Carrying around the heavy container on the slippery roofs, we sometimes stumbled and skidded, sweating profusely in the sun. We were constantly pressured by our overseer—("Faster . . . faster . . .") he must have had orders to hurry from higher up. That gave us some satisfaction. The Germans must be worried about Russian bombs.

Berke got over his illness and now was working as usual.

The Germans were going to search for arms in our rooms. Many people had guns. That was the rumor—it was certainly possible. At 322 they even bought guns from a German soldier. With all that going on, the Germans could easily have gotten wind of it. Just as a precaution, Max and I decided to hide our guns in the attic where the girls hung the laundry to dry. The building was occupied by soldiers, so they should be quite safe there. We'd get the guns back as soon as things quieted down.

Friday, September 3, 1943

In our room, after work, we were told by one of the young boys that Misha was outside and wanted to talk to Max. When Max returned, he told me what had happened. Misha was waiting with two more Ukrainians. "We are going to escape right now, this evening," he said. Max could smell liquor on his breath. Misha went on: "We know exactly where the partisans are, and you guys can come with us, but you have to give us your guns."

Max had a short answer: "The guns we don't give up."

For a while Misha tried to reason: "We are experienced soldiers, we can accomplish much more with the guns than you can." But Max would not hear of it and returned to the room.

I often saw Ukrainians armed with rifles, but the Germans didn't trust them much and probably didn't allow them to carry arms off duty.

Thursday, September 9, 1943

Things happen when you least expect them. We had been in a fever of excitement for several hours. When I came home from work, after dropping off a pail of chlorine for the girls at the laundry room, Max was bursting with the news: Misha had waited for him and announced that he'd just come back from the partisans for the purpose of taking us back there to the forest. We were to leave tomorrow evening, "but the main thing," Max said, "is that we can keep our guns." It was clear that the Ukrainians came for us only because we had weapons. They would not take along the Gutterman girls even if they had been willing to leave the rest of their family. Neither Hinda nor Golda, would consider leaving anyway, so that was not a problem.

Then, a while later, Berke came with news: A Pole he'd been in contact with for some time had also told him of a planned escape to the partisans for tomorrow evening, with an invitation for us to join them. We'd been somewhat skeptical about Misha's story, but this planned escape seemed genuine. Berke's friend and Misha were talking of the same operation. We agreed to join them and were to meet tomorrow at 7:30 in the evening in Griva, on the other side of the Daugava, beyond the bridge.

We had to work the whole next day, so there was little time. Whatever preparations we had to make had to be done right away. We'd planned a very long time for this moment, and we knew exactly what to wear and what to take along. Some of my bullets were still in the attic. Golda would get them. I had mentioned, not quite seriously, that it would be nice to have a bandolier to carry them in, and she immediately insisted on making one. She intended to work most of the night, fastening each individual bullet slot with needle and thread. I felt angry with myself for letting her struggle with that silly contraption. But she insisted on doing it.

The whole family was making every effort to help and ease our departure, although it involved leaving them. There was a feeling of sadness, at having to part, but at the same time, they understood what we must do. I believed, they even felt a touch of pride, since we were going off to fight the enemy.

Later, before going to bed, I stood outside for a while with Golda. We knew this was our last chance to be alone. The sky was clear, the stars very bright. I was overcome by conflicting emotions: the thrill, at last, of getting a chance to escape and to fight, mixed with sadness over our impending separation. We had talked, discussed, and planned for so long—now the great moment was here. We both knew we might never see each other again and were very much aware of the poignancy of the moment.

Golda looked up at the sky and said, "Every evening at nine, let's both look up at the Big Dipper over there." We found the familiar seven star constellation. "This way," she continued, "we'll think of each other at the same moment every day. If there are no stars, I'll still look in that direction anyway."

I agreed. "Wonderful idea. I'll look at it every night."

Friday, September 10, 1943

I worked hard all day. It felt strange to know that within hours we'd be away, and everything would be changed for us. Meanwhile we lugged around the heavy spraying machine over a slippery hot metal roof, pumping away furiously, while down in the street, soldiers were marching to the rhythm of their own singing, and everything seemed the way it had always been. At lunchtime, I could hear snatches of a news report on the radio through an open window: The Germans seemed to be having some problems in Italy; I was not sure what they were.

After work we rushed home—so little time! We washed and a few minutes later were at the Guttermans.

The girls had everything ready for us. Mother prepared a meal with much care, but we ate hurriedly; solemnly we drank a toast and kissed everyone good-bye. Mother said, "May God watch over you, my children." We removed our yellow stars, and we were off.

As we left the citadel, I felt well-prepared for whatever might come. I had a gun with lots of bullets, a hand grenade, and a knife. I was dressed in strong, durable clothing: Latvian military tunic, Ukrainian soldier's jacket, black breeches, German hobnailed infantry boots, and a short dark gray coat like those worn by Russian tank troops. I was particularly satisfied with my coat, made of special light material that was wind and water-resistant. I was also carrying a small package containing extra underwear, shaving kit, first aid supplies, and other necessities. Max and Berke were similarly equipped. And the compass with the map gave us an additional feeling of confidence.

We had to walk about four kilometers to our place of rendezvous, mostly over the Dombe, the main road in town, and then cross the bridge, which was guarded by German soldiers on both sides of the river. Max was the only one who looked somewhat Jewish. Not to appear suspicious, we split up, Berke walked by himself with the two of us following.

When we came close to the river, Berke stopped. Max walked over to him for a brief discussion; there was some question of how to proceed over the bridge. He returned, telling me that Berke would cross the bridge first, and it was up to me whether to go with him or by myself. We went together.

We were not challenged and in a few more minutes were across the Daugava. Our partners were not here yet. As the minutes ticked away, we began to wonder whether they would actually show up. We agreed to continue eastward by ourselves in case they didn't come. But after a while they appeared and as he passed us, Misha muttered, "Follow us."

Besides Misha and two other Ukrainians, there were also two civilians, obviously acting as guides. We continued to march east on the road toward White Russia, we Jews somewhat behind the others. After a while, one of the guides sidled up to us. "You have three guns, give us at least one." We refused and he didn't press the matter.

From the very beginning the "bandolier" under my clothing felt very uncomfortable. I removed the bullets from it filling up all my pockets.

The road was completely dark and deserted. The guides were setting a very fast pace, and we had to keep up with them. I kept wondering at the courage of these men. Here we were, a group of eight men with a few handguns, marching on the road as if Germans and Latvian police didn't even exist.

It hit me; it was Friday evening, Shabbes. For a moment, I was transported to a different, far-away world—Friday night back at home. The white tablecloth, lighted candles, the table set for Shabbes dinner and mother ready with all the special dishes as father returned from synagogue. Here on this solitary road, how far I was, in every sense, from that bright and cheerful scene!

We had been marching very fast. I assumed we were supposed to reach a specific place by a certain time. Off and on I hummed soundlessly repetitive song phrases to keep time; it made the marching easier.

As we passed villages, we were usually met only by the barking of dogs. But at the entrance to one village, there were two men in civilian clothes standing on the side of the road. We passed within a few feet of them. No one uttered a sound. I could only speculate: Were they sentinels appointed by the village? These were troubled times; fear was widespread in the land.

In our hasty departure from the citadel, I hadn't thought of taking along food. Max, though, ever the practical and experienced one, had had the sense to stuff some cooked meat in his pocket. After walking for many hours without rest, it felt good to have a few bites.

After midnight we stopped at a small peasant house. It was isolated, quite a distance from the road. We each got a slice of bread, covered with a thin layer of butter; we ate it hurriedly and were on our way again. Only now our group was augmented by a woman, a girl, and a man carrying a small hunting gun.

Saturday, September 11, 1943

We marched the whole night at the same fast pace. Since our stop at the peasant house, we had used no road, moving cross-country instead, which made marching even harder. On and on—we had to reach a certain area before daylight. We were exhausted. The three of us had worked hard the whole day, Berke had just recovered from a serious illness, and the extra weight of my ammunition didn't help. I thought to myself wryly: If we are attacked now and have to defend ourselves by crouching behind a tree to shoot back, at least I'll be off my feet for a while. But we advanced steadily, our whole group stretched out in single file, with our two guides striding confidently in front. Yes, they did know exactly what they were doing and must be very familiar with the area.

At dawn, we reached a wet, spongy area covered with small trees and bushes. We found a dry spot and threw ourselves on the ground. We had walked the whole night without rest and were to stay here for the day.

As the sun set, we got ready to leave. Suddenly shots rang out. Everyone froze; we could see men with guns in the distance. It was too far to determine who they were, and they didn't seem to move. Had someone spotted us and notified the police? The situation seemed serious; even our self-assured guides showed concern. The older one said, "Just in case we get separated, there's a small woods about four kilometers southeast of here. We'll meet there." Misha added, "We'd better have a password; we might need one in the dark. Let it be 'Pushkin'."

Stealthily, keeping our heads down, we left the area. No one followed us.

We made a lot of progress, again walking very fast, hour after hour. Berke asked that we rest awhile, but was put off with promises. We were all very tired.

Finally, sometime during the night, we stopped close to a farm. Our guides went inside and in a little while came back with two horse-drawn carts; we sat on them and off we went, galloping ahead. What a relief to be sitting and watching the kilometers fly by.

Much later a warning was passed along: "Watch out, we're coming to the narrow gauge tracks, then through the town of Opsa," obviously dangerous areas. The railroad tracks didn't seem like much, but it must have been a likely spot for German patrols. A short time later, we reached the town and everyone tensed up. We three clutched our guns. Again I was surprised by the audacity of these guides. In the midst of night, armed only with a few guns, we went galloping through the town, with metal-covered wheels making a racket over the cobblestones, loud enough to wake the dead.

After we had passed through Opsa, our guide said: "We should soon be with the partisans." About ten kilometers farther, we were suddenly challenged by an armed man. Our guide said something to him, and we went on. We had reached partisan territory! A little later we stopped at a house and, after pounding on the door, were let in, greeted, and given some food. Finally we were led to the barn behind the house to rest. I fell asleep immediately; we were all dead tired.

Sunday, September 12, 1943

When we woke up, it was midday. The house was full of men with guns—partisans. Food was cooking on the stove, and everyone was cheerful.

Misha, coming over to us with a man carrying a submachine gun, was all smiles:

"Here we are in partisan territory," he beamed.

"Now that you are here, you must turn over your weapons," said the other man.

We were confused, uncertain.

"Come, give him the guns." Misha said, "It's the rule here. You'll get them back later."

They took our guns, the ammunition, and grenades plus the compass and map.

We all had a hearty meal and something strong to drink, then went back to our carts. The village we were now leaving, Aksyutovo, was obviously under partisan control. Our guide said, "We are now going to Bobily, about eight kilometers from here."

On the road we met civilians and partisans, walking or riding in carts or on horseback. As we came closer, four or five people on horseback attached themselves to our group. I didn't know whether they knew our guides, but we were given a very warm welcome, and all rode in together at a fast trot, with the men on horses whooping it up and shooting their guns off in the air. We certainly entered Bobily in style.

Suddenly I found myself in a different world. We were in the village, and I was overwhelmed by the various sights and sounds. This being Sunday afternoon, there was a holiday air in the street. Partisans, village girls and peasants milled around. Then a group of officers rode by on spirited horses looking picturesque in their colorful uniforms—one even had a papakha (cossack sheepskin hat) on his head.

At headquarters, which was located in one of the village houses, we met Commander Antonov, and then were taken to another house, where we were to stay for now. Later in the evening, we were told to sleep in the barn behind the house. As we opened the barn door, I smelled the fragrance of the piled-up hay. We climbed on top, each one scooping out a place to sleep; it felt snug and secure inside the hay.

I tried to sort out my thoughts. We had dreamed so long of running away and finding partisans, a band of fighters somewhere in the forest. But by no stretch of the imagination did we expect to land in a place like Bobily, where partisan rule was so firmly established. It truly seemed like a dream. We'd done it. We'd escaped the Nazis and were here with partisans. With real Russian partisans. We would fight the enemy, getting a chance to pay them back, at least a little, for what they had done to us. I was elated.

Tuesday, September 14, 1943

We spent the following two days mostly resting. Another six newly arrived people were in the same house. They were all escaped prisoners of war except for one Latvian civilian. I wondered about him; he hardly ever said anything. We lounged around, walked through the only village street, and by talking with people, got to know about partisan life.

A partisan unit was called an *otryad* (detachment) and consisted of sixty to eighty fighters. Four to six *otryads* made up a brigade. Most units went by the names of their commanders; our *otryad* was called Antonov and our brigade Shirokov. Some units were named after famous heroes or even cities. Although the *otryad* headquarters was here in the village, the partisans all lived in a camp in the woods about five or six kilometers away.

The chief of staff of the *otryad* questioned each of us in great detail about our life before and during the war. The interrogation was repeated several times. I wondered why all the questioning. We were Jewish.

Surely, they must know that we would never cooperate with the Germans.

A Jewish man, Beliak, lived across the street; he had four children with him, the oldest of whom was about twelve. One was his, the rest orphans whose parents, relatives of his, were killed by the Nazis. He came from a small town in the vicinity, and it turned out he was in some remote way related to Max. He worked for the partisans and said other Jews were members of this outfit, too.

Although the shock I felt when we first arrived here was slowly wearing off, life in the village still seemed strange. We were deep in enemy territory, with the Russian army hundreds of kilometers to the east; yet, the whole area, including villages, was completely partisan-controlled. I should have been very happy. For the first time in more than two years, I didn't have to live with the constant fear that the ax might drop at any moment, that they would come for us. But just because this place seemed so much safer than I had expected, I felt some dissatisfaction. Those we left in Daugavpils—Golda, the rest of the family, and our friends—were always on my mind. Max and Berke felt the same way. What was most painful for us at the moment was the fact that our guns had been taken away from us. After lunch, while sitting on the porch, Berke said gloomily: "I saw the commissar wearing my pistol on his hip."

"I have seen it too," I said, "and the guide, the younger one, is wearing my Nagan and sporting our compass on his wrist, like some fancy watch to be shown off."

We knew by now—we wouldn't get the guns back.

After talking about it some more, we decided to ask Antonov to let us go on a mission to Daugavpils to bring back more young people with weapons.

In the afternoon, we went to a small bathhouse next to the lake. It was the typical peasant steam bath: a hut with a stove of layered stones and a kettle for hot water in a corner, plus some rough wooden steps to go up for more steam. Before entering the bathhouse, I had to witness something painful: some distance from the shore our guide was standing up in a boat holding one of our grenades. I asked one of the partisans, "What is he doing?"

"He's going to explode it in the water. It's the best way to catch fish," he answered cheerfully.

When he threw the grenade, it didn't explode. Maybe he didn't know how to activate it. I thought bitterly of the risks and the effort it took to get that grenade here.

Wednesday, September 15, 1943

We talked to Commander Antonov and asked to be sent on the mission to Daugavpils. We described the weapons our friends possessed in glowing terms, explaining that the fellows were all young and eager to fight the Nazis. He asked some questions, then promised to consider our request. We mentioned our guns, but he hardly bothered to explain much. "Eventually we'll all have enough arms," he said. That was all.

In the afternoon a partisan was sent to our house. His name was Archangelski, but he looked Asiatic, so he was probably an Uzbek. He put his army rifle on the table and said, "Come over here, I'll show you how to operate a rifle." We all crowded around the table, watched him work the lock, then each tried to do the same thing. He stayed only a short time, and I didn't feel much enlightened by the lesson.

A partisan leader and his subordinate, traveling from a different area on some mission, stopped in our village for the night. He was admired and spoken of as a hero. I saw him galloping on a horse through the street—short, very agile, with pistols hanging on both hips, and a submachine gun on his back, he looked fierce. But what interested us most was that he was a Jew. We briefly entertained the idea of asking him to intercede with Antonov about our guns, but it was immediately rejected. We knew it was a dumb idea. He couldn't interfere, and if he did, it would only make it worse for us. We were just tormented with pain about the loss of our guns.

Somewhere in the area was a family camp. Jews who were not accepted in partisan *otryads* lived together in a forest compound; many of them were women and children. During the 1942 massacres in western White Russia, many Jews of the small towns escaped to live in the forests. In the fall, the Germans launched an attack against the partisans. They failed to eliminate the partisans of that area, but managed to kill most of the defenseless Jews. A few survived. Later, more drifted in from various hideouts. Some had been hidden by peasants who refused to keep them any longer after their money ran out. Again they formed family camps. The partisans barely tolerated them. The Jews suffered from starvation and were in constant fear; without weapons, they were always in danger of being killed.

I was wondering about Beliak with the four children. He must have been of much value to the *otryad*, to be allowed to stay here in Bobily.

Friday, September 17, 1943

We began work yesterday on a winter camp. Altogether there were ten in our group, about half new arrivals and half regular partisans. We built *Zemlyanky* (dugouts) huts that are partly below and partly above ground, designed to keep warm in the winter. The place was about four kilometers away but not in the same direction as the summer camp. It was a long march, and just before reaching the site, which was deep in the forest, we had to traverse a nasty swamp with a creek running through the middle of it. In one spot, not at all visible to the casual eye, a tree had been felled over the water, which we used for a sort of bridge. An older partisan, Vassily, was more or less in charge of our party.

Golda was on my mind a lot.

"How could we have left the girls just like that?" I said to Max.

He felt bad too, but tried to reassure me: "What else could we do? You know they would not leave the family—even if we had guns for them."

It was so painful to know that just a hundred kilometers away, they were expecting death any minute, while here we were in the midst a whole army, living in a village without fear and having three meals a day. It was true that, when we left Daugavpils, we did not know what to expect. I'd had a vague idea of partisans roaming the woods, fighting all the time fiercely, hunted and always on the run; and I suppose some partisans did lead such an existence, but not here in Bobily. If only we could get to Daugavpils and bring back the whole family and our friends too. We decided to ask the commander again about the mission to bring people to the *otryad*.

Bobily was a small village; together with the surrounding fields and small lake it was barely more than a clearing in the huge forest. The road that passed through the village was also the only street. There were many partisan detachments in the vicinity, as well as in the Kozyany forest to the south of us, and they were in control of their areas. I found out a lot from Vassily. Speaking with pride, he said, "Bobily, ah—we call it Little Moscow. Even our clocks are set to Moscow time, two hours ahead."

There was also a partisan command for the whole region, which was in contact with the Red Army, and from time to time a light plane landed somewhere in the vicinity—important officers flown back and forth over the front lines. But the basic unit was the *otryad*, and its commander had almost absolute power over his people.

The important officers of Antonov's *otryad* were: Commander Antonov, a lanky man in his late twenties, and Commissar Gusheff, a middle-aged man with a fleshy face and thick neck. In addition to the chief of staff, there was also a *starshina* (literally master sergeant, but a term used for the supply officer), tall and blond. The commander and commissar wore regular Red Army officers' uniforms, but the *starshina* wore a Polish cavalry uniform and carried both a gun and a long saber.

The *otrayd* was divided into two platoons, each commanded by a noncommissioned officer. The outfit was relatively new; it had split off about a month ago from another one that became too large. It was in this manner that the *otryady* continuously multiplied. There had been partisans in this area for quite some time, but since summer, the influx of volunteers was very large—no doubt reports of the advancing Red Army had much to do with it.

We got plenty of food—beef with soup and bread, as much as we wanted, three times a day. The work was not very hard, no one rushed us. We had two horses to help us drag the trees we cut to be used as logs in the construction of the huts. At night, when we went back to the village, they were left in the forest. It was pleasant to be in the forest, but I wished we'd get a chance to fight the Germans.

We went again to headquarters to repeat our request to bring people for the *otryad*. The commissar remained silent, but Antonov asked: "Did you get to know any of the POWs in the citadel?"

"Oh, yes," I replied quickly. "We had a lot of contact with them." He again promised to consider our request. I didn't have much hope.

Saturday, September 18, 1943

As I stood with Max watching the couples dancing a waltz, I knew it was a scene I wouldn't easily forget. We'd heard the sound of music coming from the headquarters house; entering the large room, now emptied of furniture, we found a Saturday night dance in progress, mostly partisans dancing with village girls. The place was illuminated only by the faint light of a few long wood splinters made into smoky torches, stuck in the walls. It was crowded. A one-legged musician was playing on a *Bayan* (kind of accordion). Rifles and submachine guns were leaning against the walls, while partisans in their colorful and diverse outfits, with guns dangling from hips, were twirling their partners around the floor. The *starshina*, obviously very drunk, was trying to dance while his long sabre kept getting in his way. And the primitive lighting left the room in semidarkness, adding to the distinctive atmosphere, which had something exotic and exciting about it.

I was fascinated by it all, but also sad. There was one waltz that the musician seemed to be playing more than any other tune. Its haunting, bittersweet melody made me feel, in an acute way, the sorrow that was within me. We watched them for some time. After a while the dancing became more heated and vigorous; the *kazachok*, a lively dance, was being performed with lots of gusto and jumping around.

On the way back to our barn, neither one of us said anything much. Burrowed deep in the hay, I couldn't fall asleep. I could hear the music for a long time.

Sunday, September 19, 1943

We got a lot of information from Beliak, the Jewish man with the children. Besides the three of us, there were in the *otryad* another nine Jews, seven men and two women. All of them were from the area; they had escaped from small-town ghettos where they had faced certain death. The older of the two women was Pola, red-haired, in her twenties. She was a nurse, the medical officer of the *otryad*, serious, competent and highly respected. Maryusa was dark-haired, about twenty; she did the cooking for us, the workers.

Some of the Jewish men were sent on missions. Haim Pitik was armed with a long-barreled old gun, and Meir carried an *ostrezanka* (sawed-off rifle). Others were involved in the economic activities of the *otryad*, evidence of which I could see in Beliak's home: a large wool-cleaning machine took up most of the space in the main room. From the wool, they made *voliki* (felt boots) for the winter. The hide of cattle, slaughtered for food, was tanned, and turned into leather. Rachmiel, a tall middle-aged man, was quite involved in that work. There was also a Jewish tailor and shoemaker. Beliak told us proudly, "Eventually all the partisans in the *otryad* will wear the footwear and sheepskin coats we produce."

I said, "It's really impressive how well the partisans are organized, but weapons—that they don't have enough of."

"Sure," he explained. "Almost all *otryady* have problems getting enough arms. They have to be brought from *Vostok* [the East] several hundred kilometers from here and that isn't easy, I can tell you. But the Lithuanian Brigade, they have plenty of everything!"

We'd heard some talk of a Lithuanian Brigade, which had its base somewhere in the Kozyany Forest, but were not too clear about it. Beliak continued:

"There, each fighter has a Pe Pe Sha [the most desirable weapon—a Russian submachine gun with round cylinder]. They are parachuted directly to them. All kinds of supplies they get, even chocolates. And some of the fighters have also been dropped by parachute."

This information was quite exciting. Max and I were Lithuanians and Berke was Latvian, which is just about the same thing; we should ask to be transferred to that outfit.

Beliak agreed. "I think there is a good chance you'd be accepted."

I said, "Just imagine to be in an outfit like that, each with his own Pe Pe Sha and revolver!"

I thought that what we heard might be exaggerated, especially about the chocolate, but most of it must have been true, for it seemed obvious why the Russians would want to have a crack outfit of Lithuanians making a name in fighting the Germans. It would counteract, to a degree, the well-known fact that many Lithuanians and Latvians were enthusiastic collaborators with the Germans. We decided to be on the lookout for an opportunity to transfer to that fantastic unit and went home in a happy mood.

As the day came to an end, the village seemed peaceful and content. Partisans were standing around some village girls who were sitting on the grass and singing "Thestushki"—a song of many stanzas sung by a lead singer in a high-pitched voice, with the chorus repeating the same refrain.

Monday, September 20, 1943

While we were eating lunch, we heard the sound of a machine gun, barely audible, fading after a few minutes.

The culinary skills of Maryusa, our cook, were truly limited. We had beef for every meal, and she always prepared it the same way: throwing it in a kettle and boiling until it was tender enough to eat. After the scarcity in Daugavpils, it felt good to eat our fill, but still, boiled beef three times a day was too much of a good thing.

Tuesday, September 21, 1941

Today we could again hear machine gun firing, only louder. Vassily said, "The fast rattle is a German MG, the slower one is ours, Russian."

We all stopped working. After a short time, the firing stopped, but we did not get back to work for quite a while. Our conversation turned to various weapons. The Pe Pe Sha was very much coveted, but some of the older men thought it was not accurate at longer range. One veteran said, "Ah, a carbine, I wouldn't exchange it for anything. It's light, yet you can hit a man a hundred meters away." Clearly, these men didn't have much respect for a handgun. One said, "Even with a heavy caliber revolver, it's hard to hit anything from a distance of more than twenty meters."

A surprise awaited me after work—I was called to headquarters.

"Well, Sasha," Antonov said, using the name the partisans had for me, "are you ready to go to Daugavpils?"

"Yes," I answered promptly.

"Good. Misha will be in charge of the mission." He pointed to the Ukrainian, who was standing next to him, and continued giving us exact instructions. Altogether, six people would be going. Besides me and Misha there would be the same two Ukrainians and the two guides with whom we came here.

The plan was as follows: We would travel together until we reached a certain forest about twenty kilometers this side of Daugavpils. From there I was to continue on my own to the citadel to contact a friend of Misha, a Ukrainian soldier, and deliver a letter that would convince him and his comrades that I was to be trusted. I would also make contact with Russian POWs and Jews, and get as many of the people as possible to come back with me to my "escort" waiting in the forest. From there we'd all return together to our *otryad*. We were to leave tomorrow, Wednesday, and be back the following Monday.

My task would be a hard one. After arriving in that forest during the night, I would have to go on to Daugavpils by myself in order to arrive there in the morning. I'd have to contact the different people during the day and march back with all the "recruits" to my waiting escort in the evening, and then continue that same night toward Bobily.

Antonov said: "It is a very tough assignment, and you don't have to go. It is entirely voluntary on your part."

"I'll be happy to go," I answered, not even trying to calculate the total mileage I'd have to cover without rest.

"Good," he said and continued: "Now listen carefully, Sasha. Get all the POWs and all the Ukrainians you can. As for the Jews, take only those who have weapons, you understand? Don't take Jews without weapons.

"I understand." To myself, I thought, Let me just get to Daugavpils— I'll know what to do.

I guess they selected me because I didn't look Jewish, although, neither does Berke. But whatever the reason, I was happy and excited that I was the one to go. I spent the evening talking to Max and Berke. My plan was quite clear to me. I would contact the Russians and Ukrainians as ordered, but would try to save as many Jews as possible. There were many guns among the fellows when we left Daugavpils. They must have acquired more in the meantime. I knew how eager they were to escape, but I would also encourage people without weapons to flee. Even if some of them weren't acceptable to the *otryad*, it would be better that they live in the family camp and starve than wait for certain death in Daugavpils. Besides all that, my hope was somehow to procure weapons for the three of us. But my main resolve: I would make sure that the whole Gutterman family came back with me to the forest.

Wednesday, September 22, 1943

We set out in the morning. The good-byes with Max and Berke were short. We were in an upbeat mood: At last I was getting my chance. I was surprised by the warm send-off I got from Alexey, an ex-POW who came here shortly before us and with whom we'd become quite friendly. He was an architect and had lived in Moscow. "Sasha," he said with concern, "I heard what they assigned you to do. Take care of yourself and don't take unnecessary chances."

Everyone was armed with either a rifle or side arm except for me—I got only a Russian grenade. The jagged surface made it look more potent than the German egg-grenades, still, it was only one grenade. I could only think to myself of the injustice, but said nothing now. I was determined to demand a gun when the time came for me to go by myself into the citadel.

In a few hours, we arrived at the village of Aksyutovo. The town of Opsa, about twelve kilometers northwest, was under Nazi control, but here we were still in partisan territory. The house we came to was familiar—the same one we slept in when we first arrived here twelve days ago.

We spent the next couple of hours pleasantly enough, eating countless fried pork patties and drinking *samogon* (home brew). Misha first poured a little of the liquid on the rough wooden table, and put a burning match to it. It was enveloped by a fine bluish flame, a sign that the stuff was good. The men were in a cheerful mood. Glasses were refilled frequently, and the woman frying the patties kept on bringing fresh supplies. I'd made up my mind previously that I would show no weakness in any form and did my best to keep up.

There was no hurry. From here on we'd march cross-country, but even so there were only another fifteen to twenty kilometers that we could traverse during daylight; after that it would be too dangerous, and we'd travel only at night.

At last we were ready. My companions had had enough to eat and drink. The leftover patties were packed in a cloth bag, and we were off.

We spent the afternoon marching over fields and woods, without using roads. By and by, our small reserve of food had disappeared; it felt good to munch the tasty patties while walking vigorously. The narrow gauge train tracks were crossed carefully, and it was getting dark when we came to a small settlement.

The village was small and poor; the huts with thatched straw roofs, like those all over this part of the world, were scattered on both sides of the road, telling their tale of misery in the waning light. In the very first house, we got information about the German whereabouts—a Nazi unit was in a village about ten kilometers from here.

We needed food for the next day, but it was obvious there was not much of it here. Misha then split us in two, three of us on each side of the road, and told us to check each house for provisions. To me, Misha said:

"Don't let on you're Jewish."

"I understand."

The people here were really poor. And most of the time the answer to our request was: "We have just a little bread for the children—nothing more," explaining that both partisans and Germans regularly helped themselves to provisions.

It was only in one of the last houses that we discovered something decent to eat and even got to drink kvass, a kind of cider. We took along food for the trip and were on our way.

We marched at a fast pace the whole night, but it did not seem much like an ordeal. The daily walks these past weeks, to and from work, must have conditioned me for long marches. However, as the many hours passed, I felt my boot rubbing the heel of my left foot. It was not too bad yet, but I feared it would get worse. My boots were a tight fit, and now after all the walking it felt even tighter; it would take time to remove the boots, rewrap the *perchonky* (foot rags) and then put them on again. I decided to ignore it, not wanting to ask the rest of the group to stop just for my sake.

Thursday, September 23, 1943

We stopped for the day in a marsh, very similar to where we had stayed over on the way from Daugavpils; maybe it was even the same place—it was swampy with islands of dry ground here and there, and the whole area covered with low-growing brush.

It was sunny, and we spent a restful day. At last, I had a chance to take off my boots and adjust the foot rags.

In the afternoon, Misha said to me, "Sasha, we are going to stay here another night and day."

"You mean, we are not continuing on our way tonight?"

"No, we'll stay here another night and day," he repeated.

"But why?" I was flabbergasted. "We were told to be back in Bobily by Monday, why spend another day here?"

He didn't give me an answer to my question. "I am sure we can do it," he said. It just didn't make sense at all. My role in the operation was hard enough as originally planned, losing a whole day would make it much harder yet. But I did not press him for an explanation and said nothing more about it. Damn their skins, I thought to myself. I'll make it. I saw myself in my frantic flight on the road to Daugavpils back in June 1941. I knew that if at all humanly possible, I would get there and back regardless of what lay ahead. But even if we were to return to Bobily a day or two late, it still should not be much of a problem—as long as we accomplished our mission.

Friday, September 24, 1943

Our day of rest passed pleasantly. True, what little food we had was gone yesterday, and by this morning we ran out of tobacco; like the rest, I went through all my pockets and somehow gathered enough crumbs to roll one last anemic-looking cigarette. But the sky was blue, the sun felt agreeably warm, and there was a feeling of peacefulness in the air. A plane very high in the cloudless sky seemed to move very slowly because of the distance, and even this engine of destruction looked to me now more like a lazy insect than a bird of prey.

I kept thinking of Golda and of Daugavpils and was eager to be on the way. It seemed incredible that I should see her tomorrow. But then again, they might all be dead by now, so much could have happened since we left. It was hard to believe that it was really just two weeks today since I said good-bye to her.

At dusk we left our hideaway and, after marching a short time, stopped by a solitary house. Our guides went inside and brought back bread and also information which made them a little uneasy: German units were stationed at many points where no soldiers had been seen for months.

As the evening wore on, I again marveled at the guides' knowledge of the territory. We marched across country with no road in sight, yet they led us with the certainty of one walking through his own backyard. A few more times they stopped at houses for information. Suddenly the sky ahead lit up—light flares fired by the Germans west of here. We kept going. Later many more flares appeared, and after another stop at a farmhouse, I felt uncertainty among my companions. We stopped and following a brief conference, Misha said:

"We are turning back. There are Germans all over. It would be much too dangerous to continue."

I was disappointed and bitter. I thought angrily, They just don't want to take any risks.

Saturday, September 25, 1943

The journey back went fast. After marching rapidly for many hours, we stopped at a prosperous-looking farmstead. Three of us stayed outside, and the other three went in. After a while I heard a faint sound, as if a small fire cracker was discharged in the distance. Some time later our people came out leading a spirited black horse hitched to a wagon in which was sprawled a large dead pig. One of the Ukrainians said to me, "They shot the pig in the ear. That's why it didn't sound loud." We all piled in the wagon and off we went. I didn't know whether the horse and pig were taken by force. Meanwhile we were racing back. The horse was a fine animal, moving steadily on, even though he was pulling a heavy load.

We rolled into Aksyutovo during the day, stopping to refresh ourselves in the same house we started out from last Wednesday.

The room was crowded. Two partisans from an *otryad* based some distance away were caught terrorizing peasants of this area. The strangers were disarmed by our people and were being held under guard in another room. I could see their two rifles stacked in a corner (one was a Russian, ten round semiautomatic). We spent little time there and shortly afterward rode into Bobily.

Though I felt disappointed because of the aborted mission, it was good to be back with my friends. Alexey said with conviction, "Don't worry, after a while the Germans will stop bothering this area, and you'll get to Daugavpils."

Obviously something was going on: A German drive against this whole area was in progress. The mood of complete confidence and almost pastoral living we found at first was giving way to some uneasiness. Yet, there was still dancing at night at headquarters, and later, when we were wakened by a barrage of shots, it turned out to be no more than a send-off party in honor of the commander of the brigade, who was going to Moscow in a small plane.

Monday, September 27

On the way from work we met partisans riding in a cart. They were Jews. Most of our group continued on, but the three of us stopped to talk with them. They were all from Glubokoye, one of the larger towns in western White Russia, about sixty kilometers east of here. They now belonged to an *otryad* stationed in the region. Most of what they told us was all too familiar. A ghetto was set up, and because it was the largest town in the area, Jews from smaller towns and villages were brought there. From the little time we talked, I got a clear picture of the terror, the frequent *Aktionen* and constant starvation, and then in August, just a little over a month ago, the ghetto was liquidated. Some of the Jews had arms, and the Germans used artillery in order to destroy the ghetto. Still, a few, like these people, were able to escape. The saddest part of the story was that even now this handful of survivors had to experience discrimination in their *otryad*. A dark-haired, vivacious girl, whose father used to be a doctor, finished the tale with bitterness: "No matter how hard we try, we are still not completely accepted."

It seemed that even enemies of the Nazis, when exposed to virulent anti-Semitic propaganda, were often also influenced by it.

Tuesday, September 28, 1943

What was happening in Daugavpils? We worried about it. The concern for our family made us feel even closer to each other. Today, as we were returning from work, Max and I were walking on the other side of the road behind the rest. While talking about it, Max, in his dramatic way, was saying:

"Shaike, we are closer to each other even than brothers, and nothing in the world will ever separate us—except death . . . blood."

At the moment he uttered the last word, we were stopped in our tracks. Something was lying on the path in front of us—a leather belt stained with blood. It was remarkable.

"You see," Max said. "It is a sign—a sign that our bond is sealed forever."

When we returned to Bobily, we learned that the two partisans apprehended for terrorizing villagers had been executed. They were shot near that road we passed earlier, where we came upon the bloody belt.

Wednesday, September 29, 1943

There was no doubt. The Germans had opened a large campaign against the whole partisan-occupied area. We heard the sound of battle coming closer every day. I could now distinguish quite clearly the slower, more ponderous rattle of the Russian Degtyarev machine guns and the fast, nervous chatter of the German MGs; other weapons too had their telltale sounds. When the sound of firing became heavy, we stopped working and listened with concentration, as if one could gauge the progress of the battle from the various noises.

With all this activity, our hearts were hardly in the work at hand. We stopped frequently, talked, speculated, and when a discussion got too involved, one of the veterans might say: "Davai perekurom eta dela [Let's smoke these matters over]." Whereupon we'd gather around the smoldering bonfire, roll a bit of *makhorka* in pieces of newspaper, and talk continued to run smoothly.

"Ah, those battles!" Vassily explained about what was going on now: "Our lads fight bravely and against heavy odds. Sometimes a detachment of partisans is formed with fighters from several *otryady* and sent to engage an enemy unit. Our forces initially inflict heavy casualties and push them back, but then the Nazis call on massive reinforcements, forcing our people to retreat."

Although the Germans' move on our area seemed ominous, the veterans among us did not exhibit undue alarm. "It is like in the fall of '42," one said. "Then, too, the Germans attacked us, but we managed to get away. It will be the same now."

Nevertheless, I heard that many *otryady* had retreated "*na Vostok* [eastward]." It appeared that every *otryad* had a choice: to stay put or retreat east. Antonov, our commander, had decided to remain.

As we sat around the fire, talk turned to various past events. "*Na Vostok*," an area much closer to the front line, was where a huge concentration of partisans was located. It was from there that most of the arms were brought. A trip there and back was an odyssey of hardship and danger, lasting many days, with each fighter carrying back to the *otryad* three or four rifles and loads of ammunition.

Generally, in this struggle, no quarter was asked or given. Partisans, if caught, were lucky to be executed promptly. The other side got no pity either. The police chief of some small town was known for his cruelty in dealing with captured partisans. "That one," Vassily told us, "he was an inventor, always inventing new ways of torturing the unfortunates who fell in his hands. It took time, but finally our lads captured him. You know what they did with him?" Vassily didn't wait for an answer: "They put him in a cage like a wild beast—big and fat as he was, he looked like a bear. With the cage on a cart he was driven through our villages where people spat at him and abused him." After a few seconds of silence, he concluded, "His end you can well imagine."

Beliak came over to our house and said to us, speaking softly, "Tonight is Rosh Hashanah. Come over to our place and pray with us. With you we might have a minyan. [quorum of ten men]."

We readily agreed. We were treated not quite fairly by the partisans, and made to feel that we were different, and the fact that our praying would be frowned upon (if it became known) made us now feel more eager to join the other Jews. It turned out that even with us three, we had no minyan, because a couple of the men were on missions for the *otryad*. But as we stood there, repeating the familiar, age-old Hebrew passages, I was glad I was there, feeling the strong bond uniting us all.

Tuesday, September 30, 1943

So far I had yet to see the camp where most of the people of the *otryad* lived. We had been living in the village and still had our own cook—though to call Maryusa a cook was gross flattery. We continued to get beef three times a day, always prepared the same way, boiled in water with a little salt. When we first came, we thought it was quite extraordinary to be able to eat all the meat and bread we wanted. Now, our stomachs were rebelling. We did not complain, but the other partisans had begun to grumble. Not that great culinary masterpieces were requested—just an occasional change in recipes. But so far, no luck.

We three had found another way to augment our diet—berries. The walk back from work was usually a leisurely affair. We were in no hurry and rested a couple of times on the way where the ground was just covered with red berries, which had a pleasant tart flavor. We gorged ourselves on them. Berke especially was a strong believer in their beneficial effect; he'd been bothered by his stomach quite a lot, and felt strongly that the fruit helped him.

Friday, October 1, 1943

I had heard more talk about the Lithuanian Brigade.

A partisan of another *otryad* told us how well armed and organized it was. But we had to wait till things calmed down here before we could try to obtain a transfer. Battles were going on all around us, and many *otryady* had moved to the east.

I saw several officers leaving headquarters. They must have been here for a conference. One of them, wearing a beard, was very tall and looked imposing in his long leather coat. His beard reminded me of Father. Beliak said it was Commander Gromov, who was well known for his courage. His *otryad* was not far from us.

The news from the front was very good. The Red Army was on the offensive and was advancing on Vitebsk, about 250 kilometers from here.

One of the Ukrainians took a fancy to my Latvian tunic. I exchanged it with him for two shirts.

Saturday, October 2, 1943

Today was the day. Maryusa had promised to prepare something special for our evening meal. The word was that she'd have meat patties ready for us. There was also talk of future plans for the production of homemade sausage!

We were all looking forward to the special meal and hurried back from work. But just as we were about to leave the forest and could see the houses of Bobily about a kilometer away, we stopped short. A plane, [its body the shape of a rectangular frame,] was circling the village. In disbelief we all watched it make several passes, then drop a few bombs—Bobily was being bombed! So, the Germans knew this was a center for partisan activity.

Arriving at the village, we found a lot of turmoil, but no actual casualties except for a few horses killed while grazing.

There were no meat patties. Maryusa said that in the confusion of the attack, the pot with our food was overturned and ruined.

Monday, October 4, 1943

The situation was getting serious. Not only was the incident of the plane disturbing, but the sound of firing was now almost constant, getting louder all the time and seeming to come from all directions. The Germans must be trying to surround us—or, more likely, have already surrounded us.

We still went to the forest every day but did very little work; mostly we sat around the fire and talked. Besides Vassily and Alexey, we had become very friendly with the Uzbek Archangelski and a young fellow, Lolka. But I liked most to listen to Vassily, the veteran partisan, who seemed to know everything.

Tuesday, October 5, 1943

Berke stayed in Bobily this morning because he did not feel very well, but Max and I went with the others to work as usual. We hardly did anything, just sat and listened to the din of battle, which was continuous and rising to a crescendo; the fighting seemed very near. I knew that something had to happen soon.

Around midday, a messenger from our commander suddenly appeared with an order: We were to leave immediately! But instead of returning to Bobily, we were to proceed as fast as possible to the camp. The Germans were very near, and the whole *otryad* was evacuating as soon as we got back.

One problem: the two horses. It was impossible for them to cross the swamp; they had to be taken by a different route that circumvented the marsh, an additional four kilometers or so.

Vassily called out: "We need two volunteers to ride the horses back the long way." I looked at Max, he at me—there was no question: We volunteered.

Max knew something about horses, because his father used to own a horse and wagon. As for me, I loved horses, but the closest I'd come to riding one was when our family went to the country on summer visits; I'd be put on top of a horse while it was led by the bridle for watering. Max put his jacket on top of the horse, explaining, "Instead of a saddle, otherwise we'll get blisters on our behinds," and I did the same. We mounted and were off at a trot through the forest trail.

The riding was uncomfortable and awkward. The bouncing sensation was one thing, but there was also the feeling that the jacket was slipping away from under me. Then, when I tried to hold on to it, I lost my balance and fell off. No harm done, but I could imagine how funny I must have looked—Max had trouble hiding his smile. I gave my jacket to him, he had no trouble keeping them both in place, and I mounted again. The riding felt much better.

As we came closer to the road, the sound of battle became even louder. Still, we were not prepared for the scene that opened before us as we emerged from the forest and came upon the country road. It was as if a curtain had suddenly been pulled open to reveal a wide panorama, the details coming suddenly into sharp focus: refugees in horse-drawn wagons, belongings piled high and livestock towed behind; a group of partisans crouching behind a small wooden structure, firing away with automatic weapons; a rider galloping madly over a field. . . .

All that I took in within a few seconds, for in the din of exploding shells, the firing of machine guns and of rifles, our horses started to gallop. Nazi soldiers were right around here. The whole road was under German attack! As the firing went on I could hear the swish of flying bullets. (Yes, bullets really do make a sound if they pass by close enough.) But how amazing, with the horse galloping so fast, the riding felt quite comfortable. And so we rode on and on.

After a while it became quieter. There was still a lot of firing, but at least it did not seem that everyone was aiming just at us. The horses too calmed down some and continued at a somewhat slower pace, more like a canter. There were still refugees on the road, and some made as if to stop us to ask something, but we rode on. I knew how they felt and was reminded of that time in June of 1941, on the road to Daugavpils. We'd wanted to ask soldiers passing in trucks about what the situation was, but the soldiers knew very little, and as for us now, we knew even less. But as we galloped by them, we must have seemed full of purpose and authority.

We continued to see partisans, all walking in the same direction, some were from our *otryad*. Then we passed the fellows from our work brigade, waving us on. For a little while, nothing much mattered, there was just the feeling of carrying out an order well, and the exhilarating sensation of the galloping horse.

When we arrived at camp after the twelve-kilometer ride, we were complimented by the platoon commander for a job well done. Berke too was already there, anxiously awaiting our arrival. But our euphoria soon evaporated, and reality caught up with us—all we had done was ride a couple of horses to camp and risk our lives in the process. The fact was that the Nazis were all around us, and none of us three had any weapon.

Meanwhile the *otryad* was getting ready to abandon camp. We'd be leaving at dusk and we still had a few hours. It was the first time I'd actually seen this place. It was very simple, a group of huts made of branches and bark.

Throughout the camp there was feverish activity as people made their final preparations for departure. Fabric was being torn up and made into footrags. Boots were hastily repaired, and a man whose boots were completely torn was trying to fashion crude moccasins from pieces of leather. People packed the few belongings they had and checked their guns.

Beliak was not coming along; he would hide with his four children in a hole in the ground somewhere in the forest. Also a seriously wounded officer was too ill to go along. He was apparently from another outfit, and must have been an important person—a nurse and five fighters would remain to care for him and defend him if necessary.

We, the handful of Jews, were uneasy. We were tolerated when things were normal, but now in this crisis we felt a special vulnerability and danger. Haim said with concern in his voice, "They may leave us with the wounded man."

At last it was twilight. The whole *otryad* was ordered to form two lines. There were a few others besides us who lacked arms, but the rest of the men were all armed. There were also two Degtyarev machine guns, one for each of the two platoons. Food and ammunition was divided up, including the bullets I had lugged from Daugavpils.

The commander, Antonov, gave final instructions. The names of five partisans as well as Pola's, the Jewish nurse, were called out; they were ordered to stay with the wounded officer (the fighters were not Jewish). And then Antonov made a speech which was very proper for the occasion, somber yet upbeat at the same time. He told us that the Nazi enemy was making an all-out effort to destroy us and was all over the area. It would be a trying time, and hard fighting might be in store for us; some of us might not come back. But we had prevailed during last year's blockade and were sure to be successful again now. "Our heroic Red Army is advancing on all fronts," he said, "and soon the Fascist-Nazi hydra will be destroyed and our motherland freed." And then, intoning solemnly, he concluded: "Remember . . . a partisan has two loyal friends—the night and the forest . . . and these friends are with us right now."

The two lines of men, armed with a variety of guns ranging from modern machine guns to aged hunting rifles, listened attentively to the commander's words. There was a momentary hush. As I looked at the armed men standing there amidst the towering tree trunks in the gathering dusk, I was acutely aware of the drama of the moment.

Soon afterwards it became quite dark, and we left camp. Our column marched off on the *kopanka* (forest road). The two horses, now equipped with saddles, were ridden by the commander and commissar.

Friday, October 8, 1943

The night we left camp three days ago, we marched about twenty-five kilometers and camped among the trees, a few hundred yards off the road. I had expected to be on the move again that next morning, but nothing happened and we'd been waiting ever since, in a state of suspense, prepared to leave at a moment's notice.

The days were sunny and mild, the nights cold; the clearing, which I could see from where we camped, was covered with frost in the morning. We slept on the ground under trees. The three of us, lying close to each other, and pulling the coats up over our heads, kept each other warm with our body heat. During the day we could hear, from time to time, planes flying overhead and the sound of exploding bombs. When the bombs fell nearby, there was a rush of air like the swish of an ebbing sea. Several other *otryady* had also moved to this vicinity. I could see cows in the clearing and could hear their mournful mooing; their udders overflowed, painful for them, but no one bothered to milk them. They were from the herds that every *otryad* used to own but had now abandoned. I had also come across piles of hides, which had been in the process of being treated, and were now scattered on the ground, silent testimony to once high hopes.

Partisans of different *otryady* passed by here, sharing various rumors. Besides the daily bombings we heard, the Germans had also blockaded the entire region and by means of human chains were "combing" through the forest. It stood to reason that eventually they would come here too.

The three of us were often assigned to guard duty, usually for a two-hour stretch. Not too bad if it was in the evening or morning, but the time slot from two to four was rough. After managing to get tolerably warm and falling asleep on the cold ground, one was awakened at two in the morning and roused out to stand a dark, cold, and lonely watch. Last night when I was through, I had a hard time waking Berke. "I don't care what they do to me, I'm not getting up," he mumbled, half asleep. Of course, he got up and did his stint of guard duty. In the evening, though, I didn't mind it at all. The stars were bright in the clear sky. I looked at the Big Dipper, and my thoughts were of Golda. Can she really be so perfect, I wondered, or does my mind exaggerate because she is so far away, and I miss her so much?

I was given an old rifle when on guard duty and knew how to work the lock, but that was all. I had never discharged a firearm and was glad there were other guards around the camp perimeter.

Saturday, October 9, 1943

"The Germans were seen five kilometers from here!" "Bobily and the other villages have been destroyed by bombs!" This and similar talk was what I heard. Was it all true? I didn't know. I could see and hear the planes, and this by itself was most disturbing. That the Germans would use air power on us here indicated to me the importance they attached to cleaning out this area. They spared no effort in order to destroy us.

The feeling of uneasiness hadn't left me since our arrival at this spot, but today I felt especially low. I looked back with a sense of longing to the time we spent working in the forest before the evacuation, and from time to time I experienced a momentary qualm of regret, as if I had had something valuable and had somehow let it slip through my fingers. I wondered at the unreasonableness of that feeling.

The provisions we had carried with us were long gone, but we didn't starve. With all the cattle roaming around loose, there was no shortage of beef. But that's all—no bread, not even salt for cooking. I could see now how essential salt was to make food palatable. Sometimes we speared fat little pieces of raw beef and roasted them over a fire; they tasted better that way.

Sunday, October 10, 1943

As I was returning from guard duty, Max ran toward me and excitedly exclaimed: "I just saw Shmerke, your friend from Jonava, there by the *kopanka*. Come fast, you may still see him." I ran back with Max and saw Shmerke with a group of partisans just taking off. There was only enough time to exchange a few words, then he was gone, rushing to catch up with his comrades. It was like a dream, to see a classmate here in the forests of White Russia. Like Shmulke he had escaped from the Daugavpils Ghetto to Braslav. He managed to run away again when the Jews of White Russia were being killed in 1942.

In the afternoon, Antonov, our commander, made a short speech.

Among other things, he said he was aware of rumors that the *otryad* might be broken into small groups in order to enable us to elude the enemy more easily. This, he wanted to assure the *otryad*, was not true. "We will stick it out together. For what is a commander without his troops?" he asked rhetorically.

Actually the mood was better today. I even heard an old partisan say, "They might miss us, these Germans. After all they cannot cover every inch of the forest." I tried to visualize the "human chains" I guess the idea was to slip into an area the Germans had already searched.

Antonov sent out several men to get bread and information.

Tuesday, October 12, 1943

Quite abruptly, we left the camp where we had stayed almost a week. The men sent out Sunday returned early in the morning with what must have been very serious news; we were ordered to get ready for immediate decampment. They also brought back bread, and we each received a piece.

By midmorning the column stood ready for departure. It was drizzling, and a partisan wearing a heavy, long coat with sheepskin lining, asked to exchange my light waterproof half-coat for his. I knew the clumsy thing he had would be a hindrance for me, and I refused, but he insisted. "I have to be point man for the *otryad*, and for what I have to do, I need a light coat." I knew I had no choice and reluctantly made the exchange.

Shortly afterward we were on the way with the whole column stretched out on the edge of the road, hugging the tree line.

We had marched only a short distance, when we were suddenly startled by the loud rat-a-tat-tat of a machine gun. We all threw ourselves on the ground, working our way in among the trees. Clearly, we were being shot at from the road up ahead. Then there was an even louder sound of firing, and I realized it was the sound of our own two machine guns returning fire. It became quiet after a short time, and we got orders to move away from the road.

For the next couple of hours we kept trudging through the forest. When we came to a small stream, a young tree was chopped down and used as a bridge, which we crossed by holding on to overhanging branches. Finally we came to a small clearing.

The sky had cleared up and we stretched out on the grass. Antonov and the other officers were conferring for quite some time. But then they finished their talking and Commander Antonov called out, *"Yevreii syuda*! [Jews, here!].*"* When we came over, he told us that the situation was very serious; Germans were all over the forest, and we were too large a group to be able to slip through the net. He must therefore divide us into small groups. Pointing to the three of us and to four more Jews, he said that we were now on our own and to start moving. The remaining two Jewish men in the *otryad*, the tailor and shoemaker, were told to stay. My God, flashed through my head. Just like a Nazi *Aktion*—the "valued artisans" are allowed to live longer!

It was clear that the *otryad* was not being broken up—Jews were just being discarded, dumped. Antonov did not even deny it. We protested vigorously, and I said, "You might as well shoot us right now. First you took away our guns. Now you're abandoning us to the Germans."

It was no use—we were not going to be allowed to stay with them. But an order was issued, and my gun was handed to me, along with thirteen bullets. He would not return the other two pistols, and when I asked for our compass and map, I got the compass but not the map. "That I cannot give you," he said.

I felt a little better having the gun and compass in my hands, but our helpless situation was obvious. Berke asked Antonov, "Just tell us in what direction to go."

"I cannot tell you, I don't know myself. All I can say is, just evade the bullets."

So here we were, the seven of us—in the midst of a forest swarming with Germans, none of us having the least familiarity with the area. As for arms, Haim had an old Japanese rifle with a sawed-off barrel, Meir an ancient long-barreled hunting gun, and I my Nagan revolver. Quite an arsenal with which to defend ourselves against the German army.

We had no idea what to do next, but as the whole *otryad* took off, we decided to follow them at a distance. This we did, but before long our presence was noticed, and two riflemen were stationed between us and the moving column. Coincidentally, these two were Archangelski and Lionka, our coworkers at the winter camp. It was obvious that they did not relish the job of holding us back, but had no choice. And so it went on. We followed them; off and on, the two would plead with us not to follow, to go away; we ignored them. At times, the dense forest gave way to marshy terrain only sparsely covered with trees, and we could see the whole column up ahead quite clearly. They were all there, the young and the old, male and female, but we were held back by the two guards.

This went on for quite some time, and then the two in front of us disappeared for a while only to reappear a short time later. They waited for us, then Lionka said: "Fellows, you must go away. We have orders to shoot if you continue following us. Please . . . you know we have to follow orders."

We had no choice. We stopped. Night was coming. As I stood watching the last of the column disappear behind the trees in the twilight, I was overcome with a terrible rage. "You bastards! Damn you! You miserable lousy sons of bitches! I'll show you, I'll show all of you!" And though I never uttered a sound, it was as if I had yelled at the top of my voice, flinging at them, shouting out the injustice done to us and the hurt felt by me, and I felt better, much better. The hell with them, we are not through yet, I thought to myself. Though if anyone had asked me what I meant by "I'll show you," I wouldn't have known what to answer.

We were all tired; it was dark now. With no idea of where to go anyway, we decided to rest right there. We moved to a denser part of the forest and made ourselves comfortable under a big tree.

I had just fallen asleep when Haim, who volunteered to take the first watch, shook me gently. "Sh . . . quiet . . . German voices." The guttural sound of German was unmistakable. Silently we all got ready and stole away.

I thought we should travel due east toward the front line, where the heavy partisan concentrations were located. If we were to slip through the German cordon, it might as well be in that direction; besides, I'd checked the compass when we were following the *otryad* and found they had been moving in that direction too. The rest all agreed.

We made our way carefully through the forest, with me in front watching the needle on the luminous dial of the compass. Sounds of German speech had shaken us all. Now several times we thought we heard them again and were haunted by the feeling that Germans might be lurking behind any clump of trees.

Wednesday, October 13, 1943

We plodded on and on for a long time, but when it became apparent that the night would soon end, the forest began to thin out. We speeded up, wanting to reach a densely covered part of the woods where we could hide during daylight; instead, the forest ended altogether, and we were in an open field. Farther ahead I could see the looming silhouettes of straw or grain stacks—a village must be close by. Max said, "Maybe we could hide in the haystacks for the day. I used to do it back in 1941."

As we approached ever closer, there was a sudden "*Halt! Parole* [password]!" and almost immediately a machine gun opened up with a terrible racket. We ran like mad back toward the woods. Other machine guns joined in. I could see what looked like sparks over my left shoulder and instinctively swerved right. I was propelled by one impulse—to get to the protection of the trees. After an endless few minutes, I was back in the forest, still pursued by the shooting. For a while I was all by myself, then Max and Haim materialized. We stopped and waited but could see no one else. We walked a little distance in one direction, than another and called Berke's name, not daring to be too loud. No response. We were quite certain that Berke and the rest had perished under the hail of bullets.

"We blundered right into a German post," I said.

"Yes," Max said, "They must have been right behind the stacks of straw. It's a miracle we got away."

We did not dare stay too long and took off again through the forest.

The sun was coming up, and the terrain was changing from forest to marshland. Then we stopped.

"Can you hear?" Max asked.

"Yes . . . German voices." The ground was now soggy, with bushes growing on small, grassy hummocks here and there. Suddenly, it was as if we were in a bad dream: The landscape was covered with an early morning mist, and though twice we changed direction to get away from the voices, we kept hearing them and could not escape from them. We felt helpless, surrounded by an invisible enemy. At last the futility of continuing to walk became clear, and we stretched out under a clump of bushes.

The early morning was full of light, the sky bright blue and the air crisp with patches of mist floating among the bushes. It was eerie—at times no sound at all, and then we could hear the raucous voices of Germans and the neighing of horses. We could see nothing in the distance.

After a while we were overcome by exhaustion and dozed off.

I didn't know whether it was only minutes or perhaps an hour or so, but we were suddenly awakened by gunfire. It sounded as if all hell had broken loose. Machine guns were blazing away and I could see small

tufts of earth flying up in the air. "Are they shooting at us. . . ?" But
before I could complete my thought, I saw people running, darting
madly by, not more than thirty or forty yards from us. Strangely, my immediate feeling was that of relief: Partisans! At last we are not alone! I
recognized a few of Antonov's people, but most were from different
otryady. We jumped up and joined in the mad dash ahead. I thought,
We're caught in a cross fire! Then no more thinking as I merged into the
mass with its one common impulse—to get away from the murderous
fire.

Haim must have been hit after a few minutes; one moment he was
running nearby, then he was gone.

We ran. We threw ourselves on the ground, got up and ran . . . again
prone on the ground . . . and ran. Some didn't get up. The din of battle
. . . the smell of powder and whistling of bullets . . . a man lying on his
side, moaning. The ground was wet and spongy, and every step was an
effort, but we must run. . . . Way ahead a dark strip on the horizon—
forest . . . safety . . . but it was so far. Commander Gromov—yes it was
he, conspicuous with dark beard and long, black leather coat— seemed
to tower above everyone else. He was moving with measured stride, tall
and erect, stopping periodically to fire away to the left with his Pe Pe
Sha. . . . A partisan lay on his back with his legs drawn up, his face con-
torted with pain; holding in his outstretched hand a Nagan, he begged:
"Brothers, shoot me, finish me. . . !"

The sun was warm . . . fatigue and thirst . . . the heavy coat. Hold foot
an extra few seconds in spongy ground . . . immerse little plastic shaving
cup in a small puddle . . . take a deep drink of swamp water . . . and run
. . . immerse cup and drink . . . I could see the trees much closer now. . . .
I didn't see Max. . . .

At last I reached the wood. More and more partisans appeared. Haggard-
looking and winded, they flopped down on the ground. I walked on, looking for Max. A short distance away I reached a clearing and saw him.

"I was looking for you!" he exclaimed.

"I looked for you too!"

"Haim is dead."

"I thought so."

"He was hit in the temple. And," Max continued, "I saw Commander
Gromov get killed. He got hit right next to me."

"Gromov is dead?" The way he had walked there, erect, firing back at
the Germans. "What a man. . . ."

"Yes," Max said. "He was a real hero. I picked up his Pe Pe Sha."

"So where is it?" I asked eagerly.

"The commissar has it," Max answered, and explaining: "When I came here just a few minutes ago, I met Antonov and Commissar Gusev. I told them I saw Gromov getting killed. Then the commissar asked whether the sub I was holding was the dead commander's. I said, 'Yes,' and he told me to hand it over."

Groups of partisans were congregating here and there. In one corner I could see Antonov and Gusev as well as officers from other *otryady* conferring among themselves.

It wasn't long before we realized there was no safety here at all. The forest was not dense, just clumps of trees, and the Germans were still pursuing us. A small spotter plane, practically skimming the tree tops, flew over the clearing. A few minutes later, a shell hit the ground barely fifty yards away, throwing up a column of earth. Were we being shelled by mortars? The momentary feeling I'd had when reaching this clearing—that of shared danger, of all of us having just survived the latest experience, and of being allowed to stay together—evaporated quickly. We had to move away from here fast. The officers were taking desperate action, really breaking up the *otryady* into small groups. I could see three, four, five people at a time taking off, and after a while Antonov and the commissar also left with a few other officers. But we two, where were we to go? By just walking blindly, we might only run into the Nazis that much faster.

Meanwhile, the sound of firing increased in volume again.

"Let's follow these guys from a distance," said Max, referring to three well-armed fighters just moving off.

Although we followed them at a discreet distance, it was obvious they knew of us, and we were not welcome. They turned a few times and looked at us with anger. We fell back, to follow in the footsteps of another group, but left them too after a short time, before they regarded us as pests.

We found ourselves in a swamp that was running parallel to a forest from which we were being shot at.

After a while we caught up with a group of four men and a woman and followed them. At least some of them must have been officers. They were marching boldly and with purpose, strung out in Indian file, with one of them, obviously their leader, always somewhat ahead. The men were all armed with submachine guns, and the girl, blond, wearing wide tan-colored trousers, carried a light carbine. We were usually about fifty to a hundred yards from them, but surprisingly they tolerated us, neither encouraging nor discouraging our trailing behind them.

The following hours took on aspects of a nightmare. The concept of time, of how we had come here and where we were to go, all that faded. The mind was wholly preoccupied with the immediate danger and exertion: with the energy required to go on and to elude the bullets . . . the never-ending marsh, where every step called for an effort—and always the firing from the forest. Could all that shooting be directed just at me and Max, and the five ahead of us? I could see no one else. The long, heavy coat weighed a ton.

"Max, I'm throwing away the coat." I slipped out of the monstrosity and dumped it. It was easier to move now. But suddenly, "Max, Max, I had the compass in the coat pocket! Got to go back."

"Yes, I'll wait here!"

I ran back . . . was it that far? There, at last, the coat . . . quickly now . . . put my hand in the pocket . . . the piece of bread . . . no, the other pocket—yes, it was here, the compass. I was running again. . . .

"Got it, Max!"

Had to catch up. There they were, the five, in single file, firing into the forest with their subs as they moved ahead. Was it possible? Did I hear orders yelled in German from the forest?

"Max, can you hear?"

"Yes . . . orders . . . in German. . . ."

The girl was hit and fell. Her friends stopped and bent over her for a few seconds, then continued. Now only four men. We passed her motionless body sprawled on the ground, her long blond hair spread out loosely. No time to look or think. . . . Then the leader was hit. Hurriedly, they wrapped a bandage around his head, but still he continued to lead the group. Even as I struggled on, preoccupied with our desperate situation, my mind registered the striking scene: the leader with blood-soaked bandage on his head hurrying on, followed by the other three fighters, one behind the other, and all of them shooting into the forest.

Our dodging of the bullets seemed to have been going on forever. We were overcome with fatigue. But at last the shooting quieted down some. The partisans had tolerated our trailing them for a long time, and we felt it was enough. We stopped and took what scant shelter we could behind a bush. Our German infantry boots reached only to midcalf; every once in a while, the swamp water overtopped them, and our feet were soaked. We now drained out some of the water by lying down on our backs, lifting up our legs, and let it trickle out.

We didn't stay alone for long. Two Russian partisans appeared and joined us at our dry spot among the few shrubs, both strapping fellows, armed with rifles. Suddenly, as if from nowhere, a German shepherd materialized, sniffed around a bit, and ran away. "They are using dogs— the bastards," the older partisan muttered.

"Shaike, Germans!" Max shook me. Completely exhausted I'd fallen into a momentary doze, but jumped up wide awake. In the distance I saw a line of soldiers advancing through the swamp brush toward us. We ran, and immediately heavy shooting broke out. The two partisans (who had probably not been on the run the whole day as we had been) took off like hunted deer, and in minutes they were way ahead of us. The barrage of automatic and rifle fire increased in intensity; again I could hear the sound of flying bullets, and again I wondered dully, All that against us four?

We ran a while longer, but the spongy marsh terrain was just too much; exhaustion was overwhelming us. As we slowed down, Max turned to me. "Shaike, it's no use . . . the hell with it. Let's just walk— it's impossible to run."

"So be it," I said. "I feel the same way."

No chance of getting out of here alive. We stopped for a moment, shook hands, and said good-bye.

"Remember." I repeated to him the understanding we have had all along: "If I'm hit and can't go on, finish me with the gun."

"Yes," he said, "and you do the same to me."

Staying close to each other we kept on marching steadily, not too fast, not too slow, without looking to left or right; we made no attempt to dodge the bullets fired at us. Resigned, I expected to be hit any second and wondered how it would occur. Would I feel a burning sting, or would there be a sharp piercing of my body with great pain.

The other two had long since disappeared. We kept plodding ahead doggedly.

Finally we reached a narrow band of small trees and bushes, growing on both sides of a very small stream. And quite suddenly, the shooting ceased. The day was coming to an end, and soon it would be dark.

Dazed, we gaped at each other. The bewildered questions hung there in the air: "How come we didn't get hit?" and "How did we get away from them?" We walked a little farther and without warning stumbled onto the two Russian partisans. "I thought they got you," said the younger of the two, with some admiration. Looking bedraggled, they were both sitting under a tree. The older one was wounded in the arm, and his friend had bandaged him with a piece of his shirt, but some blood was seeping through the bandage. He did not have his rifle. He must have thrown it away when hit by the bullet.

The two were familiar with this area and knew of a field hospital in the woods about six kilometers from here; we decided to go there.

After trudging through the woods in darkness for hours, we found it at last—abandoned. We covered ourselves with some blankets and immediately fell asleep.

Thursday, October 14, 1943

Nothing much happened during the night; once I was awakened by a rustling sound (by now, regardless of how tired I was, the slightest sound made me wide awake). I guess partisans were passing close by.

In the morning we found that the wound of the older partisan wasn't too serious; there was no more bleeding. I saw that the "field hospital" was located in a tiny clearing with a couple of dozen sleeping places. The "beds" consisted of blankets and pillows scattered on the forest floor. I found an old black coat, apparently a woman's and slightly tight but fortunately not heavy. We also found caps for each of us, but no food. We were ravenous, and I thought of the piece of bread in the pocket of my coat I'd thrown away yesterday; I had touched the crust with my hand, but left it in my frenzied agitation over the compass. Our feet, soaked through in swamp water, and then kept warm at night with blankets, now felt as if they were cooked in our boots. We hadn't removed our boots for several days and didn't dare do it now, afraid it would be impossible to put them on again.

We left early, believing this spot to be too dangerous in the daytime. We split from the other two and agreed to meet again here in the evening.

About a kilometer away we came upon a clump of heavy, tangled underbrush and crawled in underneath. We could observe the surrounding area, but I doubt anyone could have seen us, even from a few feet away.

As the day progressed, we became more relaxed. No Germans appeared, and there was no firing in the immediate area. Even so I kept waiting eagerly for evening. Truly, as Antonov had expressed it, "The night is our friend," and I believed it was the night that had saved us yesterday. We talked again of that final chase, how we got away unscathed from the hail of bullets. We kept wondering. I said to Max, "I guess it's only in books and movies that everything comes out neatly and can be explained. In real life, not everything is so clear.

There was still daylight when, on the way back to the field- hospital, we came across the carcass of a pig. There was an odor from it and some parts had been cut away. But hungry as we were, we cut off some pieces that were all fat, believing that this part of the meat, which did not seem to smell, was not yet spoiled.

Friday, October 15, 1943

We decided to hide again in the same place as yesterday, and if everything was quiet, to meet again in early afternoon. Actually what we considered "quiet" was the usual sound of firing which we'd been hearing for many days now, almost without interruption. It had become like a normal background sound, and as long as there was no shooting in the immediate vicinity, we didn't even think of it.

When we came back, the other two were already there. What to do next? Max and I thought we should try to break through the blockade by going east, in the direction of the large partisan concentrations. The wounded partisan said:

"The *kopanka* [forest road] passes by about three, four kilometers from here. It would be a good idea to reconnoiter the area and see if we can cross it."

We agreed. He pointed out the direction to follow, and the two of us were off.

After several kilometers, the trees were not so dense, and as we moved on slowly, we could see empty cigarette packs, butts, and wrappings of German rations scattered all around. All fresh, as if just discarded. Obviously the Germans had been here a short time ago.

Very carefully we went ahead and at last could see the road through the trees. We crawled over to the edge, stretched out behind a tree and examined the empty road. We were quite certain that German patrols had it under constant surveillance, but in the darkness of night there should be no problem crossing it. We turned back.

I'd had an idea of the difficulty finding our way in the woods and had watched the compass closely on the way to the road. Now on our way back, I kept checking with it.

It was getting dark. Max said: "We should be there soon, but I think we should turn now to the left.

I looked again at the compass, "I don't think so, Max. We should get there by just going in a straight line.

"But those trees." He pointed to a clump of huge trees. "I remember, they were on this side, I'm sure we have to turn left.

We turned. After walking for some time, we realized this was not the right way. We tried to retrace our steps but got more confused. At times we thought we recognized certain landmarks that should have led us to our destination, only to get back to a spot we'd just left; things looked so different at night. As we went on, the ground was becoming marshy, and we worried that we might be moving away from our objective. At last we accepted the futility of our going on in the dark and stretched out next to some bushes, where the ground seemed almost dry.

I'd become aware of the throbbing of my right molar and felt the swelling on my cheek. Max was concerned and said he could notice the swelling getting worse every minute. I pressed the painful side of my face to the ground, and we fell asleep.

Saturday, October 16, 1943

When we woke up in the morning, Max said with surprise, "The swelling has disappeared. What did you do to it?

"I just slept on that side of my face.

It was amazing how different the surroundings looked in daylight; we knew right away that we were just a few hundred yards from the field hospital. We must have been wandering around last night within a few yards of the place.

But when we got there, our two friends were gone.

Before we could decide what to do next, a band of about a half-dozen partisans appeared, obviously the owners of this place. It was immediately apparent that they looked at us as intruders. One of them angrily snatched the caps off our heads.

"Who are you?" the one in charge demanded.

"We are from Antonov's *otryad*," and I explained how we got here with the two other partisans.

He seemed somewhat appeased and said he'd heard Antonov's *otryad* was back at their regular base, and, yes, the *kopanka* led to Bobily.

We left immediately. I was happy they did not recognize the coat I was wearing—the nights were cold. We both were doubtful that the *otryad* was back, but we decided to return there, just in case.

We went back to the *kopanka*, and after making sure no one was in sight, darted across. We made certain of the direction it was leading and after moving several hundred feet deeper in the forest we just kept marching the same way, paralleling the road, which we assumed to be heavily patrolled by Germans. The *kopanka* cut through the forest straight as a ruler, and by using the compass we had little trouble staying close to it.

The forest was pretty dense, but quite often we had to cross fire lanes—treeless, straight, and narrow strips of ground, which go on for many kilometers—and this meant emerging briefly into the open. A few times we were fired on as we ran across them, and we became cautious; we crossed only when there was the cover of brush and tall grass.

Occasionally we waded across small streams, and a few times the water reached over our boots.

"Damn these German boots," Max cursed.

It was dark by the time we got to the side road branching off toward the partisan base; we were certain it was the right place, there were so few roads here. At night we felt more confident and decided to use the small deserted road for that short distance. As we walked along gingerly without talking, something made us stop, and we both jumped at the same time behind some bushes off the road. Something was behind us. Two men passed us by, and we thought they were conversing in Ukrainian. We knew that most of the soldiers fighting partisans were German collaborators and could be Ukrainians, Latvians, or Lithuanians.

We came upon the camp quite suddenly, and though it was nighttime, the scene before us had a stark clarity like a painting—call it "Desolation." Right at the entrance, a horse tied to an overturned cart was eating oats off the ground, which had spilled from a sack still half full. The deliberate chewing of the horse sounded loud and distinct in the stillness of the night. The place was deserted, the huts all burned, the singed remnants of a few still standing. One of the flattened huts was still smoking.

We looked for some food but found only half-rotted cabbage heads in a pit. We were very hungry, and we cut some of the cores out, hoping that these might still be edible.

Again we had been lied to; there was no sign of Antonov's *otryad*. Instead, it was the enemy who must have been here quite recently.

We left after a short time.

After a few kilometers, we stopped to rest and to decide what to do next. The facts were clear to us: Nazis all around . . . no food . . . our feet in terrible condition . . . and our own "friends," the partisans, considering us outsiders—at best. We did have a gun, though, with thirteen bullets, and that made a big difference. Just feeling its weight gave me a feeling of comfort. I carried it tucked in my belt, with a piece of string tied to a little hook in the handle and the other end attached to my belt (so I wouldn't lose it). And the compass—we both had a strong feeling of trust and affection for that little instrument.

As had been the case all along, our thoughts ran pretty much in the same direction, and as if reading my mind, Max now said, "If we could only get to Daugavpils—to our girls. We could get guns . . . get the guys together. . . .

"We could organize our own *otryad*," I completed his thought. "We don't need anybody."

"Yes, but we cannot use the roads. . . "

"Max, we don't need a road. It's very simple. The Daugava flows from east to west. We're somewhere southeast of Daugavpils. If we keep going northwest, according to our compass, we're bound to hit the Daugava, which leads right into Daugavpils."

"Yes, the compass is amazing." Ever since we got lost in the forest, Max had had fanatical confidence in it. "But remember, we can use no roads at all, cannot even come close to one.

"Of course.

"Then let's move on!

Sunday, October 17, 1943

We marched through the forest all night and continued on during the day; it seemed endless. Only once did we pass several stacks of logs— the closest we came to any sign of human habitation. We kept to a northwesterly direction and rested whenever we felt a need for it.

There was evidence of Germans—discarded wrappings of food and cigarettes. But we both felt a certain confidence, unknown before last night. We had a definite purpose, a goal, and depended entirely on ourselves rather than on anyone else's directions. And the incident of last night, the fact that the two Ukrainians were walking behind us, but we became aware of them first, was encouraging. I was conscious of my sharpened senses and of being on constant alert. Even when sleeping, the faintest scratching of a small animal or bird popped me wide awake. Max, too, had felt this change. I said to him:

"If we were to meet up with somebody here, I'm sure we'd sense him first; we are the hunted.

It was in the afternoon when we suddenly reached the end of the forest. There was no thinning out of trees; just ahead of us, a few feet away, was a wide open field and in the distance a farm. I was surprised that after having walked for days and having seen nothing but forest or swamp, it should end so abruptly.

We knew the forest must be under constant surveillance by German patrols and had to wait for darkness. We crawled in under a thick clump of shrubs right at the edge and could observe the field and farmstead next to a pond. People moved around near the house, but it was too far to see who they were.

Finally our friend, the night, arrived. In the darkness, we carefully slipped away, moving to the north of the house.

Monday, October 18, 1943

We got away from the forest last night and had only a few apprehensive moments when passing very close to some men around a small fire. They were well hidden behind trees, and by the time we saw the flickering flame, we could also hear their voices, but in the inky darkness they never saw us. I was quite certain it was a Nazi patrol.

We kept going cross country, depending solely on the compass and steering clear of farms and roads. Once we came across the remnants of a burned-out house and in what used to be the cellar, we found potatoes. Most were either burned too much or raw, but some were only slightly burned and almost felt as if they were baked; we loaded up our pockets with them. I thought for a moment of the peasant family that had lived here and wondered what had happened to them. In this area, it did not take much to bring down the wrath of either the Germans or the partisans.

Our feet were in bad condition, and it was the left boot that gave me most of the trouble. In the end I decided on drastic action, I just cut open the rear of the boot above the heel. The boot lost its firmness but didn't rub anymore; that was an improvement.

Shortly afterward we crossed the narrow-gauge railroad track, which by now had become a familiar signpost for me.

We had to hide before daylight. Max thought the loft of a peasant's bathhouse would do fine. The small log structures owned by many of the peasants were usually some distance away from the farmhouses and from watchful dogs. Max had used them at times in his wanderings. When we came across a farm with no neighbors nearby, we got in and spent the whole day in the loft of the bathhouse. At one time we heard people downstairs and felt apprehension, but no one came up the ladder looking for anything.

Sometime during the day, I became aware of a certain stillness and realized that the sound of far-away firing we'd been hearing intermittently for weeks was gone. We'd gotten so used to it, it had become unnoticed, just background noise.

We decided to follow certain guidelines when entering a farmhouse to ask for food. We would stay close to the door, to be able to get away fast in case of emergency; we would ask for food firmly, neither begging nor threatening; I would keep my hand in my right pocket implying that we might be armed without actually disclosing the gun; we would talk very little and never ask for directions.

When, after dark, we entered the house, the farmer and his wife were startled at first but then became quite affable. They seemed not to have much themselves but gave us bread. Keeping to our rules, we said nothing much, but he talked about how bad things were and how "Opsa is full of Nazis.

Soon we were tramping again and quite satisfied. We had some bread in our pockets and an idea of our whereabouts. We knew we were beyond Opsa, just where we were supposed to be.

Tuesday, October 19, 1943

In the darkness it got rough whenever we had to cross densely wooded or marshy areas. But Max's faith in the compass was extraordinary. He believed in keeping to the exact course as much as possible and not looking for circuitous routes to avoid difficult terrain. "You never know how much you have to go out of the way in order to avoid those rough places," he said. And so we continued northwest, and I often checked the luminous dial of the compass, whose faint shine in the dark had come to signify to us a measure of confidence and hope.

Although I hadn't seen a map of the area, I was convinced we'd hit the Daugava, but our plan seemed so simple that I was a little concerned I'd overlooked something. But as the night wore on, our main worry was where to hide during the day. What if daylight came and we were still in the open? Sometimes we marched an hour or two without coming across anything that was suitable for our purpose.

I said to Max, "I have the feeling that to be in the open by daylight would be like finding oneself nude in a crowd of people— you know, completely exposed.

"I feel the same way. If we see the right place, let's get in, even though it may be only three or four o'clock in the morning. If we wait too long, we may not find a place by the time it's daylight. But let's look for a barn. Barns are dangerous, but it's nice and warm in the hay.

It took quite a while before we found what we were looking for. Whenever we approached an isolated farm, the dogs opened up with enough racket to wake up everyone for miles around. At last, we found the right place—no other farms around, no dog in sight, and space between the barn door and the ground, enough to crawl through. We buried ourselves in the hay, piled almost to the rafters, and experienced a comfort we hadn't known for weeks.

When it got dark—our morning—we entered the house to ask for food and got some bread and a small piece of farmer's cheese. Several men and women were sitting in the kitchen; we thanked them and left. One of the men followed us out, falling into step with us.

"Look, guys," he said in a friendly tone, "I didn't want to say anything inside, but I know you come from the forest." We said nothing. He went on, "Don't worry, I'm a friend. They say there are forty thousand soldiers in the area, and the forest is cordoned off so that even a mouse couldn't escape. How did you get out?"

We only mumbled something noncommittal.

"Well, good luck to you. I understand," he said, and went back to the house.

The sky was cloudless. I often gazed at the Big Dipper, northwest of us, the same direction we were going.

"Max, I hope nothing has happened to them in Daugavpils. It feels as if we've been away from them for ages."

"Yes, who can be sure? . . .

On and on we went, through fields and small woods, up hills and down. Once I saw two dots of lights crawling up a hillside. For most lonely travelers, a flickering light in the darkness means hope and warmth, but for us it signified both our loneliness and our danger—there was a road with a German vehicle traveling over it. Any night sound, any light or barking of a dog made us tense with apprehension.

Wednesday, October 20, 1943

We slept again in a barn and got a crust of bread from a farmer who was neither friendly nor hostile.

So far, we had received something—though not much—every time we asked for food. We both knew that this would not have been the case a year or two ago. But the Russians had been advancing and might be here soon, and the strength of the partisans had been increasing by leaps and bounds. When we entered a house, they didn't know who we were, just that we were probably armed. We were convinced that, even now, an unarmed Jew wouldn't survive long if he had to depend on getting food from farmers.

After some time we came to a lake, then to another. Each time we had to make a wide circle to get back on course.

"Max, we might be getting close to Zarasai. Remember, maps always showed that area filled with lakes."

If that was true, we might reach the Daugava west of Daugavpils and in effect bypass the city. We therefore, changed course and continued more northward.

When circling another large lake, we suddenly came upon a strange sight. A large, massive shadow appeared in the darkness,and we realized it was an old fortress. The ruins looked exactly like the pictures of old forts in my school history books—thick walls half crumbling, smoothed out by time and the elements. The place seemed God-forsaken, forgotten by time itself, with only the sound of waves splashing at the shore. I wondered about the men who, six or seven hundred years ago, fought and died defending this place. The sudden, very noisy takeoff of wild geese startled us, then the stillness returned.

For some time afterward, while marching on, the impression left on us by suddenly coming upon the old fortress lingered on. It brought up something exotic, places and things in the wide world that we had never seen and might never see.

Max said, "Shaike, if we ever survive, we will walk from place to place forever, never spending too much time in any one spot.

"Yes, just imagine, to walk like that, not having to worry about getting caught—and seeing all the fantastic things there are in the world. And how little one really needs to exist!"

We were daydreaming. Yet we really felt optimistic, and had been since embarking on our march to Daugavpils, although we were constantly alert for the dangers lurking all around us. It must have been the prospect of being with the girls, with the family. A sense of physical well-being also existed, of things working right and our bodies functioning in complete harmony with the requirements of the moment. We drank water from small streams at night and were hardly ever thirsty during the day. We never seemed to get tired as we walked, although our diet was so meager. Even our bodily functions had become adjusted to a pattern convenient to our present situation. And always there was the awareness of our sharpened senses, which reassured and encouraged us.

And then the gun. Its comfortable weight, nestling next to my body, was a continuous source of confidence.

"Max, we're damn lucky to have the gun and compass."

"Yes, and the guys in Daugavpils have plenty of guns."

It felt good to march and talk of getting together our own band, a Jewish *otryad*.

"We don't need anybody's help." I felt that we had both learned a lot these past weeks, and the obstacles to surviving in the country and forest did not seem insurmountable anymore.

"If we can just get through the next few months of winter... come spring, we'll be free like the birds!" Max said.

Thursday, October 21, 1943

"Max, we've reached the Daugava!"

We had hidden during the day in the loft of a bathhouse, but in the evening we didn't go in to ask for food, there were too many houses nearby. We kept on marching and were on the way only a short time when we came upon the river quite unexpectedly. For a moment we weren't sure: Could it be just another lake? But there was the current, and though the river was quite wide, we could see the other side even in the dark.

We were elated. For a while we stood watching the waves lapping at the shore; it was a good feeling to know we were on the right course, coming ever closer to our goal.

Max said wistfully, "If there were only a boat around here, we could row across instead of having to cross that guarded bridge in the city.

But there was no boat.

A short time later we came to a farmhouse with no other dwellings nearby. Only a woman was there, and she was quite talkative; without our asking any direct questions we found out some exciting news—Daugavpils was only about twenty-five kilometers away, and the road leading to it was not even half a kilometer from the house!

After we left, Max said, "What do you say we take the road and get there in no time?"

I agreed. "Let's go. This must be the same road we took when we left Daugavpils. The fighting in the forest was so far away. It should have no effect on conditions here."

After stomping cross country so long, marching on a regular road was child's play. The kilometers flew by, and the more we walked, the more excited and impatient we became. At one time, noticing a light ahead, we turned off the road and from behind bushes saw that it was a roadblock with soldiers standing around a fire. We made a wide circle and got back on the road farther ahead. Conditions had changed. But to us the incident was another confirmation that we could become aware of danger before it was too late.

But one big concern was always on our mind. "What if the last Jews of Daugavpils have been killed and the Guttermans are dead?" As we moved closer to the city, our feelings of elation and apprehension commingled; we became nervous, excited, and for a while even irritated with each other.

Suddenly something was moving toward us on the road, approaching very fast. The road here passed between bare fields, and we barely had time to throw ourselves into the shallow ditch. Not long after, a train of horse-drawn wagons clattered by. Every wheel rolled past just inches from my head. We assumed that these were supplies being shipped to the soldiers fighting in the forest. The encounter had a sobering effect on us—many dangers lay ahead.

Friday, October 22, 1943

At the sign of approaching daylight, we reached the suburb of Griva and realized that we had miscalculated: We'd be arriving at the bridge too early. We had expected to arrive when there was general morning traffic, so as not to call attention to ourselves, but at this hour there was no traffic yet. We looked at each other. Bad as Max looked, I knew I looked worse. We were both without caps, straggly hair uncut for months, not even combed for weeks, dirty, bedraggled. The ladies' coat I wore was belted with a wire, and Max's coat was Russian; how suspicious we must have seemed to anyone seeing us!

The bridge loomed ahead—no turning back. We must not act in a questionable or hesitant manner; no telling who might be observing us in the empty street. Max said, "Let's have our watches ready in our pockets. If the guard stops us about documents, we'll hand him our watches. If that doesn't work—shoot him, and we'll run.

We got to the bridge and were the only people around, feeling terribly conspicuous. When we passed the German soldier with the gun, he looked at us intently, but said nothing. I kept imagining him staring at us from behind, and was expecting a loud "Halt!" We walked on, our hobnailed boots making a very loud sound as we marched across the long empty bridge. But it was thus: When things were going right, even the blunders one made turned out for the best, and so far things were definitely going right.

We were now in the city, and as we walked on the embankment highway toward the citadel, we saw Sioma Pick, a Jewish boy, who worked there in the stables. He was riding by himself in a two-wheel cart and without hesitation we jumped in. Like everyone else he'd known of our escape and was now startled to see us. Without explaining too much, we implied that we were here on a mission. "Find any one of the Guttermans and tell her we are waiting behind the bushes next to the railroad track. Remember, let no one else know that you have seen us. We'll be in touch with you later." Making sure that he saw the butt of my gun and repeating our admonition not to betray us, we jumped off the cart before he entered the citadel.

Not long after, Hinda appeared at the agreed-upon place, bringing food and cigarettes. She was ecstatic at our return and bubbled with happiness. She told us there was excitement after our escape was discovered, and the Germans were very angry; some restrictions were enforced, but nothing had really changed. Also, the girls had been working on a *molina* (hiding place) the last couple of weeks, which would really come in handy for us now.

Hinda left after a while, but returned as soon as it got dark. We went through the gate of the citadel and in a few minutes were in the laundry. We were home.

And what a reception we got! Golda, Ella, Mother, and Leiser were all waiting, and the moment Hinda opened the door, they were all kissing and hugging us with great joy and happiness. A bath was ready in the other room—after all these weeks, a hot bath! We climbed in, and Ella insisted on soaping our backs. We could have done it for each other, but accepted, realizing that it was a way of expressing her welcome and affection for us.

The clothing we came with was discarded and complete fresh outfits were ready for us. We were especially happy with the warm half coats and round winter caps that had belonged to their two older brothers, kept as a remembrance since they'd emigrated before the war.

Afterward we slipped into their place without being observed. The meal we all ate together was full of talk and cheer, and everyone wanted to know all that had happened to us since we left.

We looked at the *molina*, which was under a bunk. They started building it when rumors that the Jews would be liquidated had become persistent. A square opening was cut out in the floor and a cover was fashioned from the cut out boards. The hole underneath was scraped out inch by inch, and so far there was enough space for three people, but they intended to enlarge it. The girls had to be very careful getting rid of the ground which they had carried out in small amounts. A piece of rug was placed over the wooden cover.

From what the girls told us, it was clear that the periodic scares we had always known were now more frequent. Poison was a much-sought-after commodity, and more guns had been acquired. One very sad incident occurred a few weeks ago. While cleaning his gun, one of the men accidentally discharged it and hit a young boy, who died shortly afterward. Somehow Dr. Itzikowitz managed to keep the real cause of his death from the Germans. Since we had left, tension had increased, but right now nothing could mar our happiness at being together again.

It was of great interest to us to find that people here were aware of the German offensive against the partisans in White Russia, and that many soldiers were taking part in it. Aircraft, too, were observed flying frequently in that direction.

There were two things we needed right away—a gun for Max and boots for both of us. That was Hinda's job, and I told her that if at all possible, she should get us cavalry boots—the kind that go up all the way to the knees.

Golda told me how she would look at the Big Dipper and think of me. Shortly after we left, they had heard rumors that we'd been caught, that a peasant had even seen our bodies.

"But I didn't believe any of it. I was certain you were alive. Besides," she added with a twinkle, "surely the watch you gave me would have stopped if something happened to you, and it ticked away merrily."

"Golda," I said with feeling, "if we have to die, we'll die together. I will never leave you again.

Saturday, October 23, 1943

Mother stayed home today, and Monday one of the girls would be with us. They'd decided that every day someone would stay away from work to keep us company, "to take care of us." We still didn't want anyone to know we were here. During the day and night, the door was locked. Early in the evenings and on Sunday we'd have to go down to the *molina*. It would look suspicious to have the door locked then, when people were back from work. Tonight Shmulke Palec came to visit. Listening under the floor, it felt strange to hear him discussing us, wondering whether we were still alive and, if so, where we might be now. Certainly he should know about us, but not just yet. We made a decision to wait, and I could not ask Max to make an exception. We were very concerned about the danger of getting caught here and determined to act with the utmost caution.

Sunday, October 24, 1943

This being Sunday, Max and I had to stay hidden during the day. But we were hardly suffering—one of the girls kept us company. Then, for a while both of them were with us, but the place was really too tight for four people, and there was a bit of good-natured bantering on who should leave. At last we agreed that Golda, who had been with us longer, would have to go. Climbing out reluctantly, she said in a somewhat affected, teasing voice: "You wait, there might be a time when you guys will *want* to be with me, but I won't be around. . . ." She broke off realizing what she had said. It was meant to be a teasing joke, but in our situation you don't tempt fate, and for a few seconds, none of us spoke, aware of the dark cloud obscuring the light for just a moment. Then it was gone.

As soon as evening came, and the door was bolted, we were free to come out. At supper we talked about what to do next in a tentative sort of way; we were still too intoxicated with the joy of being together to worry too much. We would have to start talking to the fellows about our plans but we wanted a few more days.

Monday, October 25, 1943

Hinda was unbelievable—she already had a gun for Max and boots for both of us! The pistol was of small caliber and had only one bullet, but she was promised more for next week. At least Max was no longer empty-handed. But the boots—I could hardly believe they were real! Brand new cavalry boots—strong, with studded soles that fit us perfectly! How she ever got them and on such short notice I could not even begin to guess.

Hinda stayed with us. A pleasant day. The flimsy white curtains, though tightly drawn over the small window, could not block out the bright rays of sun, and the room was full of light, creating an agreeable languor in the air. I thought of the sunny days and cold nights in the forest; it had been a nice fall with little rain so far.

In the evening the rest of the family came home. Ella said, "There is again talk that this place is going to be liquidated."

Max had trouble with his right foot. The place where the boot had been rubbing him during our march, became infected and developed into a real wound. Just to put on a boot was now very painful for him.

Tuesday, October 26, 1943

Golda stayed home. We were uneasy about what Ella said last night, but we'd heard plenty of rumors before and hoped the alarm would pass.

In the evening, though, our apprehension increased. There was talk that a German unit had been informed that its Jewish workers would be "removed" from Daugavpils. There was still some hope that the thing would blow over, but if this was really it, the hiding place here would be discovered in no time. Our friend, the German corporal, Liederman, knew of a place, where we could all hide, but right now the girls were concerned about us. When the moment for hiding comes, it might be impossible for Max and me to get away unobserved. They thought it best that we should be smuggled out of the compound right away and for the time being be hidden in the attic where they hanged out the wash.

They brought us to the place later in the evening. It was the building where their German unit was stationed. The attic was very large and completely bare, except for a mattress prepared for us in one corner. The laundry room, where the girls worked, was across the yard. Locking us in from the outside, they said we could feel quite safe here. The only other key was kept by the *Feldwebel* (staff sergeant); he was a "bad German," but he usually didn't come up here.

Wednesday, October 27, 1943

The girls returned early in the morning with hot tea and food. They didn't sleep in their quarters but in the laundry, and would do so again tonight. They stopped over several times and later in the day hung up the wash; it covered most of the attic. The feeling of crisis continued. Our mood was black; we felt terribly threatened. I thought of the happy days we'd just experienced and had the same feeling of regret, as in the forest, only more so—the sense of having had something wonderful, only to let it slip through my fingers—almost as if there were something I could have done to preserve it.

Thursday, October 28, 1943

Shots awakened us before dawn. Later, more shooting and no sign of the girls. We knew the end had come for the Jews here.

We felt very helpless. Here we were, locked in from the outside, in an attic filled with drying laundry, on top of a German barracks.

After a while someone unlocked the door, and like a guardian angel, Liederman appeared. He said breathlessly: "I can stay only a minute. Listen closely. The Jews are being taken away. The Guttermans are in a hiding place, and I will bring you to them in the evening. I'll be back." Then he was gone.

Peeking through a small dormer, we became witnesses to the tail end of the *Aktion* in progress and could follow the silent drama down below, on the next street. Because of the distance no sound reached us, but the scene was clear and familiar by now. There they were, the column of Jews, surrounded by gun-toting Latvians, waiting while the area was being searched for those who were hiding. How pitiful and helpless they looked. I could see myself standing there with them, waiting to take the final voyage. I whispered to Max, "There aren't any two hundred and fifty people."

"No," Max responded, "many are missing."

Even while we watched, new people were brought to the column. Like hounds, the Latvian auxiliaries scurried around sniffing out those who in desperation had tried to conceal themselves. The column was kept waiting a long time, while more and more people were brought out. And then I saw Shneier with his wife, Nehamah, and their four-year-old boy, Michele, being led by a Latvian with a gun. I had often thought of the ingenuity and luck they must have had to have saved that little child for so long a time; he was the youngest of three Jewish children who'd been alive till now. Then a sudden disturbance—a guard was running after somebody, and I realized it was David Bleier. German soldiers joined the chase; then David fired at his pursuers with his pistol. More shots . . . confusion . . .

He only has a few bullets, I thought. Another shot, and he was on the ground.

"I think he shot himself—with the last bullet," Max said.

The guards kept pumping bullets into the prone body of David Bleier—our friend. Only seconds, and it was over.

With no more Jews here, the Germans would have to come up to remove the dry laundry sometime, and it might well be today.

Where can we hide? I wondered. The place was completely empty, except for the wash, but Max thought of something.

"Look, there between the boarded cover over the stairway up to the attic, and the tin roof—if only it's wide enough to squeeze in. . . ." We managed to wedge ourselves in, staying in the same position the rest of the day.

Time passed very slowly. We expected all the time to hear the steps of the *Feldwebel* or one of his men. We smoked a few cigarettes and that helped, though lighting one, in our cramped position, became virtually an acrobatic feat. Later when darkness approached, we began worrying that Liederman might not come after all.

At last we heard steps. "Had to wait for suppertime, when the soldiers are busy eating," he explained.

With difficulty Max pulled the boot on his painful foot.

We had to go down three flights of stairs—stairs used by soldiers. "I'll go first," Liederman said, "and you follow fast behind me, a few seconds later."

We were down the steps in a flash, passing by the rooms of the soldiers, where some of the doors were open. We could hear voices and the sound of a radio playing "Lili Marlene," but met no one on the stairway.

"Now just follow me a little from behind." It was very dark. We walked fast, and in a short while we were at the other end of the citadel. Walking up the embankment I couldn't see a thing.

"Here, jump in," Liederman urged.

I dropped into a hole. Complete darkness. . . I crawled. . . "Shaike . . . here," came Golda's voice. I stood up and took her outstretched hand. I walked ahead, holding on to her carefully. I heard hushed, familiar voices. We were all together again.

Friday, October 29, 1943

In the morning, I could see we were in another attic. Very little light here, just enough to see what the place is. We were under the roof of a building built into the earthwork surrounding the citadel. The bottom of the slanting tin roof was almost flush with the top of the hill, and right there was a round hole in the roof, through which we got in last night. A tin cover lay right next to it, but we didn't dare touch it, realizing that any change in its position could be suspicious. The hole, just large enough for one person to squeeze through, was the only possible entrance to the attic, and also the place through which we got the little bit of light, besides the few chinks between the ceiling and roof. The place was large, perhaps seventy to eighty feet long and twenty feet wide. Below us were the stables for the horses of the unit for which the girls had been working.

We were all lying on the slanting concrete floor at the far wall from the entrance. Nothing at all here, just heavy wooden rafters supporting the tin roof.

In the evening, Liederman brought some food: a small loaf of army bread and a can of sardines, which we divided evenly among the seven of us.

Saturday, October 30, 1943

Since our arrival here, we had been lying in a row close together in the same position. We had spread a few coats on the cold floor, and covered ourselves with the rest, trying to retain all the heat our bodies generated. I was at the lower end, Golda next to me to the left, then Ella, Mother, Leiser, Hinda, and Max at the other end. Once in a while one of us got up and moved around some, but it was too cold. Mostly we remained under our coats. I placed a loose brick at an angle against the wall and put on it the one glove I had—it made an adequate head rest. Golda kept her head on my left shoulder. I had a hard time convincing her that my shoulder wasn't numb or painful. Every once in a while she moved over to the other side and kept her head on my right shoulder. I could stay like this forever. But at any moment someone might come sliding through the opening there at the other end, and if he advanced toward us, I would shoot. On top was a path that ran alongside the roof within a few feet of our open "entrance," and any soldier passing by might decide to kind of nose around and see where the hole led to.

But the bright circle represented not only the perilous state we were in but also transmitted what little daylight we got, and it was through there that Liederman appeared in the evening with food and water. It was truly the focus of our present existence.

Sunday, October 31, 1943

Our plans were vague: We'd try to get away to White Russia. All those Germans and their auxiliaries swarming in the forest were hardly encouraging, but we'd worry about that later. Our present worry was that we would be discovered.

We had to wait a few more days, because Max still was having trouble with his foot, and it would be too painful for him to walk. But how long could Liederman continue bringing us food? I could picture the scrounging, the "organizing" he had to do to come up with that loaf of bread every day. And meanwhile, we could hear the voices of German soldiers and Latvian girls taking a Sunday stroll on the path just outside our bright open entrance. . . .

Monday, November 1, 1943

Neither Golda nor I was superstitious, but she was familiar with many of the folk sayings and popular interpretations of dreams, and in our present condition there was an inclination to grasp at anything to support hope. I dreamed of a watch last night, and she said, "It means we can expect change—something good will happen to us."

Liederman brought strange news today. He had heard from a soldier that some Jews were still working in the citadel. We could not believe it; it must be just some crazy rumor. But he said he would try to find out for certain.

Tuesday, November 2, 1943

Liederman had no more information about Jews in the citadel. He couldn't ask too many questions, because the soldiers were suspicious of him as it was—his feelings about Jews were known to some. He told us of a snide remark the *Feldwebel* had made to him yesterday; our friend might be in grave danger.

When we each got our daily portion of food, a slice of bread with a bit of cheese or a few sardines, both Golda and Hinda argued that they were really not very hungry—we should take some of their share. Max and I usually refused.

Wednesday, November 3, 1943

Golda held in her hand the little pocket mirror—it was cracked.

"I don't know how it happened," she said sadly. We all knew that a broken mirror was a bad omen. "But of course," she continued more lightly, "all the tales about broken mirrors are just *Bobe mayses* [old wives' tales]."

I've read that people, even if they are very close—when forced to stay in a cramped condition hour after hour, day after day, with very little food and in constant fear—become irritated, even disgusted with each other. We'd been here six days, and except for a little spat between Max and Hinda, there had been absolute harmony. As for myself and Golda, we felt a great happiness in being together, even though always aware of our situation. We never got bored talking to each other, and there were always thoughts and feelings to be shared.

Tonight Liederman said, "I have heard from a second soldier that he'd seen Jews here." There might be something to it after all!

Thursday, November 4, 1943

Looking at me and Golda, Mother said in a voice with wonder in it, "After a whole week being cooped up here, you still go on about each other the way you do. . . ."

In the evening, Liederman brought important news: he had himself spoken to a Jewish man! Yes, there was a group of them working for the *Heresbaudienststelle*, and we could go and see them. Incredible!

We considered what to do next. I said one or two of us should go down first and see what it was all about, but Max thought we should all go. We all left.

After cautiously getting out of our *molina*, we came to the building where the Jews now lived. They were even more surprised to see us than we were to see them. There was Borekh Fixer and other friends, altogether about twenty people.

It turned out that a few were considered essential in the work they were doing and were not taken away in the last *Aktion*. The rest were some of those who had escaped but had had no place to go; upon hearing they would be allowed to work here, they'd returned. Now there was excitement on all sides; everyone was eager to know what had happened to us and how we wound up back in Daugavpils. Borekh told us that our escape had infuriated the Germans, and we should make sure that none of those who knew us discover that we were back. He also told us that they had heard of the offensive against the partisans in White Russia and had wondered about us.

We got the details from Borekh and a few of the others of what happened here last Thursday exactly a week ago.

Because of the persistent rumors of those last days, the fellows had a guard posted at night. Thursday, before daybreak, the alarm was sounded; Latvian police were surrounding the compound. For two years this moment, our final journey, had been anticipated with complete certainty. The reaction now of many of the people was like a spring held in check and suddenly released.

Pandemonium broke out. Many of the fellows tried to escape; some succeeded in getting away, others were killed. I guess no one knew all the details, but this much was certain: My friend the violinist David Weksler, as well as Yudl Munitz and Simonowitz, were killed while trying to escape, and as for David Bleier, we witnessed his death ourselves. Bentzl Shafir (for whom I had gotten the cognac) killed his wife and little son with his revolver, and also a young girl who begged him to end her life too. B. killed his mother with his gun and Shura Apeskin hanged himself. Someone said one of our people had climbed up on the roof, spraying bullets over the Nazis downstairs until he was killed.

Of the people who had acquired poison, some were going to swallow it at the very last moment; others took it immediately. Dr. Goldman and his sister, as well as a few more, died right there, but for others the poison was ineffective. I was sure there were other incidents that we didn't know about, nor did we know how the Jews in the city (a couple of hundred) reacted when the Nazis came for them. I also found out that among those who escaped and were not captured were my friends Shmulke Palec, Eli Gever, and Haim Gordon.

We still didn't know with certainty where those taken away a week ago were killed. The people were told that they were being taken to Kaiserwald, the concentration camp near Riga. But in previous *Aktionen* we were also told that people were taken to "a new camp," only to wind up in the ditches of Pogulianka. No, we had no hope for them.

"The *Oberzahlmeister* is coming!" someone warned suddenly. Although he had been friendly to us, one never knew. Max and I crawled under beds. We could hear from the way the German was talking to the people that he was still a friend. He then walked out to another room. Suddenly I heard something that for a second filled me with terror.

"Max," I said to him, "did you hear a woman's scream?"

"No," he answered. "I don't think I heard anything special."

How strange, I thought to myself. It had sounded faint but I was certain I'd heard a desperate scream. Could I have imagined it?

The *Oberzahlmeister* left in a few minutes. Then we saw Hinda, Mother and Leiser. I asked Hinda: "Where are Golda and Ella?"

"They went to talk to the captain of our unit. If Jews can work here, maybe we too can work again for our place." "When did they leave?" I demanded in alarm.

"Quite a while ago," she answered vaguely.

I thought of the scream. It was less than a city block from here to where the girls had gone. Could I have heard it? I must have imagined it. Their old captain had seemed so fatherly, and all they were going to ask was to wash laundry again for the soldiers.

But as time went on, concern over the girls spread and I became desperately worried. At last Max said:

"It's getting close to ten o'clock, and we have to return to the attic before curfew. Golda and Ella—if they come back . . . they might still make it to our place. . . ." I had very little hope left. We returned in despair to the hiding place, which we had left only a few hours ago with so much hope.

Friday, November 5, 1943

When we first returned last night, I still clung to a shred of hope, but as time passed, it evaporated. Then about an hour later, we heard the loud rattling sound of steel-rimmed wheels rolling over cobblestones. It was the unit's carriage, leaving the stable downstairs. It was on the way to take the girls away—I knew it as if I'd seen it happen.

The sorrow, the torment I felt the next hours—the whole night long—was shattering. I sobbed uncontrollably, only vaguely aware that I had to keep my voice down. Again and again the thought hit me that I would never see Golda again—beautiful Golda, sweet, tender, loving Golda—and I would be overcome by additional waves of grief. . . . I could not bear it. At times, I became aware that the strange choking sounds of anguish were coming from my own mouth, and could hear Mother moaning quietly, "Oh, my two bright jewels." But mostly I was conscious only of my own terrible grief—completely submerged in it, oblivious to everything else. Thoughts came and went. I blamed myself: If only I'd stayed with her all the time. I blamed Max for his insistence that we all go down, instead of just one or two of us. Once I had the thought, I should have expected that they would be taken away by carriage. I should have concealed myself and waited. . . . And for a moment I fell into a kind of fantasizing, seeing myself jump from ambush on the carriage, killing the Germans with my gun and saving the girls. But I could never get away from the terrible knowledge: they took Golda away to be killed . . . they took Golda away. . . . I was altogether one huge ball of pain and could not imagine being able to endure it.

But somehow the night passed, and during the day I became calmer, waiting impatiently for the arrival of darkness.

As soon as night arrived, I said, "I'm going to see if I can find out some details." I expected that our people would find out what had happened through the *Oberzahlmeister*.

After walking down the embankment, I became aware of someone right behind me, and then a flashlight shone on my back. Go ahead, order me to stop, I thought to myself calmly—actually wishing for it. I'll turn around and kill you. Today I felt no fear and did not care what would happen to me afterward. But whoever it was walked away, and I continued on.

Borekh Fixer confirmed what I had known all along. When the girls came to ask to be allowed to work again, the captain put them under guard; later he sent for the carriage and had them delivered to prison.

And thus did the captain repay the girls for slaving away for more than two years for his company of soldiers.

Liederman hadn't been here tonight. We believed he must be in real trouble and may have been transferred to the front line. After arresting the girls, the Germans must have suspected that he had had something to do with their concealment this past week.

Sunday, November 7, 1943

The mood here had been black. We had to take some action. The question was what? I had been completely passive; with Golda gone, I just didn't care what happened to me.

There really weren't many choices. We got a little food from the people at the *Baudienststelle*, but there were five of us, and they had little enough for themselves; besides, sooner or later we'd be caught here; with the open entrance in our roof, it was only a question of time. We'd have to get away from here and the only place we knew of was the area around Bobily. But Max had strong reservations.

"With winter coming . . . I don't know . . ." he said. "The villages were all bombed. They must have been destroyed. How would we get food? Even if we were able to get there, who knows if the German blockade had been lifted?"

But there was no choice. Tomorrow evening we were going to leave.

Monday, November 8, 1943

As night fell, one by one we climbed out through the hole, walked to the other side of the citadel and passed through the gate.

I could see all along that Max was having misgivings. As we walked toward the city, a light snow began to fall.

After a while, Max stopped and said to me, "No, it's no good. In snow you leave footprints wherever you go—and it isn't just like the two of us, slipping in here or there. With five people, it's a different story. . . ." I knew he did not mean the snow just now; that would melt soon. It was a strong reminder of the weather to come. He concluded, "We won't make it . . . let's turn back."

I said nothing, it was all the same to me.

Wednesday, November 10, 1943

Every evening either Max or I went down to see our friends and got a little food and water.

Someone said he'd heard that Liederman had been sent to the front.

Thursday, November 11, 1943

Shmulke Palec returned to the citadel. His experiences of the last two weeks were of great interest to me. This is what he told me about his escape from the last action:

The last few nights before the *Aktion*, they kept one of the men on guard, and slept with their clothes on. When the Latvians came, it was still dark. Shmulke and Michael, who also had a gun, climbed over the small brick wall, cutting their hands on the glass fragments stuck on top in the concrete. Shmulke's right hand was bleeding badly, but there was no time to worry about that. Many were trying to escape, and there was shooting. The two got out of the citadel safely, but what were they to do next. . . ? Shmulke thought of a Lithuanian farmer with whom he'd become friendly when he was in the Dukstas work camp. The farmer had told him, in case of trouble, to come to his house, which was in the Zarasai area. After a couple of days, the two were close to Zarasai when suddenly they saw about ten Lithuanian policemen coming toward them on bicycles.

Someone must have informed on them. They looked suspicious, especially Michael in his Russian jacket and boots. They took off to the woods which luckily were close to the road, and the police went after them. Shmulke and his friend started firing away at them with their revolvers from behind the trees. The policemen opened fire with rifles, but were apparently afraid to enter the woods. Or maybe they were waiting for reinforcements. Anyway, the two of them ran from there and for some time could hear the police still shooting.

For two more days, they wandered around in the woods and fields until finally they found the farm of Shmulke's Lithuanian friend. He and about a half dozen other Lithuanians were in the process of organizing a partisan band and were happy to accept the pair. But after a few days, the whole party was attacked by Lithuanian police. It was very bad; there were a great many of them and just a few partisans. Michael was badly wounded and one of the partisans had to finish him with a bullet. Shmulke's friend the Lithuanian was also killed and some of the others too. Only four men managed to get away. The house was burned. The few survivors decided to disperse and organize again in the spring. "I had nowhere to go anymore," Shmulke concluded, "so I came back to the citadel."

Shmulke and a few others who'd also escaped from the *Aktion* and returned, all joined those working in the *Baudienststelle*.

The fellows have talked to the *Oberzahlmeister* and have gotten permission for Mother, Hinda, and Leiser to work with the rest. There were now a total of twenty-six people.

The work was probably very temporary, and might be just a trap set by the Germans. On the other hand, we lived from one day to the next, and the important thing was to get through the next several months of winter. Once spring came. . . .

Friday, November 12, 1943

Our friends had heard that the "two Gutterman girls," as well as other Jews who'd been captured lately, were still being held in the prison. There was also talk that the people taken away October 28, were actually loaded in a freight train and deported to the Kaiserwald Concentration camp in Riga. This was hard to believe. They killed 16,000 Jews here in Daugavpils; why would they spare the last few hundred? Max and I were talking of making our way back to White Russia and would probably leave in a few days.

Tuesday, November 16, 1943

Shmulke had heard news that made us reconsider our plans. It seemed there was still a large ghetto with thousands of Jews in the city of Siauliai in Lithuania, and conditions there were not bad at all. He heard about it from a Lithuanian, a gentile whom he saw at work. What is more, to get there wasn't difficult. "You see," Shmulke explained, "this guy lives in Lithuania, but works here. When he wants to visit home, he hops on a freight train that passes Daugavpils at a certain time. The train is mostly empty, returning from the front, and when it comes close to his town, he gets off. The train goes on all the way to Radviliskis. There you can jump off and walk to Siauliai, about twenty-five kilometers."

Siauliai used to be the third largest city in Lithuania, but none of us had ever been there. We were surprised to hear that there was another ghetto left in Lithuania, we had heard only vague rumors of a ghetto in Kaunas. Shmulke said the man seemed dependable. Even if what we'd heard was exaggerated, it was something to be considered.

Thursday, November 18, 1943

We were told that there were now Russian refugees in the citadel. The Red Army was getting closer. I wasn't sure whether these people were forcibly removed for labor or had left voluntarily because they were German collaborators.

There was talk of partisan bands somewhere in Latvia, but the information we had was vague, and might have been only a rumor. We kept debating between Siauliai and White Russia. We had to decide which. We could be in Siauliai within a day or two, stay in the ghetto the few winter months, then be off to the woods. However, we had no details, we didn't even know where to find this famous empty freight train. And even if we did end up at Siauliai, we'd just be getting back into a ghetto. On the other hand, we were familiar with the Bobily area and would know how to get there, but with the winter upon us, the cold, the snow, and the villages probably destroyed by bombing—where would we find food? And wherever we went, we'd leave our tracks in the snow.

Our food situation was much improved. The Guttermans were making certain that we got something every day. Usually Leiser brought it over to us; some evenings we joined them. Last night we even washed ourselves from the waist up. We also suffered relatively little from the cold; we had additional coats.

Time went by slowly. We slept very little; oddly enough, we dozed off mostly in the afternoon and evening, while the night dragged on forever. Talking helped a lot.

Friday, November 19, 1943

Bad news. There were new rules now, and we could not leave the citadel. Guards had started checking documents and asking for a password at the four gates. We were thinking of using a rope to get out. We'd have to tie it up to a tree or something else close to the precipice, then slide down. The fellows promised to obtain a rope for us.

Saturday, November 20, 1943

The Ukrainian collaborators were marching somewhere—probably several blocks from here; we could clearly hear their lively marching song.

We both listened. I thought of the thousands of Jews who were slaughtered in the Ukraine during the Russian Civil War, and of the much earlier time, during the uprising against the Poles in 1648. The names of Kmelnitzky and Petlura were only too well known. . . .

I said to Max:

"They might be the ones who have been killing Jews." In Bobily we'd heard that Ukrainians were used not only for fighting partisans, but also to round up the Jews and kill them.

"The Ukrainians . . . they are as bad as the Latvians and Lithuanians," Max said. "Though I'm sure there are decent people among them too."

"Shmulke sure came across some very decent Lithuanians. . . ."

"Yeah. Of course, Varute is also Lithuanian. Remember? I told you about her."

"I know, it's the girl who saved your life."

"She certainly did. Yes. Varute Mashunaite . . . the risks she took for me . . . she certainly could have lost her life then."

Monday, November 22, 1943

How slowly the days passed! All we could do was lie on the ground, surrounded by twilight even in the brightest time of day, and gaze at our one focal point—the small circle of light at the other end. Besides Leiser's visits in the evening and our occasional visits with our friends, we still had one special thing to look forward to—cigarettes that were accumulated by Hinda in the "good times." They were a great help. These were German Army cigarettes with short hollow stems. (Someone had once said that a substance was added to the tobacco to cut down the sexual urge of the soldiers, and I sometimes wondered whether this was true). We followed a certain ritual. Max might say:

"What do you think, should we light up?" And my answer was usually "Good idea, but let's just wait a little."

We waited maybe half an hour, then Max might bring it up again, and I might counsel to wait just a few more minutes. Meanwhile there was the anticipation, the looking forward to the pleasurable event. Eventually Max would light up, take a few puffs, and hand the cigarette to me. I would take a few puffs and hand it back to him. We repeated the process a few times, until half of the cigarette was gone; then we'd put it out and save it for next time. In this way we used up only a few cigarettes a day and still had four packages left.

We had a small safety razor, a few blades, and a small piece of soap, so we shaved every couple of days. We usually went close to the opening, because so little light penetrated through the few cracks. The same little bit of water we shaved with also went for washing our faces; we had to make do with just one bottle of water a day for both of us, and could not waste even a drop of it.

Wednesday, November 24, 1943

At last the guys got us a rope, but it was quite useless. It was neither long enough nor strong enough for our purpose. We had to get another one.

Thursday, November 25, 1943

It was hard to believe, but it had been four weeks since we arrived to this hideout.

Tonight when Leiser brought our food, he had Borekh Fixer with him—we thought it a good idea that someone else should know of our *molina.*

Borekh said that a Latvian told him there were still Jews in the prison, and everyone was quite sure that the girls were still there too. I thought of Golda constantly and looked back with longing to that first week we were here.

Friday, November 26, 1943

I dreamed a lot, sometimes it was almost like daydreaming, wishful thinking while only half-asleep; other times it was a jumble of unrelated scenes. We didn't sleep much, and most nights seemed to drag on forever. Some weren't so bad—we might spend most of a night talking without stop. Our senses were probably more relaxed at night; there was less danger of someone stumbling accidentally upon our entrance.

All our waking hours, our eyes were riveted to the small circle of light at the other end; it was a constant reminder of the danger we were in. The longer we stayed, the greater the chance of our getting caught, and yet the longer one stays in danger, the more relaxed and less cautious one gets. I thought of the first time I'd hidden—in prison in July of 1941. They did not find us even when the place was searched thoroughly; then after two days we were discovered accidentally—clearly because one of us had moved while a guard was in the room. Then as we approached Daugavpils last month, because the whole march had gone well, we were not as careful in timing our crossing of the bridge as we should have been. We had to get away from this place before we gave ourselves away. But how? The gates of the citadel were all under guard.

We were both aware that, bad as it was lying here bottled up in this place, we were fortunate in having each other. Max often reminded me of how miserable he used to be, when for many weeks, he was wandering through the countryside all alone. He had had to wage a constant struggle to survive, but lack of human contact was much harder to bear than that.

We were always aware of each other's moods, seeming to sense when the other one wanted to be alone with his thoughts, and never getting on each other's nerves. And because we were so different, we also complemented one another; in many cases, what one of us lacked the other had, so that together we made a unit with a certain completeness about it.

It seemed that among the few Jews who were still in the citadel, the two of us had acquired a reputation for resourcefulness. We were talking tonight with Borekh Fixer about our predicament. At last he said, "I am more confident about you getting out and surviving than about the rest of us, even though we can move around and you have to lie in hiding." How I wish I could feel that confident!

Wednesday, December 1, 1943

It was December. We had had some cold days, but nothing unbearable yet. I knew the kind of cold weather we could expect later on, yet, we were beginning to think . . . perhaps with a few more coats. . . .

"Max, if we could just last here till the end of February, spring would then be on its way. . . ."

He replied, "I'd settle just for the end of January. . . . If we could stay here till then, the worst would be over."

The gun. I was conscious of it at all times and felt its presence in every sense. How helpless we'd have felt without it! If we were discovered, we'd die, of course, but at least we'd die fighting. And what a difference that made! I often held the gun in my hand with my index finger wrapped around the trigger. It comforted me. I wondered, if a German should suddenly appear, how close should I allow him to advance toward us before starting to shoot?

The bread that Leiser brought today was half baked. We ate most of it anyway, hungry as we always were, but a few bites of the inside part, unbaked dough, was really not edible.

Friday, December 3, 1943

I woke up around midnight somewhat shaken by a dream I'd had and told Max about it. In the dream I could hear clearly the sound of someone walking on our tin roof, then a black cat, together with little Maxik, jumped through the opening. It was strange to be dreaming of that young boy. I had only spoken to him a few times; he must have been around thirteen, and was one of those working now at the *Baudienststelle*. He had somehow managed to hide out in the latest *Aktion*.

Saturday, December 4, 1943

It was around noon, and it happened very fast. Suddenly we heard footsteps on the roof and saw something dark pop through the opening. We pulled out our guns, but immediately realized it was only Maxik dressed in a black jump-suit.

It only took him a few minutes to tell us what happened: Without warning, the Latvian police had abruptly appeared, and ordered the twenty-six remaining Jews to get ready to leave. In the ensuing confusion, Maxik slipped away. He'd heard of our *molina* from Borekh and, after some searching, found our place. And here he was. I thought of the dream.

The Guttermans were all gone. Everyone was gone. We three were the only Jews still alive in Daugavpils. I could imagine this morning's scene: The police materialize as if from nowhere . . . the fear . . . the helplessness . . . the knowledge that this was the *very* end.

Our own situation was very clear—we didn't even speak about it much. We were under sentence of death in a citadel swarming with Germans, with no way to get out and no prospect of obtaining any food. There was just a bite of bread and half a bottle of water. Leiser was supposed to have come that evening with supplies.

In the evening we divided the piece of bread among the three of us and devoured it. We had no more. We were saving a few sips of water for tomorrow.

Sunday, December 5, 1943

It was sunny outside. Soldiers and their girls were strolling on the path running parallel to our roof, and we could hear the sound of lighthearted chatter and easy laughter.

We talked a little about what had happened yesterday. The final "taking away" of the Jews came as no surprise—not only not to Max and me, but probably not to the victims themselves. What could they have done to save themselves? People lucky enough to have escaped the last *Aktion* had had no place to go. They had struggled for days on their own and when caught had been taken to prison. But those who had returned voluntarily, like Shmulke, were allowed to work, and that had given them the hope that they'd be left alone until spring. One lived from day to day. Anything could happen at any moment.

The last drop of water was gone. We gathered up the few dried crumbs of unbaked bread we had thrown away some days before, and ate them with relish.

Monday, December 6, 1943

Without food or water we cannot stay much longer. How can we get out of the citadel?

Tuesday, December 7, 1943

Maxik decided to go out, look around, and see if he could find some food. He was young and small, and might be taken as a child of a Russian refugee, of whom there were quite a few in the citadel now.

When he returned a little later, he was visibly shaken. "They almost got me . . . for that." He said, handing us a small crust of bread, and a slab of something greasy, which felt like bacon. He said no more about it, and we asked no questions. Max bit into it eagerly, but immediately began to spit it out furiously—it was brown laundry soap. What Maxik brought amounted to practically nothing, a slice of bread for the three of us, but even so in order to "organize" it, he had had to put himself in great danger. We could not expect food from that direction.

Wednesday, December 8, 1943

Nothing was happening. We still had a few cigarettes. We huddled under our coats all the time and moved around very little. Maxik lay between the two of us, so that he would suffer less from the cold. He was a good kid and in the few days since he'd been here, we had gotten to like him a lot.

We must act soon, but *how*? *How*? Since we fell in the hands of the Nazis, we'd known that there was no second chance for us. This was even more true in our present situation. Any wrong move, and we were finished. But in the end we'd have to attempt *something*. This inaction was simply postponing it.

Thursday, December 9, 1943

"The miners were trapped for many days without food or water." We were talking about a book I'd read years before, written by Zola. Coal miners were cut off by a collapse in the mine and had had to wait a long time while their comrades were digging furiously toward them, a race between their friends' arrival and death. In the end only one person survived.

"So how many days did they last without food?" Max asked.

"I'm not sure, but I remember being surprised by the length of time. It was several weeks at least."

The last time we'd had something that could be called food was last Friday. I had a continuous gnawing hunger for food, but it was thirst that was the harder to endure. I craved water constantly and could really understand why it was said that thirst was worse than hunger.

How long could a person survive without sustenance? We moved around very little and expended little energy. But in our case it was not a question of endurance, for no one was on the way to rescue us. If we waited much longer, we'd be too weak to take any action. But we could think of nothing that promised some chance of success. We could try to kill the guards at the gate. But what chance would we have against soldiers with automatic rifles? Max had only one bullet for his small pistol, and the place was crowded with troops. Yet if we could think of nothing else, that would have to be our choice.

Friday, December 10, 1943

Our situation seemed hopeless. A heaviness was hanging over us. We felt listless and drowsy. I dozed off and was immediately awake again. Sometimes my sleep seemed to be barely below the level of consciousness. Dreams. . . hazy . . . then very clear. I am on a train, in the cab of the engine. The railroad engine has water, so I drink and drink and drink, but I still feel thirsty, and the train is rolling ahead at full speed.

Saturday, December 11, 1943

It had been a week since Maxik came here. Almost a week with no food and no water. Late afternoon. Both Max and Maxik were sleeping restlessly. I was trying to think of a way out. I repeated to myself several times that we must do something fast, otherwise we'd be too weak. But my brain felt sluggish. I was overcome by an oppression of spirit and then felt a great sorrow. The Biblical outcry *"M'ayin Yavo Ezri?* [Whence cometh my help?]" came to my mind. I felt my emotions welling up in me as if ready to overflow and found myself appealing, entreating, without words, to whatever there might be in the Universe. I poured out my heart —seeing before me my parents, my brother Ruvke, my sister Nehamah, and Golda. I thought of the constant struggle and pain of the last two and a half years, and I gave myself up to a wave of grief, and wept without making a sound or producing tears.

I had never before experienced those feelings so intensely, and whatever it was did not last long. But when it was over, I was surprised at the sensation of great relief and clarity of mind that came over me. Uncertainties disappeared; I knew exactly what we had to do next.

As soon as the other two woke up, I said, "We cannot wait anymore. We've got to do something today."

"I agree," Max said. "But what?"

"We've got to try to contact a friendly German . . . Bruendl? Yes, Bruendl would be the right person." He was a soldier in charge of the horse stable where Shmulke used to work. He was known to be a "good

German," and we knew he had a crush on one of the Jewish girls who had worked for 322. I continued, "As soon as it gets dark, one of us should get out, go over to the stable, and when he is alone, try to talk to him. He might help us."

"Yes . . . sounds reasonable," Max agreed. "Who should go?"

"I don't mind going," Maxik said. "It is less dangerous for me."

He slipped away at dusk, and in less than an hour was back hardly able to contain his excitement: "I have good news!"

Rapt, we both listened as Maxik hurriedly related his amazing news: This whole week, Bruendl had actually been hiding Shmulke Palec and Sioma Pick in the piled-up hay of the stable, giving them food and any other help they needed. Just minutes before Maxik's arrival there, Shmulke had left in order to get on the freight train going to Lithuania, on the way to Siauliai.

This news was electrifying, but what was more, Bruendl was ready to help us too! He could take us through the gate of the citadel, and we could still try to get on the train to Siauliai. Or he would give us food, and we could stay where we were for another week; next Saturday the train would again be passing by in the same direction. But if we wanted to catch the train, there was little time left, and we should rush to his place immediately. All that sounded miraculous, especially since Bruendl didn't even know us.

There was no question—we wanted to get away, and worrying we might be late, we left our place in a hurry.

Bruendl lived by himself in a small room at the stable. We found him there with another soldier, who must have known about his activities. He had little information as to the details of the trip. Shmulke told him that he had to go to the Griva freight station to get the "train to Siauliai," and that it passed this way only every Saturday about eight o'clock in the evening. We also knew that the train went only by way of Radvilis-kis, from there we'd have to go by foot. We asked him to get us through the gate.

Bruendl said, "No problem, I'll get you out of here. But this trip you are going on is very dangerous. I think Maxik should stay with me. I'll keep him here. There are many refugees now, and I can say he's one of them, a Russian child. Don't worry, I'll take good care of him."

Maxik chose to stay with Bruendl.

While we talked, each of us devoured a piece of bread with cheese, and gulped some tea. We couldn't fully enjoy it. We were very much in a hurry, aware that even now we might be too late to catch the train. Bruendl gave us bread and sausage to take along, and as we were ready to go, Max said to him, "May God repay you for what you are doing for us, and may He always be with you."

Bruendl looked down at his belt buckle; embossed there were the words *"GOTT MIT UNS,—*the same as on all the soldiers' buckles—and replied, "God has been with us for a long time. It's about time He started taking care of you."

We said good-bye to Maxik and hurried out.

When we reached the gate, Bruendl said something to the guards, and we passed through. We said good-bye and thanked him again, and he replied quietly, "Good luck, be careful."

Bruendl turned back, and we went ahead toward the city.

We were on our way. We had no idea where the freight station was or how to identify the particular freight train once we got there. But we both felt confident and determined. We had our guns, compass, and each other. If it didn't work out with the "train to Siauliai," we'd turn east and march to White Russia.

We passed the city and crossed the bridge without incident, and continued by following the railroad track, assuming that it would take us to the freight station.

After some time we saw railroad spurs and, way ahead, lights. I was wondering how we could get close to the station and the train without arousing suspicion when a freight suddenly appeared, moving slowly, but noticeably picking up speed. The doors of the cars were wide open. Was it going toward Lithuania? I wasn't sure.

"Max, that might be the one." It was picking up speed every second.

"Let's jump in!" he yelled.

We ran a bit alongside, then hoisted ourselves in.

Complete darkness inside. Moving over to the end of the box car, we sat down on the floor. But before long we realized there were some people at the other end. We felt uneasy at first, but they said nothing, and we assumed they were Lithuanian workers, going home for the weekend. After a while we relaxed.

"It would be nice to know for sure that we're going in the right direction," I said.

"We could just ask them," Max said.

I walked over closer, asking in Lithuanian: "Is this train going to Rokiskis?"

"Yes, it is," one of them answered.

"Thanks." We felt relieved. Rokiskis was the next big town in Lithuania on the same line that went to Siauliai.

The other people kept to themselves, never said a word to us. Good, a longer conversation might have given us away. By traveling in a clandestine manner, they were breaking the law too, and their not knowing who we were must have made them wary also. Earlier I'd had a little hope that Shmulke might be one of them, but he wasn't there. Still, he might be in one of the other boxcars.

We ate the bread and sausage Bruendl had given us, but were very thirsty.The train stopped quite often, and after some time, one of the men jumped out at a stop. Probably we were in Lithuania. Within a short time, the rest left the train too, and we were alone. They must have lived in towns close to the border. We had a long way to go, that much we knew. I tried to visualize the map of Lithuania. I knew that Siauliai was closer to the Baltic Sea than to Daugavpils and figured it could be a distance of as much as 300 kilometers from Daugavpils. Max said, "We have to pass Panevezys—that's a big town, I know it well. Also Seduva." But like me, he'd never been to Siauliai, or to Radviliskis, where we had to get off.

Sunday, December 12, 1943

As the train kept rolling through the night, we tried to get our geographical bearings. Every time we came to a station, we tried to catch sight of the sign, but the names were all unfamiliar—except for Rokiskis, which we had passed earlier.

We were chilled through and through. While the train was moving, we often jumped around in one place to keep ourselves warm. But at those interminable stops, we had to be careful. The scurrying around of officials, the loud clanging as doors of rail cars were opened or shut, and the shouting of orders kept us constantly alert. We knew that if asked for documents or just questioned, we'd be immediately recognized as Jews. We decided that, whenever we came to a station, we'd flatten ourselves at the wall of the car next to the open door.

How smart an idea that was became clear a short time later. At one of the stations, the cars were actually inspected. Someone came over, pushed in his head and moved a lighted lantern around our car, first to one side, then another. For a few seconds I held my breath. We are caught! flashed through my mind, but, no, the inspector didn't notice us. Our precaution worked. We heard them go from car to car, apparently checking the whole train.

The train kept chugging along in the darkness. We were cold and thirsty. Every time the train came to a stop, we pressed ourselves to the wall at the open door, waiting eagerly to move again, and then we'd be jumping to the wheels' rhythm to warm ourselves. We wondered how much farther it was to Radviliskis, worrying we might pass it.

It must have been about three or four in the morning when, for the umpteenth time, the train stopped.

"This looks like a large station. Maybe this is it," Max said.

"Could be, if we could only have seen the sign!"

"Guess we'll just have to go down and find out. There's no other choice."

"OK, I'll go." I was usually not recognized as a Jew.

I jumped out from the car, walked a little, saw a railroad man and asked, "Is this Radviliskis?"

"No," he answered, "Radviliskis is very far from here," and, looking at me strangely, gave me the name of the station, a town I'd never heard of. I could imagine how suspicious I must have looked, coming up suddenly this time of night with such a question.

I went back to the car and was about to jump in, when there was a loud "Stop!" I turned around. Judging from the shiny uniform the man wore, he was someone in authority, though not of the military. Another man in a more modest uniform was with him.

"Where are you going?" he asked in Lithuanian, in a stern voice.

"To Seduva, to visit my parents for a day." I knew this was a town before Radviliskis.

"You know it is forbidden to ride on a freight train. You'll be arrested if caught again."

"I'm sorry, sir," I apologized meekly. "I will not do it again."

"Remember, if you are caught again . . ."

They left. I started to walk away. Then the train began to move, no one was around, and I jumped in the car.

Max had listened to my exchange with the official and was quite shaken. "I thought they'd got you this time."

"It was so sudden," I said. "There was no time to get scared, but I sure am lucky they didn't ask for documents."

For some time the train kept moving without incident except for frequent stops. I assumed it was for the purpose of letting heavily loaded trains pass, those going east to the front; I could hear the roar of trains rushing by in the opposite direction. But then we reached Panevezys, the fourth largest town in Lithuania, and here it was bad, very bad.

As soon as our train stopped, we realized that there was another freight on a siding very close to us. We dared not look out as we stood flattened against the wall but from the sounds we heard, we knew exactly what the cargo consisted of—a freight load of Jews. We could hear anxious voices; people were clamoring for water, and children were crying. It all added up to a nightmare.

If only our train would start moving away from this place, from the sounds! But the train kept standing, for what seemed like ages, and I had that familiar, terrifying feeling—only a few feet separated us from them, from the end.

When at last our train started to move again, we were almost limp with relief. But the invisible train with its cargo of the doomed kept on haunting us. We knew they were being taken to their death, but where had they come from?

It was about nine or so in the morning when the train pulled into a large switching yard with many diverging tracks. We had little doubt that this was Radviliskis and jumped off while the train was still in motion.

We got away from the railroad area quickly and stopped several people to ask for directions. There was a risk involved every time we spoke to someone, but we had no choice. When at last we found ourselves on the road to Siauliai, we breathed much easier.

It was a crisp and sunny morning, the temperature just below freezing but getting warmer. The landscape—fields, sparse trees, and road—was covered by a thin layer of fresh snow. Everything was white and clean, seeming to glow in the bright sun. We felt good out in the open.

"I'd rather walk on foot anytime," Max said.

I felt the same way. "You are hemmed in in a railroad car, and in daylight it's worse. The last few hours, I felt so—exposed."

The danger was real enough now too. In our knee-high military boots, identical short coats and winter caps, we were bound to look suspicious. But on a morning such as this, out in the open air, we just couldn't help but feel good.

Before too long, we came upon a fast-running brook at the side of the road and drank to our hearts' content. Right next to it Max found half a big carrot. "A good omen," he said, and in a somewhat ceremonious manner, broke it in two, handing me one piece. With a touch of solemnity we ate the carrot and were on our way.

We knew it was about twenty to twenty-five kilometers to Siauliai, and we did not have to hurry, intending to arrive there under cover of darkness. This being Sunday, there was little traffic—just here and there a peasant family, dressed in its Sunday best, riding to church in a carriage or cart. On such a fine day, the people seemed cheerful, and a few even waved a greeting to us as they rode by. Weak from lack of food and from not having used our limbs much for more than six weeks, we now tired easily and rested often.

As time passed, some of the churchgoers returned home. We thought we saw a few suspicious looks thrown in our direction; any one of them could inform the police ahead that a couple of suspicious looking characters were marching on the road. We moved off the road and waited awhile, then we continued again.

It was almost dusk, and judging by the increase in traffic, the city was not far off. Suddenly, Max said, "You know—we should really hide our guns somewhere around here, before we enter the city."

"What are you talking about!" I was flabbergasted.

"Just think, Shaike," Max explained patiently. "We are entering a big town we've never been in before. If we're stopped, these guns aren't going to help us much—they'll just guarantee our not getting out alive. It's a different story in the open country, but what chance would we have with a gun in a busy street?"

"But, Max . . ."

"Listen, Shaike, I have only one bullet in my gun, but even if I had a hundred—we would still have no chance. . . . It's true, even if we are caught without guns, our chances are none too good, and if there was no ghetto here, it would make no difference, we'd be lost either way, and I'd want to hold on to the guns. But since there are Jews here, if we are caught unarmed, there is a chance they would throw us in the ghetto, like they did with me in Daugavpils. Later, we'll get our guns back."

"I guess you're right. But my gun—it's like a friend, how can I . . ."

But in the end, I had to admit that Max was right. We were just passing a wooded area, not really a forest, just a few trees on the side of the road. We went in among them and found a tall pine towering above the others. Next to the trunk we removed the moss, dug out a hole with our knives and buried the guns, bullets, and compass in our handkerchiefs in such a way that the ground seemed undisturbed. Luckily there was no snow under the trees, and we left no tracks. I looked again at the tree, I knew that if I lived a hundred years, I would remember and be able to find the exact spot.

Back on the road we walked quietly for a while. Then Max, aware how painful it was for me to leave my gun, said, "Remember, Shaike— you can always die a hero. Everyone can. It is to stay alive, to survive— yes, that person is the real hero."

Our timing was just fine. It was twilight when we arrived at the outskirts. A uniformed man, approaching from the opposite direction, looked at us intently. We both tensed up, but when he came to us, he asked in German for a light. We offered one. Smilingly, he thanked us politely and we continued on our way. This simple act somehow made us feel good, and Max said, "It's a good sign."

By the time we were in the city, it was completely dark, and the road turned into a busy street. We now had to find the location of the ghetto, for all we knew it might have been liquidated by now. We stopped an elderly woman who told us, "Go straight, and at the second corner, turn right." A short while later we were facing a barbed wire fence and guarded gate—the Siauliai Ghetto.

Observing the entrance for some time from a safe distance, we saw a Jewish policeman (he wore yellow stars and had an arm band) approach the gate. We stopped him and said we were escaped Jews from Daugavpils and wanted to get inside. He was quite startled, mumbled something, and hurriedly walked away. We continued waiting. After a while another Jewish policeman came out and motioned to us.

"Come along with me," he said, explaining that the Jewish authorities had been informed about us by the other man. We were to go to Kavkaz, a place not far from here—once a ghetto, but now closed except for the cemetery and hospital. He was supposed to bring back a group of Jews who'd been working there and in the process would include us, too.

On the way he pinned yellow stars on our clothing and before long we were in the midst of a column marching through the gate. How he juggled the figures to come back with the number of people that supposedly left earlier, I don't know. But the guard waved us in. We were in the ghetto.

Within minutes we found ourselves sitting at a desk in a well-lighted room on comfortable chairs, gulping hot soup. These were the offices of the Judenrat, the Jewish Council. Sitting on chairs facing us were the members of the council. They were questioning us eagerly about Daugavpils and on what had happened to the Jews there. We ate the tasty soup, and told our story between spoonfuls, keeping back only the part about the time we spent with the partisans (one never knows). This went on for an hour or so, as our dishes were refilled several times. It seemed incredible to be sitting here in this warm, bright room, eating to our heart's content. And to think of where we were only yesterday!

We were surprised to find out that Shmulke Palec had not arrived yet. We hoped he hadn't been caught on the way.

Afterward we were taken to a ramshackle house and given a room with a separate entrance. It was very small, just enough space for a bed, small table and chair, and no stove for heating. But it was our own room.

When we were at last alone, we undressed for the first time in many weeks and jumped into bed; what a shock it was to see snow-white sheets!

Although it was very cold in the room, to us it felt that we had landed in the midst of great comfort. We talked a little about how everything had worked out so well, and if only the girls were with us, we'd be the happiest people in the world.

Monday, December 13, 1943

A barber came to cut our hair, which had gone uncut for four months. I felt embarrassed, knowing there were probably lice; we hadn't washed our hair for over six weeks. But he was a friendly fellow, and gave no indication that he saw any of the vermin. He wanted to know all about Daugavpils, and we in turn got some information about life here.

We talked to more people later, walked around the few streets of the ghetto, and tried to find out more about this place. People were still talking a great deal about the *Children Aktion*, which had taken place about five weeks before on what was called Black Friday. At that time, while most parents were at work, about six hundred children and more than two hundred old and disabled persons were taken away. It was a terrible shock to the ghetto and hadn't worn off yet. To us it was a wonder that there were that many children still here, two-and-a-half years after the start of war. In Daugavpils they were killed within the first few months. This really must be a very unusual ghetto.

In the evening we had a visitor, Ephraim Gens, head of the Jewish

Ghetto Police. A tall, heavy-set man, he seemed friendly as he sat talking with us. Like everyone else, he wanted to hear about Daugavpils. Before leaving, he told us about reports of the steadily advancing Red Army; and then Gens said in a pensive kind of voice:

"With all that we Jews are going through, if the Russians eventually liberate us—there will be questioning and suspicions. . . ." I knew he was thinking of his own situation. In his capacity here as an official of the ghetto, the Russians would want to ask plenty of questions, and who knows. . . ? I was pretty sure, though, that Gens was as eager for the liberation as any other Jew.

Shmulke had not arrived.

Tuesday, December 14, 1943

There were no facilities for heating our room (in normal times this place must have been some sort of shed), so today we were moved to another building.

Our new place consisted of a kitchen and another room. In the small narrow kitchen lived a middle-aged couple with two teen-aged daughters. I wondered where they all slept; there didn't seem to be enough space even for two beds. In our room was a family of four with a sister-in-law and her little boy and, with the two of us, a total of eight persons. There was just enough space for a table in the middle and beds all around. Max and I shared one narrow bed and slept head to toe.

We were still recuperating. We kept soaking our feet in hot water, and pieces of yellow skin had been peeling off them.

The ghetto was very organized, with exact lists of people who lived here. We had to register for our food rations and work assignments. The Judenrat advised us to use names that were common here in Siauliai to avoid attracting attention. My last name was now "Gordon" and Max's was "Kaplan."

In the evening, many people came to see us, hoping to hear news of relatives or friends they'd had in Daugavpils before the war. Unfortunately, we had no encouraging news for anyone. The room was full the whole evening; there was a lot of curiosity about us. Our arrival was an "event."

December 15 to 31, 1943

We were both working, Max in the shoemaking workshop, and I on the building and maintenance detail. We suspected that we were assigned jobs inside the ghetto because we were not quite trusted by the Jewish Council. When we first arrived and were brought to the offices of the council, we were asked to leave our small survival bags with the receptionist. Unbeknown to us they were inspected, and the military bandages and other objects discovered there made some of the officials suspicious. Max found out about it from a girl who worked at the council office. There were rumors about us that we were parachuted in by the Russians.

People still came to see us and asked questions; everyone wanted to know what had happened to other Jewish communities.

Max met three women from Anyksciai, the town he came from. They had been married a few years before the war and had lived in Siauliai since. They all had lost their husbands in the first months of the war, when many Jewish men were taken to prison and then shot. Here, too, as in Daugavpils, there were many women, now alone, whose husbands had been killed at the beginning of the war.

The ghetto was at the edge of town, in what used to be a very poor neighborhood. It was rectangular in shape, and its four small streets with their humble dwellings were hemmed in on the west by a large red brick building—the city prison—and on the east by the huge leather factory. To the north there was open space with a murky-looking lake not too far off, and a city street to the south, where the gate to the ghetto was located. There was also a gate directly to the leather factory. A barbed wire fence surrounded the whole area, guarded by SS troopers of Romanian *Volksdeutsche* (ethnic Germans).

It all started when I went to buy cigarettes—for the right price you could get many things in ghetto. On the way out, a woman who seemed to be around thirty and there for the same purpose, started talking to me.

"I came to see you a couple of days ago," she said, "but couldn't get to talk to you; there were so many people in the room. I wanted to ask you about my relatives in Daugavpils."

We left together. No, the people she asked about were not alive anymore, but we continued walking and talking. She wanted to know what had happened in Daugavpils and was very interested in everything I told her. She was a great listener, and we walked for hours back and forth in the few streets of the ghetto. When we said good night, she suggested that we meet again the following evening. "I would like to know your ideas about escaping from the ghetto," she said.

So we met every evening this past week. She belonged to a quite prominent family in Siauliai. Her husband was killed in prison in the early days of the war, and her little girl of three was taken away in the *Children Aktion* on November 5. Tears came to her eyes and her voice broke, whenever she mentioned her child. But she let me do most of the talking, and it was nice to have a personable older woman admiring me and being attentive to everything I said. When I told her how I felt about my gun and compass, and that I was still keeping the string with which I used to have the gun attached to my belt, she was visibly touched.

Every time we parted, she asked that we meet again the next evening. I knew that a relationship was developing, something I did not wish. Earlier in the evening, I told Max that I just didn't know how to terminate the relationship; I could not face her and say that I did not want to see her. Max said he would meet the lady at the agreed hour and tell her that I could not see her anymore.

Later, Max told me that she was very sad after hearing what he had to say and I felt bad about the way I'd handled it. I wished I hadn't done it that way, but there was nothing I could do about it now.

We got our guns and compass! It had been gnawing at me since the day we arrived here—actually not even two weeks ago. A few days ago we talked to Joseph Leibowitz, the brother of Mendel Leibowitz, head of the Judenrat, about the hidden guns, and he was a great help. Joseph was an engineer, in charge of building and maintenance but also secretly coordinator of whatever preparation for resistance was taking place in the ghetto. He arranged for me to leave the ghetto with a Jewish policeman as if being taken to work. It was the same person who had smuggled us in when we first came here. Everything went smoothly. I found the place easily, and once there it took only a few minutes to dig out our treasure. There were a few tense moments at the gate; a sudden search, a frisking for smuggled-in food was always a possibility, but the SS guard just waved us through. The guns seemed to be in pretty good condition, but we decided to give them a good cleaning and oiling.

On Sunday, as planned, Max and I locked ourselves in the workshop, and without interference, took our guns apart and thoroughly cleaned them with oil. They weren't affected much by being in the ground that short a time, and the compass, too, was in fine condition. If we could only get more bullets for Max's gun! But with time, I was sure, we'd get them.

Although it was very crowded in the ghetto, even here some people managed to make their places look clean and attractive. We visited Max's friend from Anyksciai. He had become very friendly with Shulamith, who lived with Pessia Lisitzin's family, six people together in one room. Pessia was about my age. On entering I was struck by the unmistakable feminine touch pervading the room. With imagination and good taste the few odds and ends took on a certain charm, so that an old wooden box covered with colorfully embroidered material and a small vase of wine-colored glass became an attractive coffee table, and so it went for some of the other "furniture" too. The whole room was bright and pleasant.

During the evening, several friends of Pessia's stopped by. One of them, Ita Tabrisky, was an interesting and attractive girl. I spent a lot of time talking with her and later escorted her home, actually just across the street. We spent some more time sitting on a bench under a tree and talking. It was the only house in the ghetto that was surrounded by a few trees, and there was even a swing under one of them.

Shmulke Palec suddenly appeared! We had given up expecting him anymore, but on Sunday night he arrived in the ghetto. He told us that everything had gone smoothly for him. He was accompanied by the Lithuanian fellow most of the way and was told by him how to find the ghetto. Two weeks ago when the German, Bruendl, thought he'd left for the train, Shmulke had only gone to see that Lithuanian friend of his.

Everything was going just fine. All three of us had guns, and once the winter months were over, we'd be off. We were elated.

My work was not too hard. We did various repairs, mostly rough carpentry. Joseph Leibowitz, our boss, assigned us to various locations, and Moshe Shimsher, a gaunt-faced older man, was more or less in charge of our small group. Beside him there was his son, a boy of about fifteen, a middle-aged refugee from Poland, and I.

Once in a while, we had to dig a grave in the cemetery; this was done on a voluntary basis after regular working hours. I usually volunteered as did Shimsher and the boy. For every grave we dug, we earned an extra ration of bread, which came in very handy. We had no more money to buy bread on the black market, and our regular rations were small.

Siauliai was probably the best ghetto left anywhere. Of the hundreds of Jewish communities in Lithuania and Latvia, Siauliai Ghetto was one of only three still in existence. Kaunas still had 10,000 Jews out of a prewar population of 35,000; Riga had become a camp primarily for Jews deported from Germany, with only a very few from Latvia still alive. But in Siauliai there were still about 4,000 Jews out of a prewar population of 8,000 (though many were refugees from surrounding towns, while some of the natives escaped with the Russians). But even here, enough frightening events had taken place. And when it came to meting out punishment, certain familiar procedures were followed. The details of a hanging, which were described to me, reminded me very much of the hangings in Daugavpils. The whole ghetto population was forced to witness the execution of the man caught trying to bring food into the ghetto, and here too Jews were made to perform the actual hanging. But it was the *Children Aktion*, that really left the people shaken. People still talked about it a great deal, and by now the details of that fateful day were quite clear in my mind.

In the morning of Black Friday, as soon as people had left for work, an order was issued to the Judenrat that all children up to age thirteen, as well as the old and infirm, were to be brought to the gate "to be taken to a children's home where the oldsters will care for them." Covered trucks appeared, and the *Aktion* began. It was directed by the SS, but the actual "work" was carried out by Ukrainian auxiliaries. Many of the children immediately disappeared into hiding places, but the Ukrainians pulled them out, threw them in the trucks and beat hysterically screaming mothers with their rifle butts.

We heard the most graphic details of that day from a Jewish policeman, who got into a conversation with me and Max one day, wanting to know what had happened in Daugavpils. On Black Friday, he was stationed not far from where the trucks were being loaded, and when we asked him about it, he said that he still had nightmares about what he saw that day. Being a native of Siauliai, he knew many of the people personally. He told us of mothers running after their babies, who were being dragged off by Ukrainians. But most mothers were at work at the time, and you'd see a child of seven or eight holding the hand of a younger brother or sister, maybe three or four years old, both walking quietly in front of a uniformed Ukrainian towering over them, prodding them on with his rifle to move faster. Many of the children were not even wearing coats; they had been pulled from some hiding place and not allowed to put on something warm. He told us of a little girl of about three with blond curly hair, who was walking with a small blanket draped over her shoulder. The Ukrainian wanted her to go faster but the blanket kept slipping off, and she stumbled on it several times. With anger the soldier snatched her, and the blanket fell to the ground. Tears ran down her face as she stretched out her little arms toward the blanket lying in the dirt. The Ukrainian threw her in the truck.

Later in the day, hidden children became harder to discover. Ukrainians kept going over the same houses again and again, searching ever more thoroughly, and in the process robbing everything of value, breaking up furniture, even walls. And when a child was found, there was excitement. " Hey, I got one!" they would shout. There was merriment, as the hunt went on for the little ones.

The *Aktion* lasted a whole day from early morning until late afternoon. The few mothers who were not away at work begged and fought for their children, and in their desperation some tried forcibly to follow them in the trucks. A few of them were allowed to come along, and so were Kartoon and Katz, two respected members of the Judenrat, who were also taken along "to see for themselves that the children were being well taken care of."

After the last truck left, the Ukrainians were seen sipping liquor, in a manner of people who have earned some relaxation after a hard day's labor.

In the evening, when the parents came home from work, they found their children gone, and the whole night the air was filled with the sound of wailing. About 850 people were taken away, most of them children.

By and large, the Jewish police did not cooperate with the Germans; some had even warned the mothers. However, the chief of police, Gens, brought his own child, a little girl, to the trucks. He apparently believed the Germans' promises.

I did still see a child here and there. On that fateful day, some had been smuggled by parents to their work sites, and a few, in hiding places, were not discovered.

I was told of a strange phenomenon, the jumping table, which first made its appearance in the ghetto after the *Children Aktion*. People would gather together in a room for a kind of seance, hold their hands on a small table, and wait to get answers to their questions: One side of the table would lift up and then bang down to the floor, thereby giving the answer. Mothers, holding their breath, waited anxiously to hear that their children were still alive, and the answer was usually affirmative. For a while those little tables took the ghetto by storm, and people from all walks of life, young and old, held their hands on the table and asked, "Will I survive?" It was hard to understand how quite intelligent people could have faith in a superstition so primitive, But, I guess, when the need to believe is very strong, people simply trust in anything. Anyhow, most of this absurdity seemed to be over.

There were various rumors about where the children were killed, but it was quite certain that they were all dead. Oddly, almost two months later, there were mothers who still believed that their children were alive. (It was confirmed after the war that those deported on November 5, 1943 were gassed at Auschwitz.)

Work was satisfactory. The food ration was small, but we managed somehow. I got an extra ration here and there for digging a grave, and Max sometimes got something extra at work. In the evenings we met with friends, and, in general, there was more of a feeling of normalcy, at least in comparison to life in the Daugavpils Ghetto. I should have been satisfied here. But in my mind I kept going back to that week when all of us were hiding together under the roof; we were in constant danger, and our situation seemed desperate, yet, what wouldn't I give to be back there with Golda? I now had more hope that they were all taken from Daugavpils to the Kaiserwald Camp near Riga, and that we'd find each other eventually.

There was an underground movement in the ghetto, trying to organize some form of resistance. It was called Masada, and Joseph Leibowitz was one of the leaders.

One evening, we were asked to come to the carpentry shop, which was not far from the ghetto fence. A few boards were removed from the floor, and we saw people digging a tunnel which eventually should extend to the Aryan side. We went down and could see that at some places they had used wooden supports; quite a bit of work was put in here, but it was only a beginning, a great deal more was left to be done. There was still quite a distance to the fence, and even after it had been reached, it would be necessary to dig farther until a safe place for an exit was found; also, there was the constant problem of getting rid of the dug-out ground, a large amount. But at least *something* was being done. It was not too difficult to get out of the ghetto in ordinary times, but in an emergency, when the ghetto was surrounded, a completed tunnel like this could be a vital aid to escape.

Saturday, January 1, 1944: The 924th day

Another year had passed. Two and a half years since it all started, and there seemed to be no end. Surely, it must be over soon. The news from the fronts filtering through to us continued to be good—the Russians kept advancing. How long could the Germans hold out? We didn't understand why the Americans still had not invaded Germany. There was much speculation; the feeling was that, once the Americans landed, the war would be over in a very short time.

I'd met Ita Tabrisky again and been to the house where she lived with her family. From a friend of hers I borrowed the second volume of the book *Pandre* by Zalman Schneur; I'd read the first one shortly before the war. It was good to lose oneself, even if only momentarily, in the small town of Sklar among the *horopashniks*—the so-called common, hard-working Jews in whose "child-like eyes played the power of life."

Month of January 1944

Here in Siauliai, the Judenrat, played an important role in the life of the ghetto. The head was Mendel Leibowitz, an honorable, respected member of the community. From what I heard, I was convinced that, in general, Jewish leadership had had a very positive effect on life here, although many people were critical of one or another member of the council. Lately though, things had been changing. Although Leibowitz was still the nominal head, it was Pariser, officially head only of the work-assignment office, who actually now held all the power in the ghetto.

Georg Pariser was born in Germany and came to Siauliai with his wife and two teen-aged children, a boy and a girl, shortly before the war. His wife was Christian but chose to go with him and the children to the ghetto. Like many of the men, he was imprisoned for a time and, like all Jews, went through all the hardships of ghetto life. But with his assignment to the new post, after the two council members were taken away in the last *Aktion,* he had changed his attitude. It was said that he was quite close to Foerster (the SS officer in charge of the ghetto) and his power increased from day to day. He now acted very "German," and people in the ghetto distrusted him.

The Jewish council had been administering all the internal affairs in the ghetto: food distribution, work assignments, housing, maintenance of order, and so on. It was, of course, operating within the framework of German restrictions and control but, at least in the past, had always tried to ease, whenever possible, the German-imposed tyranny under which people had to live.

There was still something cohesive about this community. Although many of the people here were from surrounding towns and some were refugees from Poland, the great majority had always lived in Siauliai, and one's social status from before the war still counted for something— it was "Dr. this," and "Madam that." I thought the effect of this was stabilizing and positive. For example, the so-called Ghetto Court, which was active until sometime last year, was highly successful in settling many disputes, simply through the moral authority of the community.

We were moved by the housing authority to new quarters on Ginkuno street and were satisfied with the change. It had become quite unpleasant in our old room. The crowded conditions were the cause of frequent quarrels within the family we lived with. In the new room, there were six of us and somewhat more space, but enough room only for one additional bed; we still had to sleep head to toe. We were used to it by now and didn't mind.

I had been to Ita's house several times. I felt welcome there, and it was nice to sit and talk with her and her brother Leon, who was about a year and a half younger. The place where they lived must have been a stable before the war, but they felt lucky to have it. Because it was so small, they didn't have to share it with another family, and there were also trees outside. Their mother was taken away at the last *Aktion,* and so was their grandfather. They lived together with their grandmother (who had hidden during the *Aktion*), Aunt Shifra, Uncle Leibl, and the wife of another uncle, killed in the early weeks of the occupation. I told them a lot about my experiences and about Golda and the Gutterman family.

We talked of a variety of subjects. Ita and Leon were both very idealistic and spoke Hebrew fluently.

"Even if we don't survive," Ita said, "I am quite sure Jews will build a country in Palestine where justice and fairness will prevail. It will be an example for the rest of the world."

We talked of Ahad-Haam and other Zionist writers. But it was poetry that she really loved; her favorites were Bialik and Heinrich Heine—she could recite long poems of theirs by heart.

I had mixed feelings about Heine. "He was born a Jew but converted to Christianity."

"But," Ita objected, "one can see from his writing that in his heart he always stayed a Jew and was never quite happy with his conversion."

She recited Bialik's poem "On the Slaughter" about the Kishinev pogrom of 1903, where scores of Jews were massacred. The poem was a bitter outcry of pain by someone who, after what had happened, could no longer pray and demanded that the heavens pray for him. It was very powerful, and though he wrote the words forty years ago, it was as if they were written about us, about what was happening right now. What a great poet he was!

We were known here as the Dvinskers (in Dvinsk-Daugavpils, we were called the Litvaks). Though few people knew actual details of our experiences, the fact that we had escaped and came from far-away made us seem heroic in the eyes of many. I didn't feel heroic, but on the other hand, our success in getting out of every jam and our smooth arrival here in the ghetto made it easy to start believing that we were "special" and would prevail in whatever we did. But I never took our good luck for granted, and I repeated my apprehension to Max several times: "I can't get rid of the feeling that we'll trip up on something small."

We had been quite satisfied with our lot here during this last month in Siauliai. The people here agree that since the Children *Aktion*, there had been no new decrees, the ghetto had been quiet,and even the frisking for food at the gate was less frequent. We knew the calm was temporary; sooner or later the ax would drop again. But we were not too fearful.

"So far," Max said, "we've never had an *Aktion* in the middle of the winter."

I got along well with my coworkers. Moshe Shimsher was a real *baal melokhe*—a skilled artisan who took pride in his work. He was conscientious and a man of integrity.

The refugee from Poland, with his blond, pointed mustache, made me think somehow of a Polish squire. I liked listening to him talk—his Yiddish had a saucy tone typical of Galicia. I had the feeling that the very act of speaking, the smooth flow of words, gave Galicianer great pleasure. But it was in the fine art of cursing that the Galicianer really excelled. When he started to swear at the Nazis in general and at Hitler in particular, he used the most colorful curses, and it was something to behold; at times I had trouble keeping a straight face.

People here were thoroughly aware of what had happened to the Jews in the Baltic States. Kaunas in Lithuania and Riga in Latvia were the only other ghettos still allowed to exist. Even in Vilnius, where 75,000 Jews used to live, there was no longer any ghetto. In addition, the Jews of the hundreds of towns and villages were all dead—killed mostly in the first few months of the war.

Many of the reports came through the Jews who worked in the leather factory, some of whom met people from different places when they came for leather goods. Sometimes SS men from Kaunas or Riga picked up leather material and brought along a few Jews to help load it. There was usually an opportunity for a swift exchange of information between the Jews working in the factory and those visiting.

What made Siauliai so different from the other ghettoes, at least so far, was the existence of the leather factory, known here as Frankel's Factory, or simply, as the Factory. It consisted of a cluster of huge brick buildings, where leather was processed, starting from raw hides and skins, and ending with the manufacture of shoes, coats, and all the other leather products. Together with the famous shoe factory Batas, which was part of the compound, it was the largest enterprise of its kind in all three of the Baltic states, employing thousands, truly an empire unto itself. In the past, it was owned, managed, and operated by Jews, and the Germans were convinced that Jews were still needed for the efficient operation of the huge enterprise.

When the Germans first occupied Siauliai, the pattern of events here didn't differ much from what was then taking place throughout the country. It seemed that here, too, the city would become *Judenrein* (clean of Jews) in short order. Jewish males were being arrested, locked up in prison, and later shot in a forest some distance away. The SS and Lithuanian officials wanted to "deport" all Jews from here, but the leaders of the Jewish community did everything possible to have this edict annulled, pointing out the importance of Jews in the continuing smooth operation of the Factory. It seemed that because of this economic reason, the *Gebietskommisar* (civil administrator of the district) in Siauliai was instrumental in allowing the Jews to remain alive until now. The usual *Aktionen* took place, but none occurred from the fall of 1941 until Black Friday.

The presence of the Factory completely dominated the ghetto, not only physically—its massive buildings dwarfed our very modest dwellings—but, more importantly, in a benevolent, life-sustaining way. The special passage and gate that connected the ghetto to the Factory was truly a lifeline for the people. The number of Jews working there had fluctuated, but at the present time was close to a thousand.

I had become quite friendly with one of the neighbors. Peretz was probably in his thirties. He and his wife managed to save their little boy of about five in the last *Aktion*—his hiding place was not discovered. I felt sorry for them. I didn't think they had much of a chance to survive with their child. But Peretz was quite optimistic. Today he said to me: " The Russians are around Vitebsk. Another couple of months, and we'll be liberated."

When I expressed my skepticism and my belief that the Germans would make every effort to kill us before they left, he said, "You are too pessimistic. We will survive. There may be more hardships when the front line moves closer, but you'll see, we will live to see their downfall."

This was not the view held by everyone here, but many people did feel that way. They knew quite well what had happened to all the other Jews, and every once in a while someone tried to escape to the countryside (most were turned in to the SD by farmers). Yet, the perception of danger here was very different from that in Daugavpils. Their own prospects of survival were somehow separated in their minds from the well-known fate of all other Jews. During the two-and-a-half years here, the Jews of Shiauliai had come to believe that their work was crucial to the Germans. The *Children Aktion* was a shock. But it was pointed out that only nonworkers were taken, and the very fact that they had been allowed to live all this time had reinforced the belief that they would survive. And some of the mothers still hoped that their children might be alive.

At the same time, many were aware that, logically, they were in grave danger. There was a lot of talk about escape, especially among young people. I believed that, for them, the motive was not just survival but revenge. I had no doubt at all that many fellows would have jumped at any opportunity to fight the Nazis.

It was Sunday afternoon, and Shmulke came over. The three of us were sitting on the bed. I could see through the window that it had started to snow, and before my eyes, the dirty brown slush was disappearing under a pure white cover. The last few days hadn't been very cold, but the warm spell seemed about over.

"It will be very cold tonight," Shmulke predicted.

I was thinking of spring—green fields and woods. I said with a touch of excitement in my voice: "Just think of it, in two months it will be the end of March, and we can be off! With three guns—nothing will stop us!" The conversation then turned to the time we spent in the forest. Less than four months had passed since then, but so much had happened. Max told Shmulke about the time the soldiers were pursuing us, the afternoon of October 13. We were still puzzled by what happened then.

"Hundreds and hundreds of bullets were flying, all these soldiers were shooting at us . . . and we just walked, we just walked away without a scratch."

I could see that Shmulke thought Max was exaggerating.

"It's true," I said. "I can't really explain why we weren't hit. The other two partisans were way ahead of us, and one of them got hit anyway."

"Someone must have been watching over us," Max said.

"Maybe, but, you know, I have a little fantasy about that incident. I know it isn't so, but I like to believe it. I imagine the soldiers having us in their gun sights; they observe how we shake hands, bid farewell to each other, and continue to march upright, without visible fear. Remember, we had no rifles, and my gun could not be seen. I want to believe that those hardened killers were touched by the behavior of two young fellows and aimed their fire over our heads. Of course, it is not so. If there had been one or two of them, maybe—but with so many, they could not all have decided to spare our lives."

At night I had often thought about the many narrow escapes we had had since the beginning of the war, some of them virtually miraculous. Many people would ascribe this to divine intervention or *bashertkeit* (fate). Probably we had just been plain lucky, but, still, many things had happened for which we had no explanation. There was my dream of Maxik bursting in through the opening in our roof, the very day before the boy appeared in our midst in that very fashion. And then my emotional experience in the attic the day we left for Siauliai. Some people would describe these as extraordinary spiritual experiences. I just didn't know. It would have been so nice to believe that one was destined for a special purpose. It would have accounted neatly for the feeling of inviolability one had. But I believed many people, maybe even most people, had that same feeling of being "special"—then the time came, and they were shot. We had escaped certain death many times, but I still thought, that, in the end, we'd probably be betrayed by some random little incident.

Month of February 1944

A group of us were sent to the forest to bring wood for the ghetto. I suppose that Sunday was the only day when the Jewish Council could obtain use of a truck. Besides a ghetto policeman, we were also accompanied by Burgin, a member of the council. It was nice to spend a little time in the countryside, and we had a chance to get food from the farmers.

One of the people I worked with was the Movie Teller. I was told that this man, a train engineer before the war, had an exceptional talent for recounting every film he had seen in the past. He was usually invited to a house for a presentation, where there was a gathering of friends. The telling might take between one to two hours, and every scene was described in complete detail. Evidently listeners became absorbed in these nonvisual films.

We heard many rumors, but one never knew what to believe. Some of the latest I'd heard: There were almost no Jews left in Poland. . . . Around Lublin was a special camp where Jews were killed in a mass production way with special killing machinery. Half a million had been murdered in this one camp already. . . . Jews who had passports from foreign countries were allowed to leave. . . .The Allies wanted to exchange Jews for German POWs. . . .

But about Lithuania and Latvia, we didn't have to guess. I had very little hope that anyone of my own family was still alive but kept hoping that Golda and her family might be in Riga.

One evening I went with Ita to visit friends of hers. A few more people stopped by. Lots of talk. One fellow said: "If I survive the war, I'll go to Palestine, I would not stay here for a minute longer than I had to." I never gave much thought to "after the war"—let me just survive. I thought this was true of most people. But the fellow was right. After what the native population here had been doing to us. . . .

Later we sang songs, or, rather, Esther, a girl with a very fine voice, sang, and most of the rest of us just hummed along.

There were many people of great talent here in the ghetto, and that goes for songwriting too. Many of the songs Esther was singing had been written here and expressed very well the grief and despair of our people. But although very sad, they were also melodic and beautiful. Especially heart-wrenching was a song often repeated, "In a Far Away Lithuanian Village," about a little Jewish boy left by his mother with a Christian family in a Lithuanian village. It was a rather long song, telling all about the pain of both mother and child as she says good-bye to him. You could not help but feel a lump in your throat as you listened.

Songs and music had always had a great deal of meaning for me, probably for most people here. In Daugavpils, in the forest, and now here—in each case, music gave expression and release to our feelings, and that outpouring somehow made one feel better.

"In a Far Away Lithuanian Village"—that song had been on my mind. I asked Peretz, "Are there many children hidden in villages?"

"A few, I guess . . . Sure, many parents tried to hide their children with farmers. But in most cases, they were either discovered by the police or betrayed by their 'benefactors,' especially after a Jew has been sucked dry of valuables and money. There are some who still take a chance and leave children with peasants. But even now, with the Germans in retreat on all fronts, a Jew still doesn't have much of a chance with the villagers. . . ."

Yet, I was thinking of Shmulke, who at different times had been helped by Lithuanians. I'd heard, too, of some priests who had helped Jews in this area, and even a couple of officials who were friendly. Surely there were some decent ones, but far too many of the other kind.

I said to Peretz, "What is it with the Lithuanians and the Latvians that they hate us so much? Before the war, sure, there was anti-Semitism, but I'd never heard of a pogrom in Lithuania, and we'd always thought that life was better here for Jews than in Poland or other countries."

"It was our misfortune—our misfortune," Peretz repeated, "that the Soviets occupied Lithuania in June of 1940, just a year before the Germans attacked. You know how the Lithuanians felt, with Lithuania having lost its independence, their hatred of the communists had no bounds. The Jews, of course, have always been accused of being communists . . ."

"But the loss of independence was a result of the pact between the Soviets and Germans just before the war."

"You know how it is—it's always easy to blame the Jews.... And then, when, just a week before the German attack, the Soviets started to deport people to Siberia, it was again the Jews who were blamed for it. Although I'm sure that, proportionately, more Jews than Lithuanians were actually deported."

"Just from our small town, maybe fifty or sixty Jews were deported," I said. "We were so worried about Father, because he was known as an outspoken anticommunist, and we were afraid they'd come for him."

"For us Jews it was always so: Woe unto us if we happened to be in the wrong place at the wrong time. . . ." Peretz said sadly.

Max told me that while he was working today, he'd seen a deer!

He said: "We all stopped working and looked through the window. From the workshop on top of the hill, you can see clear across the fence and the whole area behind."

"But how would a deer get here?"

"In the winter they sometimes leave the forest in search of food. They were shooting at him; it was sad. The deer was running behind the lake, and the Germans were firing away at him, and it was like when we were back in the forest fleeing from the soldiers. I knew exactly how the deer felt!"

"I hope he escaped."

It was said that in a Kaunas fortress, Fort No.9, Jews were made to dig out the bodies of those killed in 1941 and burn them. How could they have dug out tens of thousands of bodies?

Month of March 1944

Our Sunday trips to the forest for wood (for heating ghetto homes) had become routine. We all brought back food we bought from farmers. Sometimes, I got a chance to buy a chicken, but then I had to kill it myself with my knife before bringing it back.

Burgin of the Jewish Council sometimes came along with us. He was an interesting person. He talked loud and rough and seemed domineering and heavy-handed, but people said he was devoted to the ghetto and worked hard to help Jews, sometimes risking his own life. I heard that he was especially good at dealing with certain Germans and Lithuanians in situations where ability to think on your feet could be very helpful. But like most of the other council members, he too was criticized by some people. The complaints usually concerned the few privileges that our leaders garnered for themselves and their friends; as if it would have really made a difference in our lives were this sort of thing never to occur. In the misery of ghetto life, people railed at those closest above them.

Pariser, who, for all practical purposes, had been boss of the council for some time, now had the official title too: *Lageraelteste* (camp elder). Burgin seemed to be the only other member of the council who still exerted a measure of influence in ghetto affairs, though it was in no way comparable to that of Pariser. Pariser acted as if he was the complete lord and master, and the ghetto his personal domain.

Peretz said that when Pariser first came to Siauliai in 1939, he had seemed decent enough. When the Nazis came, he, a German Jew with a gentile wife, suffered as much as everyone else. "He used to smuggle in food, starved, worked and slaved like anyone else in the ghetto. But how he changed the minute he got authority!"

"Still, he is a Jew and must be waiting for the liberation like all of us."

"I suppose. But look at the eagerness with which he fulfills every order of the Germans, and how strict he is with the people here!"

It was the end of March, and the nights were still cold, but we knew we had to get away from here soon.

I was standing with Max next to the hospital; the barbed wire fence was right behind it. About a hundred feet away, the SS guard stood at his post, smoking a cigarette.

We looked beyond the fence, a spot we'd gazed at many times this past month. Each detail of the drab, treeless landscape was familiar to us, but we kept looking at it. Not much to see—the open space to the right of the lake became high ground and turned into a hill. We often wondered whether there were houses behind the hill.

Max said, "There is not much cover, but in a dark night it shouldn't be too complicated to get out."

"Guess the bottom strand of the wire can be pulled up high enough for a guy to crawl under."

"We should talk, though, to Joseph Leibowitz, before we make our move. He might give us some helpful advice."

I agreed.

Month of April 1944

It all started some days ago. I was at Ita's place, telling them about my Sunday trips to the forest; I told how I sometimes brought back poultry and once managed to get a small turkey. Ita's Aunt Shifra asked with excitement, "If you could bring us a live turkey—that would be wonderful. Next week, you know, is Passover."

I was startled by the suggestion: "A live turkey!"

"It could then be butchered in the proper ritual way, and we would have kosher meat for the Seder," Shifra explained, adding, "It would be a real treat for us."

I promised to see what I could do.

I was doubtful about the whole thing, but it seemed to be working out quite well. We had gone to the countryside, as usual, and I saw a very large turkey in a farmyard; he was truly impressive. But, most important, the farmer was willing to sell it for the right price. The fellows helped me arrange a hollow space, a sort of cage, under the wood of the truck, and I brought the huge bird in safe and sound. I immediately delivered it to Shifra and felt quite satisfied with myself. She was going to have it butchered in about five days, in time for the holiday.

But it turned out that the turkey was not destined to be eaten in the ghetto after all. One of the SS men discovered it just a day before the holiday. While strolling through the ghetto, he suddenly heard the *gob-*

ble gobble and followed the sound; he found the turkey and took it away immediately.

Shifra thought there would be no repercussions, reasoning that the German would probably keep quiet; he was impressed with the size of the turkey and would certainly want to keep it for himself. And so it proved.

Max talked with Joseph Leibowitz who wanted to organize a whole group to escape to the forest with us. We had some experience and guns; it was right that we should act together with the other fellows.

I was at the workshop where Max worked. Looking down from the high ground, I thought of how much of the story of the Siauliai Ghetto was all there before my eyes. The Factory, meaning work and life, was to the right; the prison, meaning death, to the left, and the lake, the open space straight ahead—freedom.

Month of May 1944

Very little change in the last few weeks. Max had talked again with Leibowitz, but we had heard nothing concrete yet.

We kept hearing of Russian advances on various fronts. There was a lot of talk of a Russian secret weapon, which was called *katyusha*, and moved from place to place on a special truck. No one knew exactly what it was, just that it devastated masses of German troops. But the city of Vitebsk, about 500 kilometers from here, was still in German hands. Yet, back in October, when we were with the partisans, it was said that "the Red Army is advancing on Vitebsk," and the city was expected to fall any day; now seven months later, it was still not taken.

It was strange that the Germans still acted with such confidence. One wondered looking at them, if they suspected their end was near.

We were both surprised at what happened today: Leibowitz gave Max a pistol, and told him we should keep it for him. It was larger than the one Max had, but there were no bullets for it yet; we were supposed to get them shortly. Leibowitz's people must have just acquired the gun. With regard to escaping, he said that plans were being made, we should have patience.

Month of June 1944

Big change. Suddenly I was in the country and living in a barn on one of the farms! The order came quite suddenly, and fourteen of us, with two SS guards, were brought here by truck from the ghetto to work in the forest. Our job was cutting down trees. We didn't know how long we'd have to stay here. At another time I wouldn't have minded it at all, but since we were getting ready to escape, I was not at all happy about being so suddenly separated from Max and Shmulke.

We were probably only twenty to thirty kilometers from the city, but because we were so isolated here, the war and the ghetto seemed quite remote, and not only in distance.

After we were here a few days, a farmer told us that American soldiers had landed on the coast of France and were battling the Germans.

We had to work rigorously to get the huge trees down, but it felt good to be in the forest a whole day and not be hungry; we got ample food from the farmers. I was constantly nagged, though, by the thought that we should have been far away by now. I also felt some compunction about logging the tall, stately looking pines, which one minute towered majestically toward the sky, and the next moment were lying on the ground, waiting helplessly to be shipped off to Germany.

After almost two weeks, instead of us returning to the ghetto, three more Jews were brought out, and among them was Shmulke Palec!

Shmulke said that the rumor we'd heard about American and English forces landing in France was true; large battles were in progress on the coast of France. He and Max had waited impatiently for my return, intending to escape as soon as I got back. Instead, he wound up here, too, and we had no idea how long we would have to stay.

The two guards were from the SS unit attached to the ghetto. They marched us to work in the morning, were with us the whole day, then marched us back; we couldn't move around much.

I was now quite used to the work. To saw through the thick trunks, we had to pull and push the heavy hand saw back and forth with considerable effort. But once a tree was on the ground, it was quite easy to chop off the few branches. The weather had been very pleasant, and time went by fast. At day's end, we were marched back to our barn, often breaking out with a song. Our favorite was a Zionist marching song. With much gusto, we sang the Hebrew words of our love for the Land of Israel, as we swung along in step, with an SS guard in front and to the rear of our small column. They, of course, had no idea what we were singing. Some of the words went like this:

> The sun's already scorching in the mountains
> While the dew still glistens down below.
> How we love you, our precious Homeland,
> In our joy, our song and our toil. . . .

There was a sense of unreality about our being here. We lived in a setting that was almost pastoral, and the very fact that we were here cutting trees to be shipped to Germany encouraged a feeling of normalcy. Yet, I was certain that events of crucial importance were just about to burst upon us; battles were raging and moving ever closer to us. With every day that passed, my impatience grew. I felt trapped, and so did Shmulke. We should have left long ago. But Max was in the ghetto, along with our guns and compass. How long would they keep us here?

June was coming to an end, and we were still here, isolated. There was talk of Russian advances, also of battles in France, but these were only faint echoes of the ongoing struggle. We had no definite news, no idea of the actual situation. The big news in the area was that after drinking the moonshine sold around here, three or four peasants had died, and another dozen had wound up with disabling infirmities.

Monday, July 3, 1944

It was night now, but none of us was asleep. The steady groaning of Mr. Lurie, interrupted only by sharp outcries, was jarring. He was lying in a cart on a bed of hay slightly away from us, but his wailing was very clear. The pain of his stomach wound must have been unbearable, but there was nothing we could do for him. He must have been delirious.

Again and again I went over in my mind the events of the last several hours. It had all happened in the blink of an eye.

We had finished work for the day and were on the way back. To reach the highway, we had to march down a forest trail in single file. Today the older SS guard led the way, followed by Lurie and myself, with the others strung out, and the younger guard following behind. As we were passing through a gully overgrown with scrub, there was a sudden burst of machine-gun fire: rat-a-tat-tat-tat! I threw myself on the ground. A number of automatic weapons, unseen, were firing at us from nearby. The shooting lasted only a minute or two. Then, in the sudden stillness, I could here the soft murmur, *"Mutti, Mutti* [Mama, Mama]" from the SS guard stretched out a few feet from me, clutching at his chest. Next to him, Lurie was lying very still. I thought, He must be dead. As I cautiously lifted my own head, I could see armed men in civilian clothes emerging from behind the ridge, and I knew they were partisans. I got up and shouted in Russian, "Friends! We are Jews!"

"So what if you are Jews," one of them responded with reproach. "You are working for the Nazis. . . ."

There was very little talk for the next minutes as the four or five partisans, who were well-armed with submachine guns, scurried around here and there. One of them shot the gasping SS guard through the head and grabbed the German's automatic rifle. I realized they were looking for the second guard, but he was nowhere to be seen. Lurie was still alive but badly wounded in the stomach. Besides him, two more of our people were hit. The partisans gave us a few bandages and were immediately gone, perhaps in search of the other guard. We bandaged up our wounded the best we could, put Lurie in the cart we used at work and took him back to the barn.

And so we had been lying, hour after hour, with the incessant moaning coming from the darkness.

It felt strange. We were in the country; there were no guards; all we'd have to do was leave, and by morning we'd be many miles away from here. I talked a little with Shmulke, but there wasn't much to say. We wouldn't escape without Max, and our guns and compass were in the ghetto. There was no choice; we had to return to the ghetto.

In general, there was little talk among the people. Each had his own thoughts. I knew that many were eager to escape, and it seemed as if a golden opportunity had presented itself. But escape from the ghetto had never been the main difficulty (at some work places there were always opportunities), it was the problem of survival in the hostile world outside that kept people back. Everyone here knew of many who had escaped and then were either caught or forced to return to the ghetto voluntarily. Besides, every one of these people had family and had to consider the reprisals that would be sure to come.

There was one comforting thought in all that had happened. I said to

Shmulke, "To think that there are Russian partisans that far west in Lithuania—things sure have changed."

Tuesday, July 4, 1944

The groaning stopped at daybreak: Lurie was dead. At least his suffering was over.

I was aware of the humiliating situation we were in, waiting to be taken back by the Germans. But we waited until midmorning, when a truck arrived with several SS soldiers. We were returned to the ghetto along with Lurie's body and found that news of the ambush in the forest had reached the people there already. The second guard had been wounded in the attack but managed to escape and get back to town.

The Russian partisans, those shadowy fighters of the forest, of whom people had heard so much for so long, had grown in the minds of many into beings of almost mythical proportion. The fact that we'd actually seen and talked to them created a lot of curiosity. Everyone wanted to hear details. It was clear that many people, especially the young fellows, could not understand why we didn't join the partisans. The fact was that we probably wouldn't have been accepted, even if we'd had the chance to ask them.

What was most important, Max was with us again. He was ecstatic. "At last you're here! I waited every day for you to get back and kept bothering the work office trying to find out when. No one knew."

As for our intentions, we'd leave the next night.

In general, there seemed to be a feeling of excitement in the ghetto.

"It is the war news," Max explained, "The Russians opened a powerful offensive on June twenty-second, the third anniversary of the war; they're making strong advances."

"Max, we should definitely lose no more time."

"That's how I feel. Shmulke is ready, too?"

"Oh, yes, we talked about it a lot."

"All right, tomorrow then."

Our plan was simple enough. At night, we'd slip through the barbed-wire fence, where the strands of wire were a little loose. The guards weren't stationed very close to one another, so we should have a good chance to get out undetected. Once on the outside, we'd continue in an easterly direction.

Today was Golda's birthday, twenty years old—if she was alive.

Wednesday, July 5, 1944

Max talked to Leibowitz, who suggested that we wait until Sunday, when he could arrange for us to get through the gate to the Factory and from there to the outside. He said to Max, "Why take a risk going through the fence, when with just a few days' wait, you can get out without any risk at all?" He also told Max that there were fellows desperate to escape and that we would be doing an important deed by taking them along.

We agreed to wait until Sunday. Max said he wasn't sure about the details, just that we'd be getting out during the day with a supposedly legitimate reason.

Saturday, July 8, 1944

We were trapped. Suddenly the ghetto was surrounded by guards; machine-guns were placed at close intervals around the fence, and no one was allowed to leave.

People talked of an evacuation order; the Russians were very close, and we were all to be shipped to Germany. At least that was what the Germans were supposedly saying to our officials.

Max and I were beside ourselves with bitterness. To get caught like that on the last day! From the moment we learned of the situation, we could not sit still and had been marching up and down the ghetto, from fence to fence, as if we might somehow discover some unguarded opening. I knew now how an animal must feel when a trap snaps shut.

Sunday, July 9, 1944

We talked with friends. We heard that some people had escaped by slipping through a hole in the fence to an adjoining linen factory, but this area was now guarded by the police and the opening sealed off. There were also about a dozen or so workers who'd escaped from the Leather Factory yesterday, they'd heard what was happening in the ghetto, and just took off—some got away, and some were shot. We kept talking about various possibilities, but nothing looked promising.

Tuesday, July 11, 1944

The people who had been living and working in the various work camps were being brought back to the ghetto. It was very crowded here. People said that the Germans were waiting for empty rail cars in order to evacuate us.

The guard around the ghetto had probably been tripled, we were debating an attempt to escape through the fence.

Thursday, July 13, 1944

The ghetto was sealed five days ago, and it was now bursting at the seams. People were streaming in from all over, and the population in the ghetto must have more than tripled. In addition to those from the work camps, the thousands who had worked at the airport in Panevezys, sent there from Riga and Estonia, were also brought here. People were everywhere.

I talked to someone who came originally from Riga. He remembered well the arrival of the Daugavpils Jews in Kaiserwald last fall, and he also told me that a small group had come about a month later from the Daugavpils prison. This was good news. It confirmed that the Gutter-mans had not been killed then. Last summer, exactly a year ago, we all went swimming—that one memorable time.

I felt as if we were suspended in midair, waiting. We kept making plans and dashing from place to place, we could hardly sit still. We were still determined to get away.

Friday, July 14, 1944

When we got up this morning, we decided that we would wait no longer. We must act today with whatever small chance we might have to succeed. We could not accept the idea of meekly letting them take us— we would not go voluntarily. If nothing else materialized during the day, we would make our attempt at night through the fence. Meanwhile we were going to explore a few more ideas. When we left our room, we took along our guns with the expectation that we might make our move without coming back to our place.

We stopped in to see some friends. We talked, going over the same ground once more. We both felt more and more restless and decided to walk over to the fence once again. I wished for night, but at the same time I was hoping that even now, some opportunity for daylight escape might arise. I knew this was not likely.

Max said, "Just as a precaution—not to look suspicious. Let's go on different streets and meet there." This carefulness did not seem really necessary, but it never hurt to be cautious.

I had only gone a short distance when I saw Pariser approaching me from the opposite direction. Coming closer, he veered toward me, said something, and when I stopped, suspecting nothing, he suddenly pushed his hand into my pocket and pulled out my revolver. The sight of the gun threw him into a rage. Shouting something unintelligible, he aimed the gun at me. I started to run. Pariser, waving the gun high over his head, yelled hysterically and began to chase me. Pariser's son suddenly appeared, trying to head me off. Without stopping I gave him a push, and he sprawled on the ground. Must get away . . . . must hide . . . . went through my mind. I kept running, and it became a kind of mad chase scene. I lost Pariser, but many of the ghetto police, not knowing why I was running, joined the pursuit. The few streets were jammed with people. I dodged and scrambled. Behind me I could hear shouts: "There! . . . There he goes!" Many people were now chasing me. Again and again I got away as people tried to head me off. But the crowds—I realized it was impossible to elude my pursuers. I thought of the few bushes around the house where we lived and made one last desperate effort. I reached the house and jumped in among the shrubbery. But there just wasn't enough cover, and again the shouts: "There he is!" I was surrounded by three Jewish policemen and led away.

From the moment we arrived at the Ghetto Police station, I felt calm and detached. There was nothing I could do anymore. I had never been in this place before, but as I sat on a bench in the busy room, with people coming and going, it all felt strangely familiar to me, as if this had happened to me before. I realized that most of the ghetto policemen sympathized with me, and I couldn't blame them for catching me; they didn't even know why I was being chased.

After some time, Max was allowed to see me for a short while. He tried to make me feel better, and as he was leaving, he said, "I'll see you soon."

240 / Sidney Iwens

"I don't know, Max. . . . I always knew I'd get caught in some silly way." If the Germans were aware of the incident, I was finished.

Hours passed. Then Joseph Leibowitz came in and explained the situation to me:

"Pariser wants to turn you over to the SS, but we've been working on him, trying to argue him out of it. You see, he got it into his head that your intention was to assassinate him. He keeps repeating, 'I was a military man, and I know. It was a loaded gun, freshly cleaned and oiled, and he was going to kill me!' He also holds it against you that you knocked his son down, hitting him so hard. We've been trying to persuade him to keep you here in our own lockup."

In the evening I was taken to the ghetto jail.

Saturday, July 15, 1944

I was all alone in my dungeon. That certainly was what it looked like: The place used to be some kind of cellar, and the few small, barred openings were at street level. The only people I'd seen so far were a Jewish policeman who brought me food, and Max, with whom I talked through the little window, the small opening with steel bars.

Max said that nothing had changed in the ghetto. The Germans were still waiting for rail cars.

Sunday, July 16, 1944

Max told me there was a lot of talk about my incident; people were convinced we had been betrayed by someone. We did talk to quite a few people of our determination to get away, and some knew we had guns. And, of course, Pariser had made every effort to prevent any possible escape. Maybe someone had reported the gun, and that was why he went straight for my pocket. I just didn't know.

I brooded about it for hours, going over in my mind again and again the fiasco with the gun. Pariser was after all Jewish too. It was so unexpected and went so fast—I just wasn't on guard. And before I realized what was happening, he had my gun in his hand. But the fact was that he got the gun from me, and I felt quite dissatisfied with myself.

Ita also came to see me. Anyone who wanted to talk to me had to do so through the barred window, by bending down all the way or kneeling on the ground; either way it was very awkward and inconvenient.

Monday, July 17, 1944

In the morning I was taken out, ordered to join a long column of people, and marched to the train station under heavy guard. At last the Germans had found transport for the Jews: A long freight train was waiting for us. I looked around frantically for Max, but they immediately started hustling us into the boxcars. Then suddenly I saw Max—he had been looking for me just as frantically. We were together again!

The cars filled up fast, and after some time, the train started moving. Max said, "I tried to get away, even in the last hours, I tried to escape, but didn't make it. I found out you'd be in this transport, so I arranged to be with you. You know, these people are all from work camps, not from the ghetto proper."

There were about forty-five or fifty men and women in our car; families were not separated. In every car there was at least one and sometimes two SS guards with automatic rifles sitting at the half-open door. The train was heading south toward Germany.

Meanwhile, with the Russians so very close, freedom was within our grasp. (We later learned that Siauliai was liberated by the Russians just eleven days later—on July 28, 1944.) But we were moving farther and farther away from it.

The relaxed manner of the guards had a calming effect on us but there was still much fear and uncertainty: What was going to happen to us? Was the guards' behavior just another deception? Now that we were on the way, we didn't quite believe this to be our last journey, but who could tell what they had in store for us?

It was a pleasant summer day. We managed to find a place near the door, and I could feel the delicious breeze. The familiar countryside rushed by: small villages, grazing cattle, peasants working in the fields. When the train stopped, we were allowed to use the station latrines.

Tuesday, July 18, 1944

Throughout the night the train made frequent stops, which sometimes lasted a long time. In the pitch-dark crowded car, we all managed to find enough space to stretch out and, off and on, fell into fitful slumber.

The morning was bright with a cloudless sky. Again, peaceful-looking fields and woods floated by, and it was hard to believe that there to the east, not at all far from here, battles of world importance were raging and approaching ever closer.

Abruptly, the mood in the car changed. We'd crossed the border—we were now in Germany. A hush filled the car as the fear and anxiety that were always there surfaced. The familiar landscape was behind us, and we were now inside that accursed, evil land. Whatever hope or half-formed plans we might have had were gone. Even if someone managed to escape from the train, he'd have no chance in this unfamiliar countryside, which seemed so well-ordered and forbidding.

But as time went on, our somber mood lifted somewhat. The guards were still not very strict, the cool breeze at the open door was pleasant, and I could not help but admire the landscape we were passing. How different these well-built farmhouses were from the thatched-roofed log houses I often saw in Lithuania. The roads were well-paved, and at the crossings I could see neatly dressed youngsters—the boys in shorts, and the girls in colorful short dresses—waiting patiently with their bicycles for our train to pass. Once in a while, a child sitting on a porch, some distance away, waved to us, perhaps thinking we were wounded soldiers returning from the front.

We had enough to eat, people who had accumulated some reserves of food for a "rainy day" were now very generous, gladly sharing with those who didn't have much. We had no idea what to expect, but everybody was quite certain that extra food would be confiscated at the entrance to wherever we were going.

Wednesday, July 19, 1944

Our train usually stopped some distance away from busy places, but not always. When it did come to a standstill in a large train station, we could see signs of the on-going war. There were a great many military personnel, some rushing to catch trains, others waiting, and always wounded soldiers. But it was the locomotives that exemplified for me the tremendous effort and singlemindedness of the Germans in the on-going struggle: huge black monsters, hissing angrily and purposefully, they carried the bold white words *"Raeder Rollen fuer den Sieg* (Wheels Are Turning for Victory)" stenciled on their round bodies.

Late in the day, the attitude of our guards changed, and we knew that we were approaching our destination. The train reached a station, and the doors of our boxcar were shut; the guards were no longer inside with us.

Thursday, July 20, 1944

The train was at a standstill for the whole night. Our mood matched the darkness inside the car. All the rumors and talk we'd been hearing lately surfaced in my mind.

In the morning, we were transferred to open rail cars on a narrow-gauge line, and shortly afterward we arrived at a station. *"Raus! Raus!"* the SS bellowed and started hitting the people who did not leave the cars fast enough. These were not our old guards, but altogether a different breed. Men and women were separated; we were ordered to form columns and marched off.

We approached a gate, where a name was spelled out in large letters: "STUTTHOF." When we marched inside the compound, which was surrounded by a double fence of barbed wire, we saw people, apparently prisoners, wearing striped uniforms.

"Everything will be taken away from us." Word spread through the column: A striped-uniform prisoner had managed to exchange a few hurried words with one of our people, proposing that he be given valuables for safekeeping, which he would later return.

The rest of the day was one long nightmare. Surrounded by SS and Polish-Aryan trustees, we were first forced to sit on the ground, then to stand for hours, to run, to march, while intermittently being beaten with heavy clubs and constantly threatened with death. Then toward the end of the day came *Entlausung* (delousing).

"Move, move, faster . . . get undressed! Take along belt only!" Clubbings . . . "Only your belts!". . . showers overhead. . . a few drops of cold water . . . "Move, faster!" We were out of the shower room, and all of us, nude, were shoved into a large room. Polish trustees standing next to tables . . . "Move!" . . . again the clubs . . . At the table I was grabbed, and in a minute my hair was cut to the scalp and my body hair was shaved. "Lie down—like that." They checked all body openings for hidden valuables. "Next . . . next . . . faster." Still the clubbings . . . naked . . . carrying only our belts, we were outside in a yard. A pair of pants, a shirt, and a jacket were thrown to each of us. A pile of shoes lay in one corner. A very few found their own shoes; most had to grab whatever was on top. No chance that our excellent boots would be left; the trustees had surely snatched them by now. "Come on, move faster!" I grabbed a pair of boots and moved on.

We were disoriented by so much brutality, and overcome by a terrible fear.

At night the kapos—prisoner trustees—chased us into a barracks. At last we might go to sleep.

Friday, July 21, 1944

We were awakened very early by a loud racket. The kapos were yelling at the top of their voices and swinging their clubs at whoever happened to be near them: "Out!" "Out!" And the nightmare of yesterday continued.

"*Appell!*" Roll call.

In a large, open space we were ordered into lines of five and counted. Then the thousands of us were recounted, then counted again, all the time with abuse, both verbal and physical.

After some hours, a long column was moved off to the side. But then an SS man came over to our line, where Max and I stood. He pointed with his stick: "You . . . you . . . one. . . two . . . three . . . four . . . five. . . ." I was the fifth in line. At first I didn't realize why we were being removed, but then the five of us were led to the waiting column, and all were marched away. Max had been next to me in line; now he had to stay with the rest.

We passed through the gate, came to a waiting freight train on a siding, and were ordered into the empty boxcars. As soon as we were in the cars, the doors were shut, and it hit me: My God, I'm separated from Max.

Shortly afterward the train began to move.

When we found ourselves in the tightly shut freight car, there was terrified silence. But as the train started to pick up speed, I could feel some relaxation of tension around me, as if people were slowly coming out of shock.

I felt very much alone and crushed by my separation from Max. In the semidarkness of the car, I was lying curled up in a corner. I hadn't talked to anybody but could hear conversations going on around me, and some remarks registered: "An attempt on Hitler's life—a Polish prisoner told me. . . ." "Stutthof is a transit camp, close to Danzig . . . did you see? The guards were Ukrainians. Kapos were all Polish. . . ." "They're taking us to work in factories. . . ." "More likely they're taking us to be killed."

"Whatever it is, can't be worse than Stutthof . . . people there are killed by gas, and the bodies are burned . . . did you see the tall smokestack?"

Saturday, July 22, 1944

The doors of our car were opened very infrequently. Although the train stopped mostly at small stations, once in a while we got stuck at one of the larger ones, and I could see several stations that were badly damaged by bombs. But the locomotives still proudly proclaimed, "*Raeder Rollen fuer den Sieg.*"

We each got a piece of bread.

Monday, July 24, 1944

The train stopped, and we were ordered to get out and form a column. Guards were awaiting us; we had arrived in the small town of Kaufering. After marching five to six kilometers, we came to a compound consisting of huts surrounded by barbed wire. Word was passed along the waiting column that we'd have to wait here because the construction of the camp was just being completed.

Suddenly there was agitation among our guards, and we were ordered into a quarry: "Air raid alarm!"

Some people became apprehensive, suspecting there was no air raid, just an excuse to get us down in the pit so that the SS might kill us from the top with machine guns. That made no sense to me; why would they drag us all the way here for that purpose? But then we heard an unmistakable drone which grew louder and louder, and after a while airplanes were flying overhead. One plane came down low, and I was surprised to see a five-pointed star on the fuselage. "It's an American star," someone said excitedly. The plane was visible only for seconds, but it was enough to send an electrifying current through all of us. I was sitting on the ground, next to some young fellows, and I could see that we all shared the same fierce joy. "I could actually see the pilot," someone said, awed. The thought of an American so close to us, even if only for seconds, filled us with irrational hope and expectation.

Stimulated, we all started to talk. I realized the fellows had all been in working camps until they were returned to the Siauliai Ghetto at the time of evacuation, but they had heard of Max and me, the Dvinsker, and knew of the incident with my gun.

The air raid alarm ended soon. Sometime later we were brought to the camp, and each given two blankets, a bowl, and a spoon. We were in our new home.

End of July 1944

For the next several days we were not bothered much. It was sunny, and I spent a lot of time outside. Our camp was located in a field at the edge of a forest of evergreens. Our ration was actually larger than what it had been in ghetto—one third of a small loaf of bread per day, plus an occasional touch of margarine; we also got soup once a day. The trees were very close to the fence, which consisted of two rows of barbed wire carrying electrical current; SS guards were stationed at close intervals around it.

The people here were all from the ghettos of Kaunas and Siauliai. How resourceful and clever some of us were! Without having left the camp, someone had already "organized" a shaving blade, then, out of wood splinters, he made a little contraption to hold it in place and was ready to shave off the beards of his friends.

The huts where we lived were round, painted green, and constructed of a fiber that is similar to cardboard but of a firmer consistency. About twenty of us were in each one. We all slept on the ground in a circle, there was very little space. I was with the same fellows I'd met the first day in the quarry, and a true feeling of comradeship prevailed in our hut. I became especially friendly with Dov Shilansky who was about my age. He was very interested in my experiences with the partisans in White Russia. He told me that like most of the people here, he was *kaserniert* in a work camp before arriving here, but while in the ghetto, he was active in the resistance movement there.

After a few days, we started working at a construction site, erecting some kind of massive structure.

The pants I got in Stutthof were infested with lice. I spent a lot of time, mostly in the latrine, trying to kill the vermin and clean the pants, but I wasn't sure I was successful. I'd been concerned that the whole hut could become infested from my pants, but then realized that many of the others had also received lice-infested garments at Stutthof.

Another worry was my footwear. In Stutthof, I grabbed a pair of boots without getting a chance to inspect them. They were of a nice soft leather and fit well, but the soles were just about gone. I'd have to do something about it.

Quite unexpectedly I found out what had happened to my family and to the people of my hometown. Nothing surprising, just confirmation of what I had expected all along: No one of my family was alive.

I met here the brothers Meir and Avram Goldsmidt, and Gershon Reibstein. They were from Jonava, but had been inmates of the Kaunas Ghetto and arrived here by way of Stutthof. They all knew my family well. We sat outside their hut, and they told me the details of how the end came to our people in Jonava.

It had happened the same way as in the other towns. I'd heard the descriptions, with some variations, before: terror and random killings in the first days of occupation; after some weeks a massacre of males, followed in another few weeks by the slaughter of the rest of the community. But now we were talking of Jonava, where every inch of the place was achingly familiar—I could see in my mind almost every house, and most of the people who had lived there.

"One of the first people to be shot was Keidansky and his sons. . . ."

Saul Keidansky, the principal and one of the teachers in our Tarbut school, with his small goatee and moustache, was a distinguished personality in the community. I must have spent hundreds of hours in his classes during my six years in that school. He and his grown sons were well-known Zionists, and the Hebrew language was his passion. I had been in their house many times and could picture the garden in the back and the many lilac trees in front. . . .

"And you remember Hannah? They lived near the railroad station. . . ."

Hannah was my age; we had been in the same class for years. One year I sat right behind her and liked to stare at her long blond hair.

"She was trying to hide . . . they caught her . . . it was a terrible death."

"And the two Zupowitz brothers, used to live on Vilnius Street. They had moved to Kaunas and served in the ghetto police there. Both were tortured to death by the Gestapo but would not give away the names of people belonging to the underground. Forty more policemen were killed at the same time."

And so it went on: "Remember . . ." this one and "remember . . ." that one, all the people I have known . . . "But most of the Jews of Jonava were killed in Geralka. . . ."

The woods we called Geralka were about a kilometer from town. It was one of the favorite places for young couples to take Saturday walks, and for us kids it was a place to roam among the trees. The gentiles would have dances there in a clearing. Sometimes on a Sunday afternoon we'd watch them twirl round and round on the grass to the tune of a polka or waltz played on an accordion.

"The men were killed around the end of July. They were taken in groups, not at one time, and told that they were being shipped east for work. But when they came close to the ditches and were told to undress, they knew. . . . Berke Fine—you know, he and his brother Abke used to play soccer with the Hapoel club . . . "

Berke Fein used to play soccer. God, how he used to play! We kids idolized him. And when there was a game scheduled, for a Sunday afternoon, between the Lithuanian Siaulistai Club and Hapoel, excitement in town ran high, it was "them" against "us"; it seemed everyone was at the playing field by the army barracks, and Berke was as fast as lightning . . .

"Yes, Berke Fein and a few more escaped and almost reached the highway, but they were all shot dead, there were so many guards. Several men threw themselves on the murderers, but of course only suffered a worse death. . . . A few weeks later, the rest of the people, were killed. It was so terrible—with the children and babies. . . . It was said that a farmer, a Pole, who lived nearby, went out of his mind after all that he saw and heard. . . ."

"And my family?"

Reibstein said: "I don't know if you are aware, but there was a fierce battle around Jonava, most of the town was destroyed by fire. After the first days, some people went to the Jewish village Alter Gostinetz, because there were few houses left in town, and also because they expected it to be safer—you know, working the land. . . . Your family went there, too. . . ."

I remembered that unusual place, a village of small Jewish farmers eking out a living off their small plots of land. Our family was in some remote way related to a family in that village, and I could remember the last time we were there, a few years before the war. We went to a wedding; and even though the village was only twelve kilometers from Jonava, arriving there felt as if we had moved back to an earlier age. The musicians were from Jonava, and we two, my brother Ruvke and I, traveled with them on a wagon pulled by a spirited horse. What fun we had! The wedding guests were all assembled and waiting as we rode in, with the horse at a fast trot and the musicians making a wild racket with their instruments. And the ceremony under the sky and the eating, the drinking and the music. . . .

Yes, Father would have thought this place to be safer. After we parted on the road to Daugavpils, my family was overtaken by the Germans and turned back. They may have not even have returned to Jonava and might have gone straight to the village. . . .

"On the day when the Jews in town were killed, several Lithuanian irregulars came to the village with a list of names, people who'd been prominent in Jonava. They took your father, three other men, and a woman to Geralka and killed them with the other people. . . . A few weeks later they brought the Jews from the village to town, and in early October, they were transported to the Kaunas Ghetto with some others who'd been caught hiding in the area, all together about 150 people. But when they arrived, it was very late at night, and they missed the *Aktion* which had taken place that day and for which their arrival was apparently timed. The next big *Aktion* took place on October twenty-eighth, and it was then that most of the people who'd been brought from Jonava were taken to the Ninth Fort and killed. . . . Your mother and little sister were among them. . . ."

Father died in Jonava, Mother and Nehamah in Kaunas, and Ruvke in Daugavpils. And Nehamah only thirteen. . . I knew enough of the details: the undressing . . . the ditches. . . .I could see it all. . . .Oh, those—those—but I could find nothing strong enough to call them in my mind, nothing that could possibly fit. . . . Mother—maybe she found just a bit of comfort in those last terrible moments by thinking, My two sons, my young and strong sons, they got away and are alive. And Father, at that moment, must have thought, There on the road—I made them go on, and I gave my sons the chance to live. Yes, they will live. But Ruvke was dead too. I alone remained now, and what chance did I have?

But *I* was still alive. Damn them all, *I* was still alive.

After a few days I again saw my friends from Jonava, and we talked about our hometown, and about the enthusiasm with which many of the Lithuanians killed the Jews. Of course, we had to remind ourselves that not all of them were that way.

Meir said: "On several occasions I was helped by Lithuanians. Once we were given refuge, not far from Jonava, by an old forest ranger. But just imagine, while we stayed a whole week in his place, where he fed us and watched over us, his sons—as he himself told us—were involved with the killings in town."

"I'm sure you remember 'Labas'," Gershon added, "the policeman, who'd greet everyone he met with Labas, he turned out to be a decent person too, and thanks to him, there are still a few from Jonava alive.

And so there were some decent people around. But nothing could change the fact that it was Lithuanians who'd been doing most of the actual killing in Lithuania, and the same facts applied to the Latvians in Latvia.

Month of August 1944

Our days started out in a frenzied rush very early—wake-up time was 4:30 in the morning. We'd run to the washhouse; there were no showers or other bathing facilities, so we washed ourselves the best we could and then on to *Appell*—roll call. Everything was "*Los, los!*" and "*Schneller, schneller!*" Roll call usually lasted a long time, often more than an hour. Then we got some ersatz coffee with our daily portion of bread and were marched off to work.

After a hard day's work, at the construction site, we were brought back in the evening, and given our portion of soup, then again we stood at Appell, which usually lasted even longer than in the morning, and then it was night.

The bread ration looked like a nice chunk. But that was all we got, no more margarine or anything else. We were hungry all the time. I often debated with myself: Should I eat the whole portion in the morning, or be prudent and save some for later? If I ate it at one time, my hunger was placated for a short while, but then I suffered until evening when we got our soup. Most of the time I was able to withstand the temptation and left some bread for later, but some of the fellows in the hut gobbled down their piece of bread as soon as they received it.

Our camp was called Dachau Concentration Camp No. 2. There were a total of eleven branches or subcamps of the main Dachau camp, each identified by a number. We were in the southern part of Germany, in Bavaria, maybe eight kilometers from Landsberg, the town where Hitler had been incarcerated in the early twenties and where he had written *Mein Kampf.*

Camp No. 1 was a few kilometers away from our camp, and the people there were all from Kaunas. A few hundred women worked there also, some of them from Siauliai. Dov Shilansky sometimes got a message from his mother and two sisters who were also there.

We heard that a group of women from Stutthof would arrive at our camp too. I thought of Golda. By now the Jews from the Kaiserwald Camp must have been evacuated to Stutthof. "Don't you dare throw away my picture," she had joked back there in Daugavpils. How little control we had over our own actions! In Stutthof I was forced to discard everything except my belt, including my "diary" and the picture of Golda. If only she were among those sent here. It wasn't likely, but I kept thinking of it and hoping.

The great majority of inmates worked on two worksites—those of the construction companies, Holzmann and Moll. "HOLZMANN" was painted on various pieces of equipment at my worksite. The work was hard but, even so, I was lucky. Moll was very far from camp, and the work there was even harder.

After marching us to work in the morning, the SS guards formed a human chain around the site. It was a huge area, and many people worked here, divided up into work brigades with different functions. The work was supervised by the Organisation Todt or OT—the paramilitary branch which was in charge of all the public work and defense projects. The people of our hut made up one brigade, and our boss at work was an OT *Meister.* We also had a kapo, who was one of our people.

Something massive was being built here, but I was not sure what it was. We knew that at Moll an underground airplane factory was under construction, and I assumed that we were involved in something of the same nature. Still, there was nothing to indicate that this was so. We dug, we poured concrete, carried steel pipe, and did all kinds of general construction work, but didn't work underground.

The fellows in my hut were really a fine bunch. Dov Shilansky was a good friend, and whenever possible, we worked and stayed together. Another fellow, Aaron Yankelewiz, reminded me a lot of my brother:

slim with blue eyes, he really looked like him and was the same age Ruvke would have been. It was always a treat when, in the evening, Spevak, who had a fine voice, sang "Mein Shtetele Belz (My Little Town Belz)" or some old familiar Jewish folksongs. We all listened intently, each with his own thoughts. I usually felt a rush of nostalgia, overcome by the sense of loss and yet also by a sense of hope.

As the days went by, I grew more and more anxious over the arrival of the women. I knew quite well that there was very little chance of Golda's being among them, but I kept fantasizing about it. I imagined the moment of her arrival, pictured every detail, and the more I dreamed of it, the more credible my belief became.

We had all been given "uniforms"— pajamalike striped pants and jackets made of thin material; also round caps.

We were also officially registered. We had to stand in line, then give our name, date of birth, address before the war, and other information to one of the clerks sitting at tables. I gave my name as "Gordon," the same one I used in Siauliai, and a random address from that town.

Each of us was assigned a number, which was put on our uniforms; mine was 84999. We were told that this was what we'd be known by, and it was to be more important than the name.

We had *Appell* at least twice a day on weekdays and three times on Sunday. Roll call sounds harmless enough, but in fact, we dreaded every one of them. We had to appear at the Appellplatz, only those in the hospital being exempt. After we formed straight lines, the procedure never varied: First, we stood at attention with our lines perfectly even— no one was to stick out; then came the ritual of *Muetzen ab/Muetzen auf* (caps off/caps on); followed by a count of the whole column and report to the SS officer in charge.

The counting by itself took a long time, because they seemed to have trouble coming up with the correct figure. But It was clear that we were assembled not just to be counted but to be terrorized. A particular torment was the ritual of the caps. At the sharp command *"Muetzen ab!"* we had to grab the caps off our heads, and at *"Muetzen auf!"* put them on again. There were about 2,000 men in Camp No. 2, and we all had to do this at the same moment—to slap the cap hard at the thigh and then slap it back on to the head, with only one loud sound heard with each motion. This up-down, up-down was repeated endlessly, often continued even after it had been done perfectly. In the meantime we were beaten, shouted at, called every dirty name in the world.

The camp commandant was an SS man as were the other Germans. There was an *Unterscharfuehrer* (assistant squad leader, a non commissioned rank) called Schreyer; he had a cruel face and was always shouting and cursing at the top of his voice. Another German was a *Volksdeutsche* who had lived in Kaunas until the war; his name was Antonas, and he used to be a carter, employed by a Jew. I heard there were people here who had done him favors back in the old days. Them he didn't beat, but he showed little pity for others and used his club liberally. When enraged, he could beat someone until the victim was unable to get up. There were others, but these two were the ones we saw most frequently at camp. In general, they all seemed to get a certain joy out of being cruel to us; they often struck people indiscriminately.

A dozen Aryan kapos had arrived here. These were German criminals who had been imprisoned for such felonies as murder and armed robbery. They were now in charge of the camp administration including the kitchen, food distribution, work assignments, block elders, and so on. One of them was the camp elder.

The women from Stutthof were also expected any day now. I had become obsessed with the hope that Golda would be among them.

We had been getting less bread and were all very hungry. Dov came up with an idea. The kitchen was at the entrance to the camp, within a barbed wire enclosure. To get our soup, we went through the kitchen building in single file, passing a huge kettle, where a ladle of warm liquid was poured into each of our outstretched bowls. We then walked out of the kitchen area through a gate into our camp proper. Today when we both got our soup, one after the other, I poured mine into Dov's bowl, then turned around and stole back into the slowly moving line to get another portion. It worked, but Dov would not accept his part of the extra soup. Although his kin did manage to smuggle some bread to him occasionally, I knew it didn't amount to much, and he must have been quite hungry. We argued about it. But in the end he made me eat it, insisting he was less hungry than I was.

I was tired and hungry, and I longed to lie down to rest for a while, but even on Sunday, which was not a regular workday, we were not allowed to do so. There was an extra *Appell* around noon, which might last several hours, and in between we were ordered to do various cleaning chores in camp while the kapos harassed us. We didn't look forward to Sunday at all, and some would rather do their regular everyday work. Here and there a work brigade left for the work site upon special request of an OT *Meister*, most often because he'd been urged to do so by his workers.

I received wooden shoes—the bottoms wood, the upper parts made of some sort of cloth. They were uncomfortable, but I was very happy to have them. My boots had completely deteriorated and had had to be thrown away.

The women arrived—a couple of hundred, all from Hungary. They were housed in huts separated from ours by a barbed-wired fence.

How I longed for a cigarette, for anything to light up. We tried something new today. An older man told me that the purple flower of the clover could be smoked. On the way home from work, we passed a patch of clover and picked some of it. I smoked it with Dov. Let's just say it was better than nothing.

We performed the "soup operation" at the kitchen only twice and then decided not to try it anymore. A fellow in front of us was caught doing something similar and beaten so badly they had to carry him away. Those criminal kapos had no mercy.

At work, Dov and I were carrying pipe, one behind the other, each with his end of the pipe on the shoulder. It wasn't easy to have a conversation that way, but we were talking anyway.

We were discussing the Land of Israel, something that Dov talked about often. Dov had always been an ardent member of Betar, and he said that the idea of an independent Jewish state was very real to him. Only by being willing to fight and die for what is ours, will the Jews have their homeland. And then he quoted, "With blood and fire will we redeem our land."

"You may be right, Dov, but who is to do the fighting? Most Jews are already dead, and as for the rest of us, the bastards will make sure that we aren't alive either by the end of the war."

"If the Jews had only listened to Jabotinsky. He talked often of the danger, but people didn't want to hear. So many could have been saved."

"But even Jabotinsky could not quite foresee the things that happened to us."

"No one could quite imagine that, but he warned the Jews that they were unsafe in Europe. After the war," Dov concluded, "the Jews will at last have their own state."

Some of our people had talked to a man from Camp No. 10, which was not far from here but much smaller. All of the inmates there were from the Siauliai ghetto, and the conditions were not as bad as here.

Month of September 1944

The grassy field we found here upon our arrival had by now been turned into one big sea of mud. With so many of us confined here, the area had been churned up into a smelly mass of slush, and to walk anywhere was hard; with every step our feet sank deep into the mud. It reminded me of the swamps in White Russia.

In the misery we lived in, the desire to smoke was very strong. Once in a while someone picked up a cigarette butt discarded by a guard. But that didn't happen often; some Germans ground the butts in the dirt with their boots when they finished smoking. When one was lucky enough to land a butt, a crude cigarette was made of rough paper and this bit of tobacco. It was usually smoked to the very end, and one almost scorched his fingertips trying to extract the very last lungful of smoke from the tiny fragment of cigarette.

After the noon break, while our group was being marched to another section of the worksite, the guard, after smoking a little more than half a cigarette, threw the rest away. Greedily I looked at the fat butt on the ground, but after a momentary struggle with myself, I did not pick it up, I will not demean myself, I thought. I kept thinking about it all afternoon. I had a craving for the soothing effect of nicotine and vividly imagined the cigarette I could have rolled from the tobacco of that butt.

Tuesday, September 12, 1944

Life was getting harder every day. This morning, my thin uniform was still damp from yesterday, and again it drizzled. I swallowed my bread ration in a few bites as soon as I got it, even though I knew I should have saved something for later. The *Appell* lasted a long time, and when we were finally on our way to work, marching in a disconsolate manner, I was wet and tired. All I could look forward to was a day of hard work, no food, again an *Appell*, and only then a bit of soup.

If only the rain would stop. Fall was almost here. Last year it was dry and sunny most of the time. It suddenly occurred to me that exactly one year ago, September 12, we had arrived at the partisan village. For a while I was lost in thought, reliving the experience of that day, the relief and joy of those first moments of arrival in Bobily, the feeling of having suddenly landed in a different world. I could see the partisan officers on horseback in their colorful uniforms, could feel the thrill of meeting other Jews in the *otryad* and the smell of fresh hay where we slept . . . Max . . . Berke.

Reliving the events of the past made me less conscious of the present dismal reality, and the time went by much faster. I decided that, for the next weeks, I would try every day to think of what had happened a year ago on that same date. This might make the present easier to bear.

Month of October 1944

Sometimes I worked the nightshift. The work was usually easier, and we were not as closely watched; but I felt even more exhausted, because we were not allowed to sleep enough during the day and were often made to do clean-up work in camp. The rain too, which had been frequent and persistent, added a great deal to the general misery. I even thought of hiding somewhere to go to sleep for a while. Those large crawler cranes used for digging came to mind; most of them were not used at night. Here and there one of the huge machines jutted out above the general construction landscape, and during the day I often looked at them—I'd never seen one back home in Lithuania. With their long necks and huge drooping jaws, they seemed like friendly beasts and would perhaps be a good place to rest in. But checking inside, I found that the engine took up all the space, hardly any room left for a person to lie down. Besides, it was too much of a risk. I could well imagine the punishment if I were caught there.

An Aryan kapo was yelling at a tall skinny man, hitting him with his club. "You have it good here! You should have been in Buchenwald. There you would have learned!" All this abuse because the man was falling behind in the marching column.

The person who earned the rage of the kapo used to be a well-known teacher in Kaunas. I could see he hardly had strength to walk and couldn't last much longer. Life here was hardest for older people and for those who were in the professions and not used to physical labor.

We often heard that "You have it good," and we knew there were places where people were tortured and killed by poison gas, while ours was a work camp; we were engaged in labor which, for whatever reason, the Germans considered important. Even so, it was a struggle to get through each day, and was getting harder all the time.

It was a sunny morning for a change. The air was cool but very clear, and I could see the mountains, which were visible when weather conditions were right. They were very far away, and they looked as if someone had painted them on the horizon. The colors varied at different times, with the hues of blue, pink, and white predominating; the view was lovely. As we marched to work, I stared at it with fascination and longing. The Alps. The Alps meant Switzerland—and Switzerland meant freedom and life.

I was in somewhat better spirits. The latest news was that the Allies had captured Paris and were making good progress across France. In fact, their armies were on the borders of Germany itself!

Last year, at this time, we were still with the partisans, with Max and Berke. Berke must have been killed in the ambush, but Max, where is he now?

We were moved to new huts, actually barracks, quite large, built of wood, and half-buried in the ground—something like the *zemlyanky* we were trying to build in Bobily last year around this time. Each barracks was called a block, and housed between eighty and a hundred people. A *Blockaelteste* (block elder) was the boss in each barracks. We slept on two tiers of wooden platforms stretching, on both sides, from the doorway to the other end, with only a narrow path for passing in-between.

Our life was changing. Jews from different countries had been arriving in camp, and many people here were not from Lithuania.

The work, too, was changing. Fewer people were being taken to the Holzmann worksite and more sent to Moll. Most of my friends were dispersed among the various blocks and worked in different places, but I was still with Dov and a few others.

Any bit of free time we could find was spent on searching our clothing for lice. The whole camp was infested with them, and no wonder—we wore the same rags all the time and had no bathing facilities. As many as we killed there were always more; it was a constant struggle.

My wooden shoes were very uncomfortable, hard to walk in, and they rubbed my feet, especially since I had no socks, only rags. Even so, I was fortunate to have them at all, for some people had nothing at all on their feet. If I'd held on to my old boots a little longer, I'd have been in the same position myself.

Our bread ration kept getting reduced. Every once in a while I'd see a cart with one or more dead men being pulled and pushed by inmates; the corpses were buried behind the camp. I didn't know how many died in a day, but it was getting worse all the time. We had an infirmary here with a few Jewish doctors under SS supervision. But not all our people died in camp. Every so often sick people were sent away somewhere; it was being said that they were killed by gas.

When we worked at night, there was a rest period, and we got what the Germans called soup, made of some kind of ersatz. I wasn't sure what it was; oddly, when the stuff was hot it was fairly thick and didn't taste too bad, but when it cooled off, it became thin like water and quite tasteless. I thought of the soup Mother used to make, how it would thicken when it grew cold. We were all quite sure this stuff had no food value at all, but at least it was something warm I could put in my belly.

Tonight we ate our soup in a small wooden barracks. It was nice to be in a warm, lighted place and out of the cold drizzle that had been soaking us through and through. But as soon as we finished gulping down the liquid, our OT overseer chased us out. His name was Max; he was short and fat and had almost no chin. "Out, you lazy dogs!" he yelled and, following us out, continued shouting a variety of obscenities from *Scheisskerls* to *Schweinehunde* to *Saujude*, all enunciated with much obvious satisfaction.

We walked outside in the rain, shivering in our damp, thin clothes, while he followed us saying, "What worthless shit you all are!" In contrast to us, he had his tunic wide open at his thick neck, and as he stood smoking a cigar, his whole stance proclaimed that he, a German, was made of wholly different stuff from us. After five minutes he went back into the building, where he would, no doubt, sit at the hot iron stove with sandwiches and coffee, leaving us in the hands of the kapos to endure another five hours of hard labor in the cold and wet. He was not really as bad as some of the others; he seemed to be one of those little men who suddenly find themselves with power over people and enjoy every minute of it.

I met Gershon Reibstein, who took me to his barracks. He worked for the *Sommerkeller* (summer cellar) and so did Meir. The workplace was the envy of everyone—a huge food warehouse, which distributed food products to many of the camps. Almost all the people who worked there, about twenty in all, had a chance to grab an extra bit of food, once in a while. But Reibstein, because of his specific duties at work, was in a position—most exceptional— to "organize" food consistently. He gave me a piece of bread.

The conversation in our block was about the Moll worksite.

"The most that you can last there," I heard someone say," is five weeks. After that, you are dead."

"You are wrong," his friend responded. "It's more like three weeks. At Holzmann you may last five weeks."

"At Moll, when they pour the concrete, you know—if someone falls in—he stays there. . . ."

I'd heard much about Moll, but so far I'd been able to avoid working there. Lately, though, it was touch and go every morning. After *Appell*, when all the small work commandos were formed, the rest were all marched off to Moll. The trick was to get into one of the smaller units. So far I'd been successful, but this was getting harder and harder to accomplish.

These last few days people were brought here from Czechoslovakia and from the city of Lodz in Poland. I watched a column of Slovak Jews, a sight I hadn't seen in a long time. The people looked the same as before the war. They were dressed in suits and overcoats and showed no sign of undernourishment. Until a month or two ago, they'd still lived in their own homes. It was the opposite with the people from Lodz. They looked emaciated and weak from years of uninterrupted starvation. They now came here from Auschwitz. But for more than four years, until a couple of months ago, they had lived in the Lodz Ghetto, where at one time there had been some 200,000 Jews.

I might have heard of "calories" before, but if so, paid no attention to it. Now, though, the word had a great deal of meaning for us, and we all talked about it.

Our bread ration had been reduced again, and a loaf of bread was now divided into eight portions; we kept wondering how many calories that might be. With the soup you could not be sure of anything; sometimes it was just a thin warm liquid. If one was lucky, there might be a piece of potato or vegetable. In any case, according to a doctor who lived in our block (only a few doctors practiced medicine and lived in the hospital, the rest worked like everyone else), we were probably getting one tenth of the calories our bodies required.

Month of November 1944

Now that we had been living in our wooden barracks, it was somewhat warmer at night, but during the day we all suffered a great deal from the cold.

Today, as usual, we were already chilled to the bone by the time *Appell* was over. Later, after our work brigade delivered wooden boards some distance away, we had to wait in a yard. It was gray and cloudy, and the cold wind went right through me. The thin stuff we were wearing was just no protection from anything, and every part of my body yearned for a bit of warmth. I looked longingly at the radiator of a small auto. I knew the water in the radiator got hot when the auto was driven, but although it had been standing there lifeless, with an irrationality born of despair, I hoped I might still find some warmth there. We were not supposed to move from the place, but slowly I shuffled over and touched the metal. It was, of course, ice cold.

Five people of our camp were taken to Camp No.1 and executed by hanging. The crime of the offenders? They'd been caught wearing underwear crudely made out of blanket material or some other kind of cloth.

I had a surprise. A truck with inmates from Camp No. 10 stopped for a few minutes close to where I was working. Shmulke Palec was among them! I found out that there were only about 600 people in their camp, all from the Siauliai ghetto. Even now some of the ghetto leaders—Burgin, for example—were in positions of power inside the camp, but Pariser was not there. Conditions in No. 10 were much better than in any of the other camps in the area.

We were all issued brightly colored overcoats, probably belonging to some European army or police force. Although the material was quite thin, we were glad to have them; they were better than nothing.

Every day people died here—how many I didn't know. But those whose end was near were easily recognizable. Some got swollen up and walked around with puffed-up faces. But most became extremely thin, just skin and bones with a certain empty look in their eyes, which seemed to become very large. When a person reached that condition, he was called *Musel-mann*—a name brought here by the Aryan kapos. It was sad, but most prisoners who had not yet reached that stage tried to think of them as little as possible. But in our own barracks, there were about half a dozen people whose suffering was very hard to ignore. They were barefoot. I looked at their swollen, purple-colored feet and could well imagine their torment. The increasing cold had begun to cover the puddles on *Appellplatz* with a thin layer of ice, and we had already had some snow. These people slept close to the entrance, and every time we ran to *Appell*, I saw them huddled together, waiting until the last possible moment before hobbling out to what was obviously an extraordinary torture: standing barefoot on the freezing ground as long as everyone else. They were all German Jews and spoke only German. They had probably arrived with one of the later transports, I knew nothing else about them. How much longer could they last now that it was growing colder every day?

A transport of Hungarian Jews was brought here. They had lived in comparative freedom until last spring when they were abruptly deported to the Auschwitz extermination camp. Now they all looked like *Musel-manner*.

The work at Moll was very hard. But it was the distance we had to cover to get there and return that made it unbearable. It was very far, maybe six kilometers. Lately, I wound up there quite often, though luckily not every day. This was how it went yesterday. . . .

As usual, we were jarred out of our sleep by the banging of metal and the hysterical screaming of the kapos—"*Aufstehen! Raus!*"—the daily wake-up call. The suddenness of the brutal sounds never failed to have a jolting effect as we jumped up to face another day in Camp No. 2.

It was so very early, and I hadn't had enough sleep, but there was no time to think much. I ran outside to get my bread ration, and devoured the few bites of bread with black ersatz coffee, standing in the cold. It only took a couple of minutes. There was the usual agonizing: The voice of reason told me, "You have to leave at least something for later, remember the long day ahead of you until you get the soup." But on the other side was Terrible Hunger, and reason had a tough time; it was a toss-up. Today I managed to leave a tiny piece of bread in my pocket.

The *Appell*—it went on and on. I caught sight of one of the barefoot men of our barracks, his face distorted in a grimace of pain, as he kept jumping from foot to foot. As soon as *Appell* was over, there was a rush

of people to the various work commandos. Those who had their established work places were lucky, but most of us who didn't, had to play a
grim game of chance every day. We milled around, we began pushing
and rushing toward an area where we hoped small commandos were
being formed. Kapos cursed, clubs were swung. But eventually I wound
up with the majority—the Moll work brigade.

After more counting and rushing around by kapos and guards, our
column was at last on the way. By now we had been up a long time—
felt like hours—but it was still dark when we left camp. Time went by,
our long column kept moving ahead, then it was daylight. Two German
boys passed us on bicycles probably on the way to school, and I
wondered for a moment what they thought of the hundreds of ragged,
exhausted men they saw. I was tired and hungry, and the thought of that
small piece of bread in my pocket nagged at me constantly. But I
remembered the days when I succumbed to temptation and swallowed
the few bites in the morning. I knew I wouldn't feel less hungry, just
guilty and worried that I'd have no food until evening. Still, the pull of
that morsel of bread was so strong that twice I was ready to pull it out—
I even touched it with my fingers. But today I was successful in fighting
off the terrible temptation after all.

At last we arrived. The site was enormous. We were sorted out by
several kapos, along with other columns that had already arrived earlier
from Camp No. 1. A Kaunas Jew from No. 1 was in charge here, shouting orders in a rough, loud voice. There was pushing and jostling around
as people tried to position themselves to be chosen for an "easier" commando. The kapos swung their clubs, and after a while we were all assigned to our various work places.

The kapo led us to the main worksite, which was a gigantic cavity in
the ground. Standing at the rim for a moment, I looked down at a
tremendous hole from which enormous bites of earth had been scooped
out and removed; it was the future underground aircraft factory. It was
so big that the people and equipment down on the bottom looked like
children's toys. I thought with contempt, The stupid Germans! How can
they expect to finish this before the end of the war? We were led down a
long earthen ramp to the bottom, and our workday began.

Our job was to smooth out and grade a stretch of ground with spades.
The OT people and kapos dashed around, shouting, *"Los, los, bewegt
euch, schneller!* [come on; bestir yourselves, faster!]" I felt lucky, not to
have wound up with some of the "bad commandos." But even so, it was

very hard work. The kapos yelled and cursed, and every so often we got clubbed by them.

The long day stretched ahead of me—the weariness, the hunger, the cold—like an unending road. How would I ever get to the end of it?

I glanced with envy at a fire the kapos had built for themselves in a large steel drum. Then I started thinking of Daugavpils: a winter evening . . . Golda and I in the laundry room by the fire . . . the glowing embers. . . . I lost myself in thought, and time moved much faster.

The half-hour break for lunch amounted to little or nothing. I swallowed the bite of bread and didn't feel one whit less hungry. In the afternoon the shovel seemed to weigh a ton in my hands. I thought of the warm soup awaiting me at camp. One never knew. Tonight I might find something solid in it, something that had a few calories.

And again I began to daydream. These other people—did they daydream as much as I did? Perhaps some did. But no one else had a Golda in his life. I was certainly luckier than most. How would I ever get through the day without her? She was with me always, and all I had to do was plug in one of many episodes, of which I had a large memory supply, and I was far away from here. . . . Poor Golda, she might not even be alive anymore, and still she was with me, aiding me, helping me endure every single day.

At last it was dark, and we were ordered into columns again. The guards who were part of the *Postenkette*—cordon of guards— now surrounded our column. After some counting and recounting, we were on the way.

There was still the long way back to camp, and that was no small feat after such a long day, but there was the soup to look forward to and at last the chance to stretch out and rest.

Too soon, my hopeful mood evaporated. It was such a long way; we were just too exhausted and weak, and the wooden shoes made walking difficult. The guards tried to keep us in straight lines, but in the darkness they had to give up. We shuffled along in broken lines, every step an effort.

When I heard some commotion in the back, I knew what it meant: Someone had collapsed. Whenever a man died or just collapsed and could not move anymore (and that happened on every trip) he had to be carried back to camp on a makeshift stretcher. Anyone nearby stood a good chance of becoming one of the stretcher bearers. The very thought of having to carry someone now was enough to make me shudder. I sped up, and got to the front rows.

It was late, and we seemed to have marched for hours, at last we were in view of the camp. But as we entered the kitchen compound, there was a sudden wailing of sirens: an air-raid alarm. The lights went off, and we were plunged into darkness. We were told that we could enter the camp proper and go to our barracks, but if we did so, we would not be allowed to return for soup. If we wanted to get the food, we had to stay right here and wait for the all clear. Each of us had to make an agonizing decision: go in and forgo the warm soup we had been looking forward to all day, or wait here, with no way of knowing how long the alarm would last. Most of us stayed. I could not think of giving up the soup, but some of the people were just unable to stand it any longer and went to their barracks.

The Allied planes passed our area on the way to bomb larger cities. They never dropped any bombs here—I wished they would—but they would have to return before the all clear sounded, and it took them a long time. More people gave up, and went inside. And still I waited. It was cold, I was beyond exhaustion, but I wasn't going to give up the calories, especially after having waited so long. It was very late, and the camp had been asleep for a long time when we finally heard the all clear. Lights went on in the kitchen, and after a while, we got our portion of soup at last. It was tepid and not very thick, leaving me hungry and dissatisfied.

While we were standing at the evening *Appell*, a prisoner was brought by a guard and made to stand at attention. We were told he had been captured while trying to escape from the work site. They beat him for a long time and then made him stand in between the two rows of electrically charged barbed wire. He was a young fellow, and as I looked at him, standing there without a coat, trembling, his face stained with blood, I wondered how long he could survive in the cold and snowy night.

Later in the barracks, people talked about him. We assumed that he had slipped through the guard chain during the day and that he would be kept standing until he died. Before going to sleep, I went over to the fence again. He was still standing on the same spot. I tried to imagine what was going through his mind.

Next day I was astonished to hear that the boy had been allowed to stay alive after all. He had apparently convinced the Germans that he had not tried to get away, he just fell asleep at work, waking up after his commando had left. You never knew with the Germans.

In the four months we had been here, much had changed, and not only the amount of food we got. When we first arrived, there was still a feeling of community among us; we were all from Lithuania, from the ghettos of Kaunas and Siauliai. The kapos were well known and were former friends and acquaintances. But with people dying at an accelerating rate, the composition of the camp population had been changing rapidly; the kapos were now our chief tormentors. The most vicious were the German criminals, but some of the Jewish kapos were not much better.

A hierarchy among the prisoners was much in evidence—which was encouraged, at least implicitly, by the SS. The great majority starved, worked, and died, but a small privileged class was also in existence. Those various functionaries who ran the camp under the authority of the SS, or were our kapos at work, helped the Germans keep us in a constant state of terror. Most of them did it in a most brutal way and were compensated with food and other privileges.

We all dreaded the *Appell*, but today's was certainly one of the worst. It started out the usual way, with *Muetzen ab* and *Muetzen auf*, the counting and recounting, and with kapos running around shouting and striking people with their clubs. But more than the usual time passed, more counting and more harassing. We could see there was some problem, and as time went on, we became aware that there was one person too many. The irritation and anger of the kapos and *Unterscharfuehrer* kept increasing, translated into a cascade of blows. And it was only after about two hours that the mystery was solved at last. A *Musel-mann* who'd been reported dead—he did not wake up and looked lifeless to his comrades—had somehow pulled himself up, after everyone had left the barracks, and dragged himself over to *Appell*. I heard a little scream. Meir told me later that the Aryan kapo, Willy, was so enraged that with a few blows of his club, he killed the man. "Now the numbers will balance," Willy said.

Month of December 1944

The misery here was increasing every day. I swallowed my piece of bread early in the morning, unable now to hold back any part of my ration. It was just beyond my power to withstand the terrible craving. Twice more, while on the way back from Moll, we were caught by air raid alarms as we approached camp, and once I went to sleep without the soup; it was beyond my endurance to wait. The cold, the hunger, the lice, the *Appelle*, the mud and the rain and the hard work—I got some relief only in my daydreams about Golda and in some other fantasies.

I saw Gershon.

"How are you doing?" he asked, looking at me closely. I said I was OK, but he seemed concerned.

"So you work sometimes at Moll." It was more a statement than a question.

"Not that often. I got out of it today too."

"We'll have to do something about that," he said as the orders for *Appell* were being shouted out.

We called it the *Scheisserei* (the shits)—severe diarrhea, the condition that precipitated dying in most cases. We looked at it more as a final stage in the deterioration of the body, rather than the actual cause of death. A *Musel-mann* who had become very weak and emaciated with that particular "look," got the runs. He could keep nothing inside, and at times could not even make it to the latrine. After a few days he died. That was the course it ran. Sometimes it took a little more time, sometimes a little less.

I spent most of the day in a warehouse fixing wooden racks. This was the *Sommerkeller*, the dream commando of the camp. A carpenter was needed there, and Reibstein arranged for me to get the work. My job was not only inside—a rare privilege—but in a place full of shelves containing a variety of foods. I had to be careful—Germans were always around—but I did manage, besides chewing bread, to swallow mouthfuls of sugar and even a bit of margarine. In the afternoon I was sent to a noncommissioned officer's quarters to repair a stuck window. Eventually I got it loose, but the German who was watching me must have seen that I was no expert.

After work I was told not to return the next day. I don't know whether it was because my work was unsatisfactory, or because they only needed someone for one day. The next day it would be back to the usual hell, but at least I had this one great day, and I was thankful for that.

There had been a change lately—and for once, for the better. Our commandant had been killed in an air raid while home on leave, and the new one was apparently more human. Perhaps it was the swiftness with which the camp was emptying that had something to do with the change in attitude toward us. Lately, there had been no new arrivals while the dying continued unabated. The cart filled with spindly bodies was a familiar sight at camp. Every day many died here, but others who were sick were sent to die at camp No. 4—the "camp for the sick," from which no one ever returned. At any rate, the soup lately seemed thicker and more plentiful, and the *Appell* didn't last so terribly long.

I was now working in a new commando where I hoped I could continue a long time. Our work involved sorting potatoes that had been stored in the ground and covered with a roof of straw and earth. We had to dig them out, remove the rotten ones, and load the rest on trucks. Already on the first day, we each managed to bring a few spuds into camp, and I had myself a feast. I cut them in very thin slices, roasting them until tender on the hot metal of the small iron stove in our barracks. Surely, there could be nothing in the world so good as sitting near a hot stove and eating roasted potatoes!

The job was arranged for me by Reibstein and other fellows of the *Sommerkeller*. I didn't not know any details. But in this place, if one had food, he had power and influence. Most used it for their own advantage only; a few helped others as well. But Gershon Reibstein risked his life daily for the sole purpose of helping friends.

Most people in my commando were from Kaunas, and so was our kapo.

After I'd worked at potato sorting for a week or so, it was announced that our camp was going to be closed, because there weren't enough people left. We were to be distributed among the sister camps in the area. I didn't know what would happen to our "potato commando" and was very uneasy. How galling it was for this to happen now—just when I got the new job and after the change for the better in camp conditions.

Monday, January 1, 1945: The 1290th day

So, 1944 had departed. I thought of the end of 1941, the scare we'd had that New Year's night. How long ago it seemed now. Surely war could not last much longer, but hadn't we thought so for a very long time?

We were dispersed among the various Dachau satellite camps, and I was now in camp No. 11, close to the town of Landsberg. This place looked very much like No. 2. The same tormentors were here: our old big-shot kapos, *Unterscharfuehrer* Schreyer, Antonas. Luckily, our commando continued to function from here, and I was still working at potato sorting. Dov Shilansky was able to transfer to No. 1.

Month of January 1945

The majority of the people here were brought from Auschwitz. For a long time I had heard frightening tales about what was taking place in certain camps; judging by the details I heard now, none of it was exaggerated. But as usual with the Germans, you just could not figure them out. Thousands of people were killed in Auschwitz every day, but last fall when the advancing Red Army approached that area, prisoners were evacuated, and many of them were here.

The barracks, as in our old camp, was built partly below ground, with long, double-tier, wooden platforms on both sides, and a very small, round iron stove in the middle. I slept on the upper tier. In our hut there were about ninety inmates, brought here from many countries of Europe. Besides me, there was only one Lithuanian. Many are from Poland and Hungary, as well as from Romania, Germany, France, Greece, and probably some other countries; at least one person was from Italy. My neighbors to the right were an older man and his son—from Paris.

I was usually called Litvak or 999, the last three digits of my number. No one here knew my real name, except for Yanek, a fellow from Poland who slept to the left of me.

Most of us spoke Yiddish, although each in the dialect of his country of origin. But there was also a babble of different languages. Some of the Hungarians and Romanians of the so-called educated class didn't speak Yiddish at all, and some of the Polish intelligentsia spoke it very poorly; the German Jews spoke nothing but German. Still, in general, communication was not a problem; most of us spoke more than one language and knew German—except for the Greeks and the one Italian, who spoke neither Yiddish nor German.

At work most days we were able to "organize" a few potatoes, on occasion only a single one, and sometimes nothing at all. One day we had to deliver a load to camp and had a real chance to fill up our pockets. After work I was able to cook them and ate almost all of them. I knew I shouldn't, but for once I wanted to eat until I felt no more hunger. That was impossible—I could not imagine ever not wanting to eat. In my case, the control mechanism that told me when to stop eating simply didn't work. I ate too much and had to run to the latrine several times.

Five people in our commando were replaced by new workers. No one was talking, so I could only surmise what's been happening: Our commando was considered one of the best in camp, and people with influence were trying to get their proteges in. Why I was not replaced, I didn't know, but I suspected that the fellows from the *Sommerkeller* must have made a strong effort on my behalf.

Electrifying news! Golda was alive! At least she was last summer, when Mark, one of the new fellows at work, last saw her. He was from the Netherlands, but had spent some time at the Kaiserwald Camp. I asked him whether he had ever met a girl from Daugavpils named Golda Gutterman, and to my surprise he answered, "Yes, I remember her well." He described her to me and said, "She used to talk to me about you."

"Do you remember anything specific she ever said about me?"

"Yes, a few times she remarked sadly, '*Wehr weisst wu zeine beindalech zeinen yetzt.*'"

"This is just what Golda would say!" I told him happily.

Conditions here were pretty much what they were in our old camp before it got better. Here, too, the SS men walked around with whips and the kapos with clubs—it didn't take much of a transgression to get whipped. My personal circumstances, however, were much improved, due to the potatoes I was able to "organize." Of course, I might have gotten caught any time, but meanwhile I felt wealthy and lucky. I usually ate them baked, but once in a while I exchanged some for bread. Either way,

I had something extra most days. And after the news I got of Golda, I was full of hope.

The prisoner hierarchy here was much more pronounced than in Camp No.2. The brutality and viciousness even of Jewish kapos knew no limits. Perhaps that was because we had so many toughened camp veterans from Auschwitz. But some Lithuanian Jews were just as bad. Hanging over them was the reality that since they themselves were also inmates, their benefits and rights could be withdrawn at the slightest whim of an SS man. They had to keep proving themselves constantly. Even so, a few of them tried to be humane when possible, others fulfilled their duties as tyrants with much gusto and, I suspect, enjoyment.

Not all of the privileged people were equal in the power they had and the benefits they received. But there was a sort of understanding among most of them, concerning exchanges of favors, sometimes not only for themselves but for friends and proteges as well. That applied, to some degree, even to tailors and shoemakers, who worked in camp. For example, it was quite natural that a shoemaker who had fashioned a pair of leather boots for an SS man should expect extra food and sometimes certain favors from his pleased German master.

Sleeping across from me were about half a dozen men who always kept together. I believe they came from the Bedzin-Sosnowiec area in Poland. One of them, who seemed to be a teenager, had quite an extraordinary voice. He often sang at night after the lights were turned off when we were all in our bunks. I'd never heard anyone sing so enthrallingly as this boy did; the sad melodic Jewish folksongs tore at one's heart. But the song he favored most was "Gypsy Love," which he sang often, with great feeling. It was truly a beautiful song.

Month of February 1945

The "potato commando" was dissolved—no more work. I was back at the bottom.

I was again working at jobs of many kinds, having to depend on my luck every day. But while the work was unpredictable and changed from time to time, the intense hunger for food was always there, unrelenting in its ferocity. In Camp 11 our rations were distributed in the barracks, not in the kitchen, and it was all in the hands of the barracks chief, the

Blockaelteste. Ours was a Jew from Hungary, with reddish blond hair, who must have been about forty or so. He was a very religious man; I often saw him praying—he even wore a prayer shawl. (I could not imagine how he got it here; he certainly must have had a lot of pull.) All the same, he was not a nice man, to say the least.

To pour a ladleful of soup into an outstretched bowl seemed like a simple enough feat. But there was more to dispensing soup than that, a lot more. When the two men would carry the soup vat into the barracks, we would already be waiting eagerly, people hovering around with their eyes fixed on the precious liquid. The barracks chief would stir it around a bit, while we all looked transfixed, at the solid pieces that floated up to the top. Once in a while there was something that even looked like a scrap of meat, but I was never quite sure—nothing like that ever landed in my bowl. The first to get their portions would be the *Blockaelteste*'s cronies; they were the ones who got the best morsels. There was a fine art to the process of stirring the soup and then pulling out a ladleful that contained the best there was in the huge vat. Usually, the farther back one stood in line, the less chance there was to get a piece of potato or some other unrecognizable vegetable, but there was no certainty. Everything depended on the man with the ladle. He determined what you would wind up with. Sometimes there was some soup left over after all the portions were meted out, and a few lucky ones got seconds. Since the *Blockaelteste* hardly knew me, I wasn't one of the lucky ones.

I suppose the German SS were all needed at the front. Our guards now were of the Hungarian SS, their uniforms were different. They may have been Hungarian *Volksdeutsche*.

There were some bad apples among us, but not many. What was more surprising was how much decency still remained, and sometimes one came across it in a most unexpected way.

I was in a column of about fifty people being marched to a different work location when a group of prisoners approached us from the opposite direction. As they came closer, I recognized Joshua Lutzewski who'd been with me in the same hut, in Camp No. 2, and was transferred to No.1 last December. From the way he smiled, I knew he noticed me, too, and in the split second that we passed each other, he pushed his hand into my coat pocket and was gone.

What he put there was a cigarette! My God, *a whole German*

272 / Sidney Iwens

cigarette! Even if he managed to keep from smoking it, he could have
exchanged it for bread. But instead, he gave it to me, though we had
known each other only a few months. Of course, I was happy to get it, I
hadn't smoked a real cigarette since Siauliai, but it was his act of
generosity and selflessness that made me feel good all over.

At *Appell* today I stood next to the only Italian fellow here. He was
trembling. It was probably harder for him to take the cold than for us
who came from a colder climate. Whenever I saw him outside, he
seemed to be freezing. He could hardly communicate with anybody and
was trying to tell me something; I couldn't understand him, nor did he
grasp what I was saying to him in German. I felt sorry for him.

I had had a running sore on the ankle of my left foot for some time.
Although I'd rearranged the rags on my foot and the shoe didn't rub me
there anymore, the sore refused to heal. There were also several sores on
my neck that did not dry up. Malnutrition, I suspected.

The free time we had on Sunday or in the evenings we usually spent
trying to free ourselves from the hordes of lice. We sat half-naked, some
of us with only a blanket around our shoulders, checking the seams of
our clothing and squashing the vermin between the nails of our thumbs.
For a while I itched somewhat less but I knew that as hard as I worked
at delousing, I could never eliminate them completely. In a short time it
was as bad as before. Yet, I kept on hunting them. I had the feeling that,
if I ever stopped, they would eat me alive.

Most of the time I'd managed to avoid beatings, but however careful
you were, it was hard not to get hit. This morning there was some pushing as the work commandos were formed, and the chief kapo struck out
with his club left and right. I was standing quietly but got hit on the
shoulder anyway. Nothing unusual. But certain people got hit repeatedly.
I wasn't sure what made them such tempting targets. As for me, I had
learned certain rules of demeanor back in Daugavpils; I made myself as
inconspicuous as possible and never looked a Nazi straight in the eye.
For such "insolence," at the time of the *Aktionen,* you could have been
sent off with those who were to be shot. Here you could be beaten, and
in our weakened condition, the result might have been catastrophic.

It was logical that, as time went on the daily death rate should increase. *Scheisserei*, still remained the most common prelude to the end. To a few, death came right here in the barracks, to some in the hospital, but to most it was the *Scheunensblock*, a barracks where *Musel-manner* were sent; no one returned from there. Sometimes men on their last legs were shipped off to "sick camp," also a one-way trip. It was curious, that *Musel-manner* got so little sympathy from other inmates. The kapos and bullies among us treated them with derision and contempt, while the rest of us just avoided or ignored them.

Four people in our commando, where I've been working for about a week, each received a package of Russian *mahorka*—stem tobacco. This had never happened before. I guess it was among supplies captured from the Russians. (I used to smoke it in the partisan village, Bobily). The Germans didn't like to smoke it, so during our unloading of gravel and mixing concrete, the OT *Meister* said he'd give the tobacco to the "good workers." As it turned out, this grand prize was given in an arbitrary fashion, and I was very disappointed not to have been among the lucky ones.

Because people in other commandos were also recipients of this prize, the exchange rate for that tobacco dropped quite low, and in the end I was able to get a package of tobacco in return for my portion of bread. I knew it was not wise and thought of the calories I'd be losing, but the piece of bread had been so small lately—just a few bites—while that tobacco, if I was careful with it, could last for days. Anyhow, I wouldn't do it again. This I promised myself.

The ration of bread still presented me with my daily struggle. I'd been feeling guilty about the tobacco, and in an effort to be sensible, I decided to divide my ration in several parts and make sure to eat bread at least twice a day.

After about a week, I was surprised by how well my new system worked. Not only did I eat bread more often, but I actually managed every day to save a tiny piece of my ration, and in my pocket I carried around bread that amounted to almost a daily ration. Although I could swallow it in a few seconds, that morsel made me feel almost wealthy and more self-assured: I had a reserve of bread. The fact that I saved something, even a crumb, made my hunger more tolerable. I usually ate the older bread and kept the fresh and was surprised at the ease with which I could keep to my strict regimen.

But after I had accumulated more than a portion of bread, I ate up my whole reserve. Not because I had trouble controlling myself, but because I'd started worrying. There had been thefts in the barracks before, but last night a portion of bread was stolen not far from where I slept. I shuddered when I thought that it might happen to me and decided to take no chances. No, I wasn't any less hungry, but at least I had those few calories in my own stomach.

Yanek told me about Auschwitz-Birkenau; he was there for a year and a half and worked at sorting the belongings of new arrivals. Many former Auschwitz people were here, and I heard the stark facts of the selections, the gassing, and the crematoriums. But Yanek told me some details of what went on at the unloadings, of the hundreds of tragedies played out there every day, haunting stories. And this went on for years! Truly, even if someone should survive the war and tell about Auschwitz, no one would believe him.

On the way to work, we were stopped at a railroad crossing while a passenger train passed by. As the cars went clattering past, I could see people in their seats facing each other, and a man sitting comfortably reading a newspaper. I had a momentary thought: How splendid that would be! To travel in a train and leisurely read a newspaper!

Actually it was hard to think at all about "after the war." I just wanted to survive, and my dreams were mostly of how to put something in my stomach. Once in a while there was some talk in the barracks about what one would do if he survived. But it seemed to be half-hearted. Hunger took up most of our thoughts, dreams, and emotions.

Some mornings I woke up just moments before those early-morning wake-up calls. I had a vain hope that there would be some minutes left to me before the sudden banging and brutal shouting. It happened only rarely, but when I did get those quiet moments, they were the only time when I belonged to myself. Everyone was still asleep, and I, covered with blanket and coat, for once felt snug, almost warm. Usually, though, I was disappointed, for almost the minute I awakened, all hell would break loose, and I was abruptly thrust at another harrowing day at camp.

We had a selection. All the inmates had to stand in line while several SS men inspected us; those who were in very poor physical condition were taken away. We were told they were going to a "recuperation camp," but we all knew that no one came back from wherever he was being taken. We were all pretty thin, but I suppose this too was relative. In general, I trusted no hospital, infirmary, or sick camp. It was obvious that they only spared us at all because we were needed for work. The minute one admitted to being in some way incapacitated, he was as good as dead.

I noticed some men whispering together secretively. Yanek said he'd heard that they'd killed a dog at work and brought it into camp. I was very envious.

I could think of nothing but food. Even fear, even the acute awareness that I might be murdered at any moment, receded into the background. All concern was centered on food.

It was Sunday, we could rest a bit. I watched the Greek fellows, whose bunks were close to mine. They looked different—tall and dark and always jabbering excitedly. I had to remind myself that they were Jews. I couldn't understand their language, but I could tell, by the way they were smacking their lips, that they were now talking about food. One of them tried to tell me in broken German all about the different foods they used to eat in Salonika—the sausages, the meats, the cakes, the pastries, and other delicacies.

There was no more "Gypsy Love." The boy who used to sing so beautifully was moved away. A pity. Someone said the Germans liked his singing so much they gave him a job in the kitchen.

I exchanged my portion of bread for a full bowl of potato peels and was glad for the opportunity. The fellow said they came from a German kitchen and really, the potatoes had apparently not been peeled too skimpily. They had to contain more calories than the small piece of bread, but what really appealed to me was the volume. I could almost feel them swelling up in my poor shrunken stomach.

Behind the barracks, I put the peels in a can with water and put the can on a small fire I'd made from scraps of wood. We were not allowed to use the small stove inside. With great anticipation I watched the water get hot, and impatiently waited for it to boil. Suddenly, our Hungarian block chief appeared.

"Put out the fire and take the stuff away!" he yelled.

"But I've seen other people do it. Just—just five minutes more, a couple of minutes . . ."

"Put it out immediately, or I'll dump your junk on the ground!"

I had no choice. I stamped out the fire, cursing him in my mind: Damn you a thousand times.

And this man prayed with fervor several times a day—with prayer shawl yet. How was one to understand somebody like that?

With great bitterness I went to my bunk and ate the raw potato peels. At least they were warm. Surprisingly, they did not taste as bad as I had expected.

On my way to evening *Appell*, I ran into Reibstein.

"Shaike, I haven't seen you for so long. How are you?" he asked with concern.

"Fine."

"Why don't you ever come to see me?"

I said nothing.

"Stop in my place after *Appell*. Be sure to come."

I knew what he meant. If I'd gone over to his barracks from time to time, as some others did repeatedly, I'd have been receiving bread from him. But I couldn't do it. Reibstein had done a great deal for me, I wouldn't be around anymore if not for that stint with the potato brigade, and I had often thought of him with gratitude. But to push myself on him like the others, would be the same as begging—I couldn't beg. But now that I was asked specifically, I did go.

It was as bad as I'd expected. At least half a dozen people stood around, obviously waiting for a handout, while I hung back, feeling awkward. After a while he noticed me and called out, "Ah, Shaike, why are you standing there like that? Come here." He gave me a piece of bread. We exchanged a few words, and I left.

Even as we were becoming more and more emaciated, our lice were getting fatter, more ferocious. Truly, they tortured us constantly.

At work today, the cold, hunger, and exhaustion were as usual, but the itching seemed worse than ever. I had a momentary flash: If I die here, at least, that the lice will die with me. I suppose I'm their—sort of world, I mused, and when I'm gone, they'll be gone too. That would be some consolation, but I knew it wasn't so. When I died, the lice would just move to someone else.

Month of March 1945

Quarantine. Our camp was sealed. No one was allowed to leave for work. We were told there was an outbreak of typhus. Small wonder, with all these lice around.

Weeks were passing and nothing was happening. We were shut off from the outside. At first not having to work seemed like a dream come true. But more people died of starvation now than before.

Our ration was reduced still further, much of it just plain mold. Each piece of bread had two shades, a layer of the usual sand-colored bread and a layer of green, somewhat powdery mold. The proportion of bread and mold depended on luck: the dividing line usually ran at an angle, as the mold ate the loaves in an uneven way. It was not unusual to wind up with as much as half the ration consisting of the green stuff. I heard that the mold did no harm and was even used in some drug, but there were no calories in it. Some threw it away, others ate it. I not only ate my own but sometimes took it from people who were afraid of the mold. It had a sweetish kind of taste.

We spent a lot of time on our bunks, experiencing a general feeling of lassitude. No one had any idea how long we we'd be kept shut away. We also didn't know how widespread typhus was here. Although we could rest all we wanted, I felt quite weak; so did most of the other people.

I was lying on my bunk watching a man gnawing a bone. As one of the cronies of the block chief, he'd gotten it in his soup. This bone was not the kind to be easily ground up with one's teeth, nor was it as hard as stone; it required hard work to extract its juice. It held me like a magnet; entranced, I was unable to take my eyes away as the man went on and on, working with his teeth. I was hoping that, when there was almost nothing edible left, he'd throw it away, since he always got extra food. Would I have picked it up? Yes, if no one had seen me doing it. But he went on and on. I kept watching and I thought: Just like a dog. I'm watching that man the way my dog Rex used to watch me back home when I ate supper. And only last fall, I would not pick up the cigarette butt the German threw away. . . . The man still kept on with the bone, and at last I turned away.

Hunger. How was one to describe our kind of hunger, an all- absorbing yearning for food? The need to put something in one's belly—the craving of the body for any kind of nourishment—was so strong that other normal concerns lost their urgency. We had a single desire—food.

I felt tired all the time. The weather had been good; I walked over with Yanek to a barracks where the roof had a southern exposure. The bottom of the sloping roof was flush with the ground; all we had to do was just lie down on it and feel the sun's warm rays. I got to know some fellows, and we talked about different matters. Sometimes we reminisced about the "time before," which now seemed so very remote, or about a war rumor that filtered through to us even now in our isolation. We knew that the situation of the German army was getting worse all the time. We conversed quietly, without much passion.

I suppose man is both very strong and very vulnerable. After years of being in the hands of the Germans, I often marveled at how much one could endure when he had to! On the other hand, we were absolutely at the mercy of their whims. All they had to do was cut our ration just a little, and probably an additional twenty men would die every day. If the next day, they'd cut out the bread, maybe another fifty would die. And if they gave us an additional few ounces of bread, many people would continue to live. It took so little to make the difference.

As the days went by, I seemed to get weaker; we all did. We still came to the roof. Mostly, we just lay in the sun. I was baffled by the fact that at times it took an effort just to talk. Surely it doesn't take much energy just to move one's mouth!

There was a rumor that we were to receive Red Cross packages. But we'd heard plenty of glorious rumors before, and the events predicted never did come true.

But miracles did happen after all. We actually received packages! "Package"is probably not the correct description. What each of us received was one small can of sardines, one can of evaporated milk, about a pound and a half of cube sugar, and a package of twenty cigarettes. The women got a can of sweetened condensed milk instead of the cigarettes.

After receiving our treasure, we all returned to the barracks, sat down on our bunks, and feasted our eyes on the unbelievable wealth we'd just acquired. What to start with? The Frenchman said, "You have to make two holes in the can of milk."

Someone had a nail and made a hole with it in the lid. He tried to drink it, but the milk did not come out easily.

"You've got to make another hole,"the Frenchman insisted. He was right; two holes let the milk flow easily.

Many of us used the nail to punch the holes. When I put my mouth to the can and started to drink the thick savory liquid, it felt as if life itself were pouring into my insides.

Yesterday I only drank the milk. Today I ate the sardines. The sugar I kept in my pockets; from time to time I took a cube in my mouth and sucked on it. I had decided not to smoke the cigarettes. I could not see myself using up, in this manner, something that was of so much value. Until yesterday, one could get more than a loaf of bread for them. Now that everyone had some, the exchange rate dropped precipitously, but I intended to hold onto them until supplies were used up, and then exchange them for bread at a decent rate.

In the afternoon it was announced that everyone would receive a supplement of one more food item; I came away with another can of evaporated milk.

Something terrible happened during the night—someone stole my cigarettes. I had kept them in the pocket of my pants, concealed under my head rest, but when I woke up in the morning, the cigarettes were gone. Obviously someone lifted them while I was asleep. I had not even opened the package, dreaming of the bread I'd get for it. That dirty rat, whoever it was!

It must have been done by someone who knew where I kept the cigarettes, someone who'd been sleeping near me. I had a strong suspicion but could't prove it. My neighbor, the old Frenchman, had been puffing away like mad. Was he the one?

The loss of the cigarettes ate at me the whole day, and I became more and more convinced it was the Frenchman. Still, I could not accuse him openly without proof, but from the hostile way I acted toward him, he must have become aware of my suspicion. In late afternoon, he came over, handed me a somewhat wrinkled cigarette box, and said:

"I couldn't help myself. Temptation was too strong. Here, that's what I have left."

Inside were eleven cigarettes.

I felt quite disgusted. I wasn't going to take any more chances. I smoked the eleven cigarettes myself.

After three, four days, the glow that had engulfed the camp the moment we got the packages was fading fast. I held on to a few cubes of sugar a little longer and then was back where I'd been before, living on a few bites of bread and some soup.

Month of April 1945

Quarantine was lifted. It had lasted more than a month.

On the way to work, we passed some dandelions. Someone said the leaves could be eaten. I picked some and ate them.

Lately we had been hearing the sound of planes flying overhead almost every day and were sure they were American. Even here, evidence of the bombing that German cities were experiencing was visible. A work commando of about twenty of us was taken to Landsberg several times to clean up the rubble after the bombing.

Another big surprise! For the first time since our arrival in Germany, we had a chance to take a shower. We were marched off to the delousing facility at Camp No. 1, and while we were in the shower room, our clothing was being treated with intense heat. I hoped all the lice were killed.

Someone stopped in from the neighboring barracks to tell us that the American President, Roosevelt, had died; the Germans had been passing the news around with much glee. But it wasn't going to help them; their end was near. Too bad about Roosevelt, though. As long as I could remember, he had been the President of America; he was always known as a good person and a great man. But his death could not possibly help the Germans much. Let them gloat.

The end really must have been near. At work one day a guard watched me struggle to dump a wheelbarrow heavily laden with dirt. No one else was around. Handing me a piece of bread, he said, "It won't last long for you anymore. Soon I'll be in the position you're in now."

We went to work the same as always, and the SS were still as threatening as ever.

We had waited so long for our deliverance—for the defeat of the Nazis. I tried to imagine how it would come about, what they would do with us at the very end; the Germans were so unpredictable. Would they shoot us or try to dispose of us some other way? There could be a lot of confusion and chaos at the end, and that might be of help to us.

I said to Yanek: "We've got to run if we see that they mean to finish us. Remember, just because someone shoots at you doesn't mean he'll hit you—run like the devil. . . ."

Meanwhile, the only indications of battle were the many planes flying overhead. We knew few details. The general camp routine continued, and our main preoccupation was still food. We were as hungry as ever, and people got the runs and they died.

I hadn't seen Reibstein since the time when he had asked me to come to his barracks.

I walked by a large rubbish heap, which hadn't been there before. Somewhat to the side I noticed a small prayer book on the ground. Back when we were children, if a prayer book accidentally fell to the floor, we'd pick it up fast and kiss it. I felt a twinge, seeing it abandoned in the dirt, and picked it up. Small, only about three by five inches, but thick and printed on very thin paper, it contained prayers for many occasions, something that a religious Jew might take along on a trip. I wondered what the owner was like as I was putting the little book in my pocket.

Monday, April 23, 1945

As the day wore on, our feeling of nervousness and expectancy kept increasing. There was no doubt—the Americans were coming closer and closer, bringing either deliverance or death at the hands of the SS.

Late at night, maybe eleven or twelve o'clock, someone threw our barrack door open and shouted:

"The kitchen is wide open! The guys are helping themselves to the food!"

I took off like mad, finding the kitchen unguarded and unlocked. Inmates swarmed all over, but by now there was hardly anything left, except for a few potatoes. I managed to grab two.

My hopes rose. If no one bothered guarding the kitchen—was freedom at hand...? But as we returned to the barracks, I could see the SS guards at their usual posts.

Tuesday, April 24, 1945

Since early morning, there had been confusion and uncertainty. They counted and recounted us, ordered us into marching columns, but then made us wait again. The talk was of evacuating us—where and how no one knew.

At last, we were told that we were being evacuated by foot. We were warned to keep in line and that we would be shot for any infringement of the usual rules; the ill and weak would be transported alongside in vehicles, together with the hospitalized inmates. But very few admitted to being sick, and some who could hardly stand up refused to accept the offer of transportation.

An extra bread ration was issued to us, and at last around ten o'clock, we left camp. Surrounded by many SS guards, our column of perhaps 2,000, stretched a long way. They wanted us to walk fast and kept urging us on:

"Five in a row! Five in a row! Keep in line! Faster!"

For a while we kept up, but after a few hours all the shouting and hitting with rifle butts could not keep the column in orderly lines. Finally they gave up, but were still very strict about our keeping up with the column, and were ruthless with anyone who fell behind.

Later in the day I saw the same scene repeated quite often: a man, unable to walk any farther, lying on the side of the road, and being threatened and beaten by a guard, who was trying to make him get up. I had to move on and could not see the outcome. Sometimes I heard rifle shots, but I also saw a few people who had collapsed from exhaustion, being thrown in a truck traveling in the same direction we were.

The guards kept hurrying us on. I was very tired.

At last it was night, and we were led to a low-lying area, which was marshy and wet and had a small stream passing through it. When the guards took up positions on the high ground surrounding us, some people were alarmed. "This might be the place where they'll finish us all," I heard someone say.

There was a rumor that we were being led to the Swiss border to be exchanged for Germans, but we didn't believe it. We didn't trust the SS at all; they might shoot us down any time.

On arrival here, a kapo had said, "A truck with bread is on the way. We'll get our rations tonight." To my surprise, late at night, we each received a slice of bread.

Wednesday, April 25, 1945

We were on the road since early morning without food or water, straggling along in broken lines. I knew none of the people around me. Everyone seemed to be on his own, absorbed in the aches and pains of his body. The guards had completely given up trying to keep us in any marching formation.

I thought of past grueling marches when I learned that one can go on for a long time just by putting one foot in front of the other. But now . . . many ended up in the ditch. How weak we all were....It was our lack of food . . . and the damn wooden shoes . . . the aching feet . . . the sores. . .

We were led along roads that were little traveled and passed very few villages. At one point, I found myself near the end of the column. Behind me on the empty stretch of road, a German civilian on a bicycle was drawing nearer to us, and way in the back were stragglers with guards urging them on to catch up. As the German came closer, I could see in his wire basket two loaves of bread. I kept walking, but the next moment—commotion. The German, with a startled expression, was standing next to his overturned bicycle; the loaves were on the ground, and a pile of men struggled to get at them. He must have tried to give it to us! flashed through my head. I dove into the midst of the mound, and for a few seconds became part of the clawing, intertwined mass; I managed to tear off one small piece of bread and push it into my mouth. Then an SS guard started hitting us with his rifle butt, and for a split-second, I was aware of the scene and seeing it as an observer: the men hurling themselves at the bread . . . fighting each other . . . tearing at it. . . . Within a minute all was back to normal, and we speeded up to catch up with the rest.

I still had my two raw potatoes. There had been no chance to make a fire last night. From time to time I thought of eating them raw but kept postponing it. I told myself that, when we stopped for the night, I'd get a chance to cook them. Meanwhile, having the potatoes in my pocket gave me a bit of hope, of expectation. I kept seeing before me the soup I'd make of them.

Thursday, April 26, 1945

We spent the night in a quarry and were again on the way in the morning.

I kept on plodding ahead with my eyes riveted to the ground. . . . What did I expect to find? Still I kept looking, searching. I picked up a tin cigarette box—it was empty. A little later, I found a three-inch pocket knife with two blades and a corkscrew. But it was food that every fiber of my body cried out for—food. . . .

We passed through a village. People offered us water, but the guards wouldn't allow us to take it.

The street narrowed, and we passed close to the houses. We were overcome by a frenzied desperation. Ignoring the threat of being shot, some dashed into doorways, hoping for food. I, too, darted in through a door, and found myself in an enclosed porch. I saw a flat wooden box with some greenery—might be salad leaves or just flower plants. . . . I grabbed a handful of the long, slender leaves, crammed them into my mouth . . . zoomed out again. The street was filled with the frantic mob, and the guards, in their effort to keep order, shouted and cursed hysterically, threatening us with their guns.

We had reached the end of the village. It was calmer. I noticed a civilian standing at a doorway, motioning. Five of us scrambled over, and each got a boiled potato.

Late in the afternoon we came to an abandoned camp. We were ordered into wooden barracks with three-tiered bunks. I still had my two potatoes and the prayer book I found next to the rubbish heap.

Friday, April 27 1945

We were up early. The bunks were actually more comfortable than the ones we'd had in our camp. But I felt tired—as if I had never rested at all. My feet and legs felt heavy, they were swollen.

Limping along, dragging our feet, we were back on the road again. Mind dulled by exhaustion and hunger, gaze fixed to the ground, I was driven by the one clear thought: To fall back, to stop, means the end. . . must go on.

After some time we were stopped at a camp, and word was passed throughout the column: "Whoever is too exhausted or too sick to continue may stay in this camp."

I had only a few minutes to decide. I knew that to admit to being weak was always dangerous. But if I continued marching, I'd wind up in the ditch. I had no more strength. I stayed at the camp, and so did many others. The rest continued on their way.

The camp, called Allach, was packed. I was told to go to a barracks, which I found so crowded that there was no place to sit down. We had received no rations since the first night on the road, and there seemed to be no chance at all of getting any in this camp.

Outside, people were milling around, most looking like *Musel-manner*. An inmate hovering over a small fire was cooking something in a tin can.

My potatoes! I thought excitedly. "Can I use the fire after you're done?" I asked.

"Yes, in a little while."

What luck. I got water in my tin dish, and with my newly acquired knife, cut up the two potatoes into small pieces, then waited anxiously. The few pieces of wood could not last very long, and I could see no way of getting any additional kindling. At last he was finished and walked away with his can. But as I was about to put my dish on the fire, two brothers appeared; they were from our camp, and I knew them to be bullies.

"Wait!"one of them said with authority. "We're going to use the fire first—then you can have it."

Of course, the fire would be burned out by then.

I jumped up and snarled at them: *"You-just-try-to-come-any-closer . . . !"* They looked at me for a few seconds with blank uncertainty, and then walked away. I had always avoided any confrontation with potential for violence, but now—the expression on my face must have left no doubt about my determination. At any rate, I was not bothered again, and at last was able to eat my precious potatoes.

I spent some time resting on the ground next to the barracks, which were large and built of concrete. From people who were seated next to me, I learned a little about this place. Allach was also a branch of Dachau, and only about eight kilometers from the main center. It had been a camp for Aryan prisoners, and they were still there. But during the latest evacuation, Jewish prisoners from various camps, who were unable to march any longer, were dumped at Allach also. We were allowed to use only a few of the barracks, and most of the camp was off-limits to us.

Later, knowing it would be dark soon, I went back inside the barracks but could find no place to lie down. The floor was completely covered with stretched-out bodies. At last I found a spot on a table, with just enough room to sit down. It was uncomfortable to sit with my legs dangling, but I spent the whole night sitting on that table.

Saturday, April 28, 1945

In the morning there was no change. People moved around aimlessly. I kept to myself. I didn't know anyone here. I had seen no Germans inside the camp since our arrival.

While at the outdoor latrine, my gaze fell on the row of half-undressed, squatting men. They were skin and bones, with practically no buttocks. These men are almost *Musel-manner*, I thought to myself. Then I looked down at my own legs, my thighs, and touched my buttocks—only bones. I looked the same as the rest . . . strange, I hadn't thought of myself in that way.

In the afternoon, a rumor: "The war is over." But a while later I heard the sound of far-away explosions, and I knew that the war was still going on.

When it got dark, I found a place to lie down on the floor, but didn't dare leave for fear of losing it. To be on the floor was better than sitting on a table, but I could not sleep much for there were no lights, and people on the way out had to step over our prone bodies. In the darkness I was stepped on quite often. Every once in a while I heard an outcry of pain, as one or another of those heading for the latrine stumbled over sleeping people.

Sunday, April 29, 1945

Inside the camp there was no real authority, just some kapos and bullies, who still had their strength; it was best to stay out of their way.

How long could I go on without food? How long had it been since I last ate bread? Five days? I didn't have much strength, but after a while I could no longer sit in the barracks. I tramped around outside—searching, looking. I moved away from the milling crowds toward the fence. No people there. At the hospital building, I stopped abruptly. On the ground, next to a trash can, were a few chicken bones. The source of the bones was apparent: An overflowing garbage can. The lid could not quite conceal a bundle loosely wrapped with newspaper, now partly open; it was crammed with chicken bones. It was hard to believe but shreds of chicken had been left on them. Certainly, they must have been discarded only minutes ago; otherwise someone else would have discovered them by now. What luck! I crammed them into my pockets and slunk away from there fast.

Careful not to be noticed by anyone, I chewed on the soft bone of a wing. I was in seventh heaven!

Shells had been exploding since before noon, becoming increasingly louder. I thought: Artillery . . . the battle must be moving nearer.

In the block someone said that the guards outside the fence had disappeared earlier, but now were back again at their posts.

In the evening the explosions sounded closer, and the firing went on without stop. I found a place to sleep on the third tier of a wooden bunk. The crowd must have been thinning out, many people died every day.

During the night, there was an ever-increasing crescendo in the sound of the battle. It seemed that our camp lay between the two opposing forces; I could clearly distinguish between the two sides in the cannon duel. Some shells might have fallen inside the camp or near it, but I was beyond fear, absorbed in grinding and chewing my bones. I did it deliberately and with relish. During the day I ate stealthily, concerned that my windfall might be noticed. But now, enveloped by the protective darkness, with the luxury of a bunk, I felt contented and relaxed, chewing away. A few explosions sounded so loud I felt certain that the shells had landed in the next barracks.

Sometime in the night the shelling quieted down, and I fell asleep.

Monday, April 30, 1945: 1409th day

In the morning we found that shells had hit the hospital during the night, destroying part of a wall. Several patients were killed and more wounded.

Outside, people shuffled around, weak and hungry, minds set on their desperate need for food.

Someone said, "I heard American soldiers are at the gate."

Another rumor? I wondered.

I walked to the gate. There, a file of about twenty inmates moved quietly in line past three tall soldiers in khaki uniforms. Each inmate, as he passed, kissed the hand of one of these bewildered-looking soldiers. *They Were Americans.*

I went to the end of the line.

The Days After

We were liberated. After nearly four years the miraculous happened, our tormentors were gone. But at Camp Allach there were no sounds of jubilation, no shouts of joy. We, the remnant, who in spite of everything, outlasted those who were to destroy us, were barely alive. Enfeebled, half-crazed from hunger, we held on to life by a thin thread. Indeed, in many cases that thin thread snapped the following days, as the death rate in camp continued unabated.

That very first day, some of us walked out of camp in search of food. Not many people lived in the area, but when I and two other fellows found a house and walked inside, the people cowered in alarm at the sight of us. They stared at us, and their faces expressing disgust mixed with fear, kept repeating, "We didn't know . . . we didn't know anything. . . ." But we only wanted bread . . . we walked out. The American soldiers tried to be helpful, but the war was still going on and they had neither the resources nor the personnel to do much for us. Though well-intended, the meal of macaroni and chunks of fat meat, which was prepared for us the second day after liberation, was a disaster. The heavy meal made people very sick and the dying went on at a fast pace.

After a few days, I too became ill. I felt very weak and could barely muster enough strength to crawl out of the block. Hour after hour we'd lie in a long row next to the building, hoping that the pleasant spring sun would bring us back our health. And then, because disease was so rampant here, I yet again experienced a quarantine, our camp was closed up. Armed American soldiers were patrolling outside the fence and no one was allowed to leave.

The days went by and I did not feel any better. A few times I considered going to the camp hospital for help, but had been told by those who'd been there that not much could be done there for us anyway, and so I didn't go.

Although it seemed to take a long time for me to recuperate, eventually I started feeling stronger. After more weeks passed, I decided to get away from Allach where there was still so much death and disease. Of course, I was eager to start searching for Golda immediately. I knew she'd been alive in Stutthof last fall. However, a lot could have happened since then. And what of Max and all the friends? Who of them was still alive?

The escape from camp was dangerous. I heard that one of the men had been wounded by a guard while trying to get out. I crawled through the wire fence in the darkness of night and found a clump of bushes a short distance away, where I lay waiting for the night curfew to end.

The hours of waiting went by slowly. While lying among the tangled branches, I kept thinking of all those countless times when I'd been lying concealed, heart pounding away, pulse racing, knowing full well that discovery meant certain death. It was different now. I knew that even if I were discovered, my life wouldn't be threatened, there was even somewhat of a tingling sensation in the perceived danger. Yet, I felt a touch of bitterness, it had been weeks since our liberation, and still. . . . But suddenly I noticed the sky in the East starting to brighten, soon it would be morning, a bright sunny morning . . . and I was free. I will find Golda. And I could feel exhilaration swelling up in me. . . . I could see myself reaching the road just a few hundred feet away and walking toward the city, the big city of Munich, and beyond Munich there was the wide, beautiful world . . . full of mystery and unfamiliar joys . . . and yes, I was free.

I am the only survivor of my entire family.

No one of the Gutterman family survived.

They were actually deported to Riga, Kaiserwald Camp, in November of 1943 and from there in 1944 to Stutthof Camp. Their brother, Leiser, was shot in Kaiserwald while trying to bring in food for the family. In Stutthof, the three sisters refused to part from their mother and lost their chance of being transferred to a work camp, where a more reasonable chance for survival existed. The first of them to die was Hinda. While she was standing at *Appell*, the string of the pendant Max had given her broke. She treasured that tiny plastic disk with his engraved initials. Frantically, she looked for it in the deep mud. When a kapo ordered her to stand up straight and began hitting her with a club, she refused and continued her desperate search. The kapo hit her until she collapsed, and Hinda never recovered from the beating. Although I never learned the details, Golda, Ella, and Mother also died in Stutthof.

Max lives in the United States.

After we were separated at Stutthof, he was sent to Muehldorf, a camp in the south of Germany, east of Munich. He was liberated by the American army.

Berke lives in Israel.

Just as we were certain that Berke was killed when we stumbled upon the German outpost, so he too was sure that Max and I had died in the same hail of bullets. He later managed to join up again with Antonov's partisans and continued fighting in their ranks until the area was recaptured by the Red Army.

Shmulke Palec lives in the United States.

Haim Kuritzky lives in Israel.

Dov Shilansky lives in Israel and is currently speaker of the Knesset.

I married Ita Tabrisky. We live in the United States and have two married daughters and five grandchildren.

Of the roughly 16,000 Jews who were in Daugavpils when it was captured by the Germans, less than a 100 survived. Among those who perished were all my other friends, those from Jonava, as well as the citadel, ghettoes, and camps.